CHRISTIANITY AND THE STATE

BY

S. PARKES CADMAN

A series of lectures delivered before the Pacific School of Religion, Berkeley, California, during the Spring of 1922, upon the Earl Foundation

New York

THE MACMILLAN COMPANY

1924

Set up and electrotyped. Published March, 1924.

Printed in the United States of America

To

MR. AND MRS. HARRY ANSON MOODY

OF DOUGLASTON MANOR, PULASKI, NEW YORK

IN GRATEFUL RECOGNITION OF

THEIR UNFAILING KINDNESS TO

THE AUTHOR

"WHERE there is much desire to learn, there of necessity will be much arguing, much writing, many opinions; for opinion in good men is but knowledge in the making. Under these fantastic terrors of sect and schism, we wrong the earnest and zealous thirst after knowledge and understanding which God hath stirr'd up in this City. What some lament of, we rather should rejoyce at, should rather praise this pious forwardness among men, to reassume the ill deputed care of their Religion into their own hands again. A little generous prudence, a little forbearance of one another, and som grain of charity might win all these diligences to joyn and unite in one generall and brotherly search after Truth, could we but forgoe this Prelaticall tradition of crowding free consciences and Christian liberties into canons and precepts of men. I doubt not, if som great and worthy stranger should come among us, wise to discern the mould and temper of a people and how to govern it, observing the high hopes and aims, the diligent alacrity of our extended thoughts and reasonings in the pursuance of truth and freedom, but that he would cry out as *Pyrrhus* did, admiring the Roman docility and courage. If such were my Epirots, I would not despair the greatest design that could be attempted, to make a Church or Kingdom happy."

JOHN MILTON: *Areopagitica.*

PREFACE

This volume contains the substance of several lectures delivered during Lent, 1922, at the Pacific School of Religion, Berkeley, California, upon the Earl Foundation provided for that purpose. I trust their essence harmonizes with the religion of inwardness and freedom which was first revealed by our Lord in Galilee, and afterward proclaimed by His Apostles throughout the Græco-Roman world. I have intended the position these lectures assume, the ideals they defend and any modifications they suggest, to be subordinate to the teachings of that great religion, the center and life of which are in "Jesus Christ, the same yesterday, today and forever."

Faith in Him, with the rights such faith includes, should not be left at the mercy of external authority, however deeply intrenched. Neither should it be subjected to the vagaries of theological controversy, however sincerely waged. Nevertheless, its historic, institutional and doctrinal forms in the Christian Ecclesia, and also in some phases of the nominally Christian State, are of first rate importance as testimony to the indispensability of original Christianity itself. I have therefore emphasized the characteristic benefits derived from a scrutiny of organized religion in its relations to the political State.

The treatment of so vast and intricate a theme in a necessarily fragmentary manner exposes the writer to the charge of naming subjects which are not explored with thoroughness and precision. The omission is in part enforced and in part deliberate. In so far as it is the latter, it is prompted by the hope that what is here set down may induce the reader to define afresh his personal knowledge of the annals of Church and State. For other but equally cogent reasons, the separation between theology and the science of history has been respected. One can, in the words of Hazlitt, "endeavor to feel what is good, and to give a reason for the faith that is in him," without carrying the selections into the troubled area of doctrinal differences. It must also be owned that in the case before us criticism has been animated by one's devout gratitude for the lasting gains that Christianity has conferred, not only upon the State, but upon the whole course of civilization. That gratitude has perhaps neutralized the consciousness that much so-called religious history is prejudiced in statement, prone to exaggeration and irreligious in temper. A salutary change makes recent contributions conspicuous by contrast, and may well be a prophecy of Christianity's renewed approach toward the unity of the Spirit in the bond of peace.

The patient survey of broad historical spaces, the analysis of their component elements, the reappraisal of premature judgments, the accurate observance and description of famous individuals or leading events are the tasks of competent scholars who enjoy literary leisure. Yet ministers involved in an incessant round of clerical duties need to understand the interactions of Church and State. They should be able to give an account of nationalism and internationalism, as these have affected the history of the Faith which is ordained for the purification of human society. They can be confident that there lies deep in the hearts of all Christian people a keen desire to apprehend at closer range the historic achievements of their religion. The Psalmist's preference is still dear to them: "I have considered the days of old, the years of ancient times. I will remember the years of the right hand of the Most High. I will remember thy wonders of old."[1] Nor is this practice the less commendable because it exhorts us to hopefulness, forbearance and a more comprehensive charity. At every stage of the retrospective process we see the better future arising from the dying past; the entwining

[1] Psalm LXXVII: 5, 10, 11.

of what has been with what is to be, the persistent continuity with which opposing theories and parties complement each other.

Science, as Dean Stanley observed, may direct the preacher to wider horizons. Philosophy may penetrate for him profounder springs of thought and action. Poetry may kindle in him loftier fires and enrich his speech with more telling phrases. But history should rivet his attention and concentrate his energies because it aids him in the solution of those ever recurring problems which were seldom more insurgent than they are now. It was said of Richard William Church by one who knew him intimately that had he been "less strenuous in his effort to be just to all men, he never could have borne the part and left the mark he did." The historical spirit was the finest result of his consecrated scholarship. It was felt "in the way he spoke of men, in the weight he gave to the considerations which might fairly weigh with others, in the large allowance he would always make for the vast diversity of men's gifts and opportunities, for the inscrutable depth of every human life, for the unknown hindrances and difficulties and discouragements through which those who seem to advance slowly may be winning a heroic way."[2] If we can but imitate the example of Dean Church, we may cherish the expectation that the unification of Churches shall precede that of States, and that righteousness and good will shall yet abound in the earth. To this end, Christians of every persuasion will have to realize afresh the forms, and use the means, and value the lessons of that living Ecclesia which enshrines the power and wisdom of the living God.

I am deeply indebted to the Reverend Herbert B. Workman, Litt.D., Principal of Westminster Training College, London, England; the Reverend Oscar L. Joseph, Litt.D.; Professor Thomas Sharper Knowlson; the Reverend William

[2] "Life and Letters of Dean Church," edited by his daughter, Mary C. Church, p. xx ff.

S. Winans, M. A.; and the Reverend Albert S. Morris, for their generous assistance in revising and correcting the manuscript of these chapters. I also gratefully acknowledge here the very considerable help and guidance I have received, not only from the volumes mentioned in the Bibliography and the references, but from contributions in "The London Times Literary Supplement," "The London Spectator" and other ably conducted and responsible journals. Many valuable ideas and suggestions have been obtained from the two weeklies named, which are competent guides in historical matters.

S. Parkes Cadman.

Central Congregational Church,
Brooklyn, New York City.
October 15, 1923.

CONTENTS

FIRST LECTURE

THE TWO VOICES

"Oh! we're sunk enough here, God knows!
 But not quite so sunk that moments,
Sure though seldom, are denied us,
 When the spirit's true endowments
Stand out plainly from its false ones,
 And apprise it if pursuing
Or the right way or the wrong way,
 To its triumph or undoing."

ROBERT BROWNING: *Christina.*

"There are, it may be, so many kinds of voices in the world, and no kind is without signification. If then I know not the meaning of the voice, I shall be to him that speaketh a barbarian, and he that speaketh will be a barbarian unto me."

I Corinthians xiv. 10, 11.

CHRISTIANITY AND THE STATE

FIRST LECTURE

THE TWO VOICES

The world outlook is one of darkness and despair to materialistic interpreters — Those who reckon with God and immortality, in the light of our Lord Jesus Christ and of all history, reach a more adequate conclusion concerning human destiny — The chronic antagonism between these two views constitutes the problem of the ages — The voice of Faith is more vibrant and penetrating than the voice of Fear, because inspired by the Gospel of the Incarnation — The economic situation should be viewed from the standpoint of eternal justice and love — A reappraisal of the manifold issues of war is an urgent and timely demand — The Church must offer the final solution of the problem of world peace — Secularism ends in a *cul de sac,* while the spiritual idealism of Christian believers leads to the City of God.

THE world wears a tragic aspect for those who mistake their own unbelief and despair for a universal state, and who speak as though humanity had fallen into irremediable ruin. To them the past is a series of blunders and crimes encumbering the present with their fatal heritage; the future foredoomed to failure. This thoroughgoing pessimism, which has always pervaded some minds, was greatly intensified and diffused by the late war. Notwithstanding the sufferings that war inflicted upon guilty and innocent alike, it has left peace exceedingly precarious. The spirit of Nationalism has revived and there seems to be no exorcise for it. Armaments are being adapted to more deadly methods of conflict. Dissensions prevail between the conquerors and the conquered. Civil strife is imminent in not a few countries, and in nearly all lands antagonistic groups imperil the safety of the State. Religious or racial prejudice poisons the life of communities and cities. The tenacious retention of wealth is countered by greed for its acquisition. Capitalists and industrialists think in terms too restricted for the public good. Strikes and lockouts, riots and conspiracies, terrorisms and massacres kindle further discontent and anarchy. The Christian habit of life is often forsaken; and men are too much confined to their own resources, which, though immense, are never enough for their actual demands. The combative instincts that produce war-mentality show few signs of abatement in some leaders of public opinion. The law of our Lord that we should love our enemies is abrogated. The Mosaic law, "An eye for an eye, and a tooth for a tooth," governs in its sinister insistence the claims and counter-claims of classes and nations. Christ obviously intended His law to prevail in human intercourse; but those who are infected by the virus of militarism, either construe that law under nullifying limitations, or openly disparage it. Their enemies have only to be sufficiently brutal to justify brutality everywhere, and thus release Christian peoples from an obligation proclaimed by the Church as an essential of their Faith.

In truth, warnings against war are heard on all sides, and its irreparable disasters are vividly portrayed. But too many politicians and statesmen and the majority of soldiers of high rank believe it to be inevitable. This separation of the pacifist from the military mind resembles that of the Hellenistic States, which for centuries squandered their manhood and their treasure in civil strife. Rejecting the counsel of a few enlightened patriots who foresaw the fatal consequences of the policy, they renewed their quarrels, and within seventy years from the time the remonstrance was made, all these States had succumbed to the sword of Rome. A similar fanatical devotion to war at the risk of national and international well-being is rampant in certain groups of our own time. Their contention is that forcible self-assertion is the one needful, concrete, victorious quality. War is life, and when the will to fight ceases, life ceases. Concord through justice is an iridescent dream. Right and the freedom that right bestows are well enough for the individual, but they are only beguiling fancies so far as intercourse of States is concerned. Unrepentant nationalism comes into the picture before us, and protests against even elementary measures required for the world's peace. These opinions imply the denial of an intelligible moral purpose in history. Those who hold them maintain that since every form of civilisation is of brief duration, armed violence in the struggle for survival is the sole possible alternative. The very dead are invoked in behalf of the bomb and the bayonet which dismissed them out of life. Friends and foes who now rest together on the battlefields of Europe and Asia, and in the depths of the sea, could they speak, would bid all peoples seek peace and pursue it. But the departed are exploited by responsible officials of the State and by its citizens who still believe in retributive emotion, and in the efficaciousness of brute force. The monstrous iniquity which robbed them of their youth is placed beneath the sanction of millions of the slain who cannot disown it from their graves. It is not surprising that some writers detect, as they believe, the evidences of ultimate decline in the white race. The sophistication of human life, the abandonment of its real values, its appetite for carnal things, the credulity of its cults, the complexes injected into it by the irreconcilable elements of cities and of hostile States are enumerated at length to prove that modern civilization is slipping toward the gulf.

These aspects of human life admittedly give point to the pessimist's plea. Notwithstanding the better self of nations, they seem to be dedicated to flagrant evils. His complaint is upheld by the lack of leadership in nearly every realm, and by the resultant babel of advices which frequently expresses the shattered state of the contemporary mind. Ideas that devour one another fly abroad as swiftly as swallows, and in as many directions. The voice of Despair challenges the voice of Faith. It tells us that none is wise or brave enough to analyze and remove the ills that vex the world. Many philosophers, psychologists, biologists, moralists, journalists, and occasionally, clergymen, make common cause with radical skepticism about the impossibility of future good. Science, which has done marvellous things, is left comfortless in their midst because of its materialistic conclusions. It traces man from his genesis in organized matter only to leave him stranded in a universe which is slowing down. In all life there is no valid refutation of death; infinite, silent, lifeless space is its final goal. Man is on a blind bypath ending in pitiful and brief delirium, in dust and then — nothingness. The speculation vouches for Schopenhauer's description of life as a "uselessly interrupting episode in the blissful repose of nothing." We are told to set our house in order by denying all forms of existence other than those guaranteed by physics and chemistry. Palpable material characteristics and qualities are preferable to any of the imaginary existences vaguely defined as spiritual. Ghosts, gods, souls and the religions that cluster around them are outcasts among advanced thinkers. The intelligent creature who has delved into these mysteries of the physical universe is himself no more than a cunning combination of protein molecules. Speculative analysts whose books are widely read, deal with the incalculable expenditures of cosmic energy extending through aeons, the duration of which was but momentary when measured by the chronometers of the creative process. They insist that the outcome will be chaos; that the comparatively insignificant solar system in which our planet is a minor star has already banked its fires for the approaching night. The reasoning mind that interprets the cosmos is only love's labor lost. Pen and ink Napoleons of this species of scientific materialism and philosophic pessimism gravely inform us that the progress man has made is a lure, like that of the carrot hung in front of the ass to coax him along. Thus do the apostles of annihilation preside at the obsequies of our dearest hopes and swell the chorus of despair.

This extinction of the higher forms of existence leaves its lower forms in possession of the field. What further systems and worlds, forms of life and intelligence, may be evolved by the ceaseless revolutions of matter and energy are entirely conjectural. It is sufficient to know that destruction is the sure assignment of those that we observe. Not all scientists and thinkers, however, demand so abject a surrender of reason and morality. A large and influential school concedes that the ideas of God, righteousness and immortality must be retained. The conceptions of physical knowledge are not comparable, it is said, with those that postulate the supremacy of spiritual realities. And although there can be no scientific basis for religion, and faith must always remain the sole source of religious development, it is not to be treated lightly, nor cast aside. Science tolerates it as not necessarily incompatible with the knowledge derived from logical deductions that deal with facts originating in sense perceptions. Perhaps we should be thankful for the mercy which relegates religion to a realm equal with that of scientific research. Small as such mercy is, it measurably neutralizes the insolence of the materialistic theories that have been mentioned.[1]

A different kind of pessimism is purveyed by publicists and authors who before 1914 assumed that the march to Paradise had well begun. Since the march into Belgium they are sure of nothing save the arrest of a progress they once described as automatic. The printing press pours out volumes of a more or less biological complexion, which maintain that whatever becomes of his physical being, man's moral decay has set in. As humanity increases in quantity, it proportionately decreases in quality. Works upon racial decadence are seriously

[1] Cf. for a more extended view of this issue, Sir Henry Jones: "A Faith that Enquires," especially Lecture VI upon "Scientific Hypothesis and Religious Faith."

received. The cave man and the crowd man loom up in the apprehension of readers who know little about biology except these dismal lucubrations. Economic disaster naturally follows upon the heels of social disintegration. Political problems, we are assured, have outstripped statesmen who are not less capable than were their predecessors. But the obstacles to efficient administration exceed all previous dimensions, and few precedents are obtainable for their removal. Moralists depict the oncoming orgy of animalism to which some fiction and drama cater. Premillenarians believe the present order is anathema to God, and can only be cured of its diseases by His miraculous intervention. Highly colored prophecies of the approaching end of the age play a prominent part in the religious rituals of despair. It haunts Church and State, its statements are cleverly concocted, its inferences sound plausible even though their note is stormy. Ears that are deaf to the New Testament Hope or heedful of insensate force are captured by its doctrine.

Learned men who do not accept its teachings often rely upon the laboratory rather than the soul of man for his rejuvenation. They assume a self-assertive concrete universe for which secularism is the living air; from which the spiritual elements of life are excluded as an insoluble enigma. Prevalent moral formulas, says an American professor of philosophy, are based upon the adolescent thinking in which romanticism predominates. But the time is at hand, he informs us, when individuals who have to make ethical decisions will desert priests, ministers and melodramatic religious revivals for scientists who can give them directions about conduct derived from ascertained realities, and not from imagination. Theological dogmas may for the moment reduce the strife between flesh and spirit, and render first aid to a much bedevilled world. But ultimately they are productive of childish experiments which benumb brain and conscience. So this self-appointed successor to Plato and to nearly all moral philosophers since Plato, pronounces the

Christian solution of the human problem ineffective and negligible. A second category of similar opinions resorts to chemical affinity for its solution, and regards the human mind as no more than instrumental in the biological adjustments which that affinity effects. This assumption is vehemently assailed by more responsible scientific scholars as altogether unwarranted. But the majority of the school before us is convinced that the powers of eager upward living are not directly due to Deity, but to the germ plasm. Their hopes are fixed upon the further release and use of atomic energy, which, they assert, is at least coördinate in rank with ethical and religious beliefs.

What are the values of the Church, of the Bible, or of the annals of both, from the account of creation in Genesis to the present hour, as compared with those attending scientific discoveries? The query confounds natural with moral phenomena, and falls into abeyance because of the concession accompanying it that men must be morally meritorious to benefit by science. If they refuse to safeguard its terrific forces by their good behavior these forces will surely turn again and rend them. The concession need not be labored; it is as a flood of light in a dark and dangerous cavern. The one continuous Ecclesia in Judaism and in Christianity was instituted by God, and the Bible written by her prophets and apostles under His inspiration, to instill the moral meritoriousness which scientists themselves desiderate. They ask for it because they cannot produce it, and also because they realize that their best work is condemned to ignominious uses without it. Academic chatter about man's achievement of amity within the domains of scientific knowledge is a mere beating of the air. Laughter often unifies society better than logic, and love regnant in its heart will go beyond the most erudite mind to solidify and elevate the race. Faith is still the greatest foe of human ills. The germ-plasm has its mission, but it cannot transfer man from the perishable to the imperishable.

This pessimistic onslaught, animated as it is by materialistic ideas, does not appear to advantage in the present crisis. It wills the actual and achieves the fantastic. Those who direct it are frequently prisoners of their own culture and can scarcely conceive of any other. They display the fastidious narrowness which often characterizes the so-called liberal mind. Ever and anon one is reminded by their violent egocentricity that few persons are so completely at the mercy of their own vanity as those who enjoy a limited reputation. They freeze the enthusiasm of youth, undermine the spirituality of maturity, and turn candor to cynicism. The ironic complacency they manifest toward the Church and her Gospel is ludicrous in view of the fact that the masses, young or old, who seem indifferent to her overseership also reject the particular education advocated by her unfriendly critics. The choice with the average person is not between religion and learning; still less is it between the Pentateuch and Darwin. It is between God and unsafe pleasures or illicit gains; between art, science, philosophy, and the pugilistic ring or the film pictures. If there is today little popular inclination toward the Church, there is still less toward the Academy.

II

Let us take the flesh and leave the bones of the controversy. It is as old as Christianity itself, and drew down upon the classic period of culture the Apostle's dictum that the world by wisdom knew not God. If, as Professor Bliss Perry says, no man can understand America with his brain, how can he with the same instrument understand the Deity? One is driven to believe that the other-worldliness which George Eliot chastised would be a welcome relief from the this-worldliness that is too much with us night and day. Events outpace thoughts, thinkers agitate themselves to no purpose; we have heard enough from scientists of a sort; mankind is not disposed to march to their music indefinitely.

After all, the physical universe recedes and disappears. Its philosophies move in a cycle; the spiritual interpretations of life crowd into the places those philosophies vacate. It is our duty as Christian teachers to center real knowledge and real progress in the sense of God and Immortality, for want of which even Greek wisdom came to grief. The duty is best discharged by ministers who realize the impermanence of the visible fabric, and the futility of resting all human hope and fear upon it. The smallness of the earth, a mere pin-prick of light and heat within the barriers of immeasurable space, reminds us that only as we discern in its fleeting shadows the spiritual factors of the Eternal Will are we qualified for the ministerial office. The preachers and theologians of yesterday who insisted that mortals were but strangers and pilgrims here below, were nearer the truth than modernists who associate their fate with the fluctuations of physical environment. The question of questions, as Dean Inge assures us, is not the betterment of this present world, but whether the race that inhabits it is vitally united to the unchanging love and holiness of its Creator.[2] The outward man and all around him dies; the inward man is renewed daily. Our supreme, solemn confession should be that of the Psalmist: "Before the mountains were brought forth, or ever Thou hadst formed the earth and the world, even from everlasting to everlasting, Thou art God." [3] So long as the believing mind finds the law and the goal of being in Him Whose loving-kindness is better than life, man's environment is subjected to that law. In that mind the die is cast, the goal is discernible.

Hedonistic theories are set up against the melancholy idea that life is the exorbitant price to be paid for death's release. They construct Utopias in which godlike creatures wander free of all restraints and inhibitions. Education renders political government superfluous; religion is supplanted by hereditary law, qualified by vigorous birth-control. To be

[2] "Outspoken Essays": Second series, p. 54, ff.
[3] Psalm XC. 2.

Big thing — perfection of human nature in its physical not its spiritual — old truth presented in modern lang.

sure, we should encourage education, sex hygiene, model dwellings, suburban retreats, and whatever else contributes to man's physical well-being. One lingers fondly over Mr. Wells' vivid descriptions which forecast what good may be in the future. Long distance audition, wireless telegraphy, the release of radium, mansions for all, slumless cities and light work that charms the worker are sumptuous if empirical framings for the oncoming race. But will its members be blessed or cursed by these manifold inventions? Will its obstinate questionings of sense and outward things be obliterated? The reply depends upon human nature itself, and whether it will be ruled by reasons which essentially are no reasons. For it is a true story, of which many are heedless, that riches or poverty, success or failure, greatness or obscurity, are really small and unimportant things in the presence of a man's soul. As he thinks there, so he is, whatever be his outward state. Probably Mr. Wells would now admit that an Arcadia from which poverty and distress were banished, in which bodily health and prosperity were enthroned, must be the by-products of man's moral and spiritual development. Even at that, it would not become the pledge of his highest good, nor furnish the things his soul's growth requires. While the view prevails that the world is crass matter without any influx of spirit, he will have to encounter those periodical convulsions which no earthly paradise can avert.

> "Just when we are safest, there's a sunset touch,
> A fancy from a flower-bell, someone's death.
> A chorus-ending from Euripides,—
> And that's enough for fifty hopes and fears
> As old and new at once as nature's self,
> To rap and knock and enter in our soul,
> Take hands and dance there, a fantastic ring,
> Round the ancient idol, on his base again,—
> The grand Perhaps! We look on helplessly.
> There the old misgivings, crooked questions are" [4]

[4] Robert Browning: "Bishop Blougram's Apology."

Notwithstanding Mr. Arnold Bennett's assertion that real life consists in the "full smooth-running exploitation of the whole machine" to the daily satisfaction of the mechanic, its noblest estimates and deeds have been nurtured by a monotonous discipline repulsive to these tamer days. Profound experiences of pain and labor have delivered men and women from moral death, revealed their real character, won them a reverence which no mere "smooth-running exploitation" of life has gained. Sacrifice is always a great and moving spectacle. The entire Western world was made possible by its supreme exemplification. The sterile fallacies of the pleasure seekers, or of those experts in conciliation who evade resistance until they lose their force, will not stabilize the individual or society. Emma Calvé speaks for many of the elect when she tells of the sorrow in whose sunless depths her song was reborn. The toil and the grief that upset easy circumstances also release unsuspected reserves of fortitude and courage. Even if life's problems are insoluble, and some are, it is possible for the initiated who have endured hardness to get clear comprehensive views of it as a whole, to see society, not as a finished product, but as a spiritual fabric, always growing, never complete. Many of the constituents that form it are either non-existent or not yet existent. Those who would rebuild it must reflect that its factors are elusive as the air, "unfathomable in their motive forces, exhaustless in their range, and incalculable in their results." [5] Gibbon's observation should be remembered that few individuals, however talented, "are capable of discovering the nice and secret springs of action which impel in the same uniform direction the passions of the multitude." But we may be sure that the voice of one crying in the wilderness that the Kingdom of God is within men, is more trustworthy than the thousands of siren voices which assure us that one man is as good as another, even when he is good for nothing. In the spiritual organization, therefore, which society really is, the

[5] " Cf. " The Times Literary Supplement," London, May 24, 1923, p. 437.

spiritual man is the chief determinant. Emphasize as much as you please the necessity for humane and efficient social appliances, but emphasize even more the moral resistance within men and women, which must be superior to every outward pressure. Otherwise, though those appliances encompassed mankind, it would be devitalized in their embrace.

The bearing of these issues upon the general situation has been clarified by some first rate minds in various realms. Their response to the true and guiding voice of Faith is free from the moroseness that so often accompanies the response to the voice of Fear. Undismayed by the rapid intellectual advances or the moral disasters of our age, they perceive that its accredited adventures favor a religion which is reasonable as well as mystical in character. They refuse to allow their efforts for the betterment of society in Church or State to be hampered by those who simulate honesty of thinking only to strangle it if it contradicts their peculiar ideas. We should not hastily infer that these hopeful spirits are, as yet, a predominant group. On the contrary, the pessimist who sees too much and believes too little is not abashed by those who feel that they have an ancient charge to keep in a new fashion. The pulse that bounds in them is flabby in him. He possesses no satisfactory hypothesis of human nature, and the lack of it explains his impatience with its will to live, to believe, to act beneath the guidance of that common sense which is the distilled wisdom of the race. There is no place in his system for the transcendent human movements that are frequently traceable to divine intervention in troubled days. He looks upon his fellow men as Daudet looked upon Renan's brain, which he said resembled a cathedral used to house hay and cattle. It retained its sacred architecture but submitted it to ignoble ends. The pessimist fails to perceive that few persons are fools from all points of the compass. The prevalent egotism which is idolatry's lowest form, and from which he is not always exempt, disturbs him. He not only regards the age as wrecked and leaderless but as separated from all past ages, and enshrouded in portentous mystery.

So wise an observer as Mr. Benjamin Kidd believes that we are witnessing the first phase of a transition, the eclipse of which rests upon every land. It cannot be ascribed, in his opinion, to the open or clandestine guilt of any single State, nor can it be given a fixed duration. It is a genesis in itself, with an infinite progression ahead. No reasoned knowledge of East or West has even the methods of thinking required for its explanation. The colossal outlines of so weird a speculation remind one of the oppressive sculptures of Oriental temples. It has their unrelated expressionless cast of immobility and remoteness. Its rhetorical description of the present age as "the strangest flower that ever grew in the fields of Time" is suggestive, but nothing more.[6] These misgivings are rife among literary leaders and churchmen. Those who in the repercussion of the late war consign the race to perdition are given to proposals which would be logical there. Those who for the same cause speak of it in terms befitting heaven seem oblivious to the fact that its life has to be lived out on earth, where "Truth is the daughter of slow Time," and few things are more deliberate than real progress. Their sensational outlook warns us that experimental treatment is the key to every period. Not the results of any definite experiences in any age, but the sum total of all experiences, past and present, historic and personal, is the controlling factor of the human story.[7] When authors or preachers forsake the experimental for the sensational interpretation of life, they are certain to indulge hectic ideas and fabulous predictions concerning it. Yet what are their qualms and fears, their ill founded anticipations and hopes, but registrations of the larger life, the lifting horizons, ever on before, to which they have not been accustomed?

[6] Benjamin Kidd: " The Science of Power," p. 3. ff.
[7] Cf. J. B. Bury: " The Idea of Progress," p. 5.

Layers of Civilization and debt to previous ages –

The majority of men and women who plod along prosaic ways may not be aware of the steady accumulations of heredity and of history which create life's changing scenes. But they are keenly aware of their relation to the past. The stultifying idea that they are cut off from it is instinctively set aside. Previous civilizations did not exist for our sole benefit, nor did their economies die in giving birth to ours. The debris of former generations is not so much "filling in" of the gulf over which our generation proceeds to its foreordained supremacy. The cocksureness of these conceits flatters our pride and vanity, but a moment's reflection condemns them. It is an open question whether ancient Greece or Judæa does not now exercise a far more pregnant influence upon the world than any modern State. The true distinction of our age is that it forms a single layer in Time's strata, and few conceptions are more misleading than those which attribute to it excessive importance either for good or evil. But to conceive of it as a part of the whole of that human history which from first to last has been an indivisible unity, is to liberate beneficial social and political ideals. There is one law, one life, one element, one destiny; and the seemingly static differences that contradict this oneness are slowly giving way. What the forbears were, the children are; they stand and fall together. If the brotherhood of the race is honorable, so are we; if we are dishonorable, so is it; if other nations squander the soul's heritage we are the poorer; if we enrich it, they are the richer. They live in us as we live in them; there is no life divided in the succession of its eddying forms. One flesh, one blood, one story, one strife, one defeat, one victory—this is the underlying secret of the human drama. Scan it where you will, there shine the righteous to cheer our darkness, there cower the profligate to dim our prospects.[8]

[8] Cf. "Henry Scott Holland. Memoirs and Letters." Edited by Stephen Paget, p. III.

An era of materialism

III

At the same time none must forget that neither praise nor blame, human good nor human evil, closes man's case with his Maker. "Not mine own fears, nor the prophetic Soul of the wide world, dreaming on things to come" determines its fate. A divine justice and a divine love which burn ere they transform have to be reckoned in the process. In man himself there is a residual greatness which is not too familiar to a materialized era. The sidereal universe is apparently unique in its grandeur and sublimity. Yet how ephemeral it becomes when compared with the astronomer who watches it. Likewise the thinker who, as Pascal did in his last years, looks into the perfect law of liberty and continues therein, shows us the duality of human life and human nature. "Man is a reed, but he is a thinking reed, and all his dignity lies in his consciousness." The eternal silent spaces, the absurdities of life, the brutality of death cannot quench that consciousness. The happiness he pursues is evanescent as the dew; the lower levels he frequents have no rational terminus. Even an Asiatic nomad knows full well what he wants, and is glad to get it. But once he has tasted of the powers of the world to come he will start the prayer wheels on which a million petitions revolve daily to satisfy the longings of his heart for freedom and for rest. These realities have no relation to the contemptible brochures on success that deal with getting and spending. They belong to the soul which, once "secure in herself," said Addison's Cato, "smiles at the drawn dagger."

The homeless Pilgrim, tossing upon the North Atlantic in a rude and ill found ship, is doubtless a far less congenial spectacle for lovers of luxury than Cleopatra in her gorgeous barge floating on the unruffled Nile like a burnished throne. But the humble Pilgrim came out of great tribulation to be the builder and maker of Commonwealths, whereas the haughty Queen glided on to self-murder and the destruction of a vast empire. The fascination of sensuous delights does not deceive God-seeking spirits. The Pilgrim temperament is averse to the hole and corner existence of the prosperous, the well-fed, the bovine. It does not too readily accept those vulgar social estimates that are often repeated but seldom weighed. It understands that prosperity, lightened of scruples, kills far more virtue than deserving poverty on a daring quest; that the abundance of this world's goods is still a vexation, since life does not consist therein. It prefers the music of existence played in major chords, with the overtones of victorious suffering enveloping it. Its delight is in the steep rugged ascent. It believes that to breast the heights heroically makes the heroical man. The voice that summoned Abraham from plenteousness to pilgrimage has resounded in courageous hearts at various but appointed seasons. It was heard centuries later on the Babylonian plains; and centuries later still, in the hill country of Judæa and Galilee. It should be heard by those of our generation who know many things, but understand few things with the wisdom which is insight.

It is the voice of Faith, whose resonance drowns the discordance of the voice of Fear, the lamentations of which are now all too prevalent. It bids us hope and see our hope frustrated, then hope again. Listen to its trumpet note in the opening words of the original Gospel attributed to St. Mark. The author quotes the unknown seer of Israel's exile:

> "Behold, I send my messenger before thy face,
> Who shall prepare thy way;
> The voice of one crying in the wilderness,
> Make ye ready the way of the Lord,
> Make his paths straight." [9]

This prophet viewed all preceding ages as a prolonged preparation for God's approaching entrance into history. The Evangelist applied his rhapsody to the revelation of God in

[9] St. Mark I. 2, 3.

Jesus Christ. The exposition of Christ's mediatorial sovereignty does not belong here. But what does belong here is the fact that countless multitudes have never known what life was until they knew it in His life. The too long delayed enforcement of His ideals also belongs everywhere: of truth as opposed to falsehood, of freedom as opposed to tyranny, of peace as opposed to war. These are the hall marks of the Faith which He ordained; the revelations of the God and Father who ordained Him. It is men's degraded conceptions of that Father's nature and purposes which have inflicted its more deplorable evils upon society. And the question is opportune, why the luminous spiritual experiences that attended the creation of the Church and inspired the writings of Holy Writ should not make a fresh contact with the present stage of civilization.

Students of the past who compare it with the present are aware of the Providence which has been "the great corrector of enormous times"; "the shaker of o'er rank States"; often using very unlikely agencies to advance causes that seemed weak beyond words. We have already noted that the visible fabric vanishes, which is an implication that the invisible realm remains. The spirit in man subsists with marvellous capacity for adaptation, while all else takes its determinate leap and disappears. The wider range of his intellectual faculties has resulted in a lopsided knowledge which reports that during the last one hundred and fifty years the human race has literally been rediscovered. Its numbers have grown to one thousand six hundred and fifty millions of people now living on the globe, whose diversities in color, language, social habits and religion create the differences from which most international differences spring. Twenty-five languages are spoken in Europe; forty-five in Asia; and the remaining sixty which swell the total to one hundred and thirty are spoken in America, Africa, and the Islands. The present number of independent States is about sixty-five; of which twenty-seven are in Europe, eighteen in Asia, twelve in South

America, and eight in North America. These statistics bring out the extraordinary human complexity of the modern world and the necessity for an ordered observation of its requirements. The complexity is furthered by the advance of modern learning, some of the ill effects of which have been noted. It has grown ten times as fast as in the period between Cæsar and Napoleon, and one thousand times as fast as in pre-historic days. Upon the authority of Professor Karl Pearson, the product of this tremendous activity is in many instances worthless. The age in which we live has been a series of dissolving views, in which recent economic and material gains were half obliterated by their swift succession. In the physical sciences alone radioactivity has shown us what unsuspected energies are bound up in the minutest particles of matter. But in organic chemistry a single worker may at any moment stumble upon a substance at the verge of related compounds, that will be infinitely more potent for good or harm than any now in operation. The atoms thus chemically treated are arsenals in disguise.

Under these novel conditions races and nations recently far apart have been jammed together without previous preparation. The pace is killing; it strains to their utmost tension every educational and religious machinery; the forms of yesterday are the relics of today.[10] Yet I cannot but believe that these wonders have brought us to the threshold of a renewed intimacy with their Creator; and one which is absolutely necessary to their right use and direction. The French savant, Madame Bisson, is convinced that if human intercourse and knowledge are to proceed to advantage, they will have to cultivate the spiritual side of life. She insists that further deference to the materialized metaphysic already mentioned will be inimical to the general welfare, and the French Academy has given her protest respectful attention. In other words, she solicits for France and for mankind

[10] Cf. G. M. Trevelyan: "British History in the Nineteenth Century," p. 13, ff.

the voice of Faith which proclaims an Ideal Order behind all history, and an All Holy Being whose nature necessitates that Order. Whatever may be said about her protest, it can hardly be questioned that the vilest modern evils have arisen, not from ignorance, but from knowledge wrongly interpreted and fearfully misapplied. Whoever doubts the need of one visible universal Society in the Church, or the moralization of the Ideal of the State, few, I think, will doubt the benefit of that deeper and invisible unity which finds its outlet in a common love of the living God, and of His sensible creation.

These conclusions are reached by what J. B. Mozley termed reason working on a higher plane. Nevertheless, they have substantial grounds on lower planes. The monarchy of public opinion is always difficult to deal with, because it cannot be called into the open. Its rivulets for the last half century have flowed into devastating currents, while the men and women who prided themselves on keeping in touch with it have been unaware of its real drifts. Seemingly great things have been observed; seemingly small things have escaped observation. What was viewed as important fizzled out, while so small a matter as a pistol shot blew up half the world. A civilization thus exposed condemns itself, and justifies insistence upon its regeneration. These conclusions also bespeak courage. They prevent in men the mixed determination for betterment which is afraid of ridicule; the vanity which will not endanger a rebuff; the faint-heartedness due to a sullen pride that must be sure of its ends before it will risk its means. True courage challenges that patronage of religion which is the armor of half-witted spirits who cannot read the signs of the times. It abolishes the dread of life, which visualises its terrors ahead and ready to pounce, or even suspects that its Author may turn out malignant. Such courage means more than one can tell in a world of cross purposes, where so many people find their resolution to do well in the well-doing of the few. It is "valor without vengeance," as Dr. A. J. Lyman happily expressed it; apart from which no goodness is altogether secure, no wickedness is seriously threatened. Yet courage cannot be entrusted with the values of civilization unless it is united with patience, fidelity, and the spiritual vision which knows those values when it sees them.

The belief that the man who heeds the Divine Voice, and forsakes all else to follow the right as he sees it will be backed up by God, is of immense service to morals and to faith. His course may appear imprudent or even fanatical, but its wisdom has been repeatedly demonstrated by a historic religious experience which is far more vital than the formulas in which it has been expressed.[11] Deeper than the fear of penalty, higher than the hope of reward, stronger than any motive in life, is the assured confidence that the Moral Sovereign of the universe sustains every just and righteous cause.

IV

The courageous servant of God will not make his intellect the slave of his heart, nor blink disagreeable realities at the biddance of his emotions. But he will remember that instinct often outvies knowledge; that love is the height of good, the hate of ill; and that peace and progress come, not by unaided reason alone, but also as the outflowings of a brave, believing spirit. Principal L. P. Jacks pertinently states one feature of this discussion. "On the surface of things there is discord, confusion and want of adaptation; but dig down, first to the center of the world, and then to the center of your own nature, and you will find a most wonderful correspondence, a most beautiful harmony, between the two — the world made for the hero and the hero made for the world."[12] This statement elicits sympathy even from the

[11] Cf. A. Seth Pringle-Pattison: "The Idea of God in the Light of Recent Philosophy," p. 87.

[12] L. P. Jacks: "Religious Perplexities," p. 61.

arrant coward. It is idle to suggest that he relishes cowardice, or its accessories — fear and unbelief. He and the rest of men are on the side of the spiritual hero. Society favors the angels. Controversies about nebular or materialistic hypotheses leave it cold. It looks upon naturalistic theories of the universe, if it knows them at all, as irrational attempts to explain it. The younger social groups are keenly aware of the new world which is being evolved out of its disorders. The older groups desire a bond of religion and morals that shall be sufficiently strong to anchor their drifting lives. Spiritual problems, always formidable, are encircled by the craving of old and young for an energizing faith which enshrines courage, justice and right living as the integrating forces of society. Everywhere, so far as I can ascertain, love is esteemed the light of human existence: love of goodness, of reality, of progress, of one's fellows, and above all, of one's Maker. It is generally recognized that the New Testament Gospel exalts such love, and regards humanity as the field fertilized by God for its regenerating seed. Men ask for it in manifold ways, not the less religious because of their variety. And we have it, not primarily as a philosophy, a theology, an institutional method, a law; but incarnated in a living Person with whom all souls can commune.

Christian truth is summed up in Christ's Person; Christian character in His example; Christian morality in His teaching. Obedience to Him recreates human nature. The rebellious, the desperate, even the inhuman, as well as those who do a little conventional good with their superfluous means, and live apparently blameless but unoccupied lives, have been transformed by fellowship with Him. Not belief, therefore, in a metaphysical Absolute, nor in a Deity to be sought and found by reason alone; but belief in the God who was in Christ reconciling the world unto Himself, is the dynamic of all Christian creeds and of all Christian Churches. He is made known to them as the "God who lives in the perpetual giving of Himself, who shares the life of His finite creatures, bearing with and in them the whole burden of their finitude, their sinful wanderings and sorrows, and the suffering without which they cannot be made perfect. . . . And thus, for a metaphysic which has emancipated itself from physical categories, the ultimate conception of God is not that of a preëxistent Creator, but, as it is for religion, that of the Eternal Redeemer of the world. This perpetual process is the very life of God, in which, besides the effort and the pain, He tastes, we must believe, the joy of victory won." [13] Whatever He may be as the Absolute, "existing in solitary bliss and perfection," the God of the Christian revelation is the Father of all spirits, Who manifests Himself in His Son to their varied stages of imperfection. He is, in the words of Earl Balfour, "A God Whom men can love, a God to Whom men can pray, Who takes sides, Who has purposes and preferences, Whose attributes, howsoever conceived, leave unimpaired the possibility of a personal relation between Himself and those Whom He has created." [14]

Hebrews, Catholics and Protestants who in the joint discharge of common duties, have at last found it possible to live together without regarding each other as natural enemies, can approach the problems of our age in the light of their personal relation with the universal Father. "They have been obliged to recognize that truth, honour, purity, justice, manliness, are neither the growth nor the privilege of a belief in special formulas; that men can disagree in religion without wishing to destroy each other." [15] The difficulties to which Industrialism (which involves Capitalism), Militarism, and Secularism give rise are shared by right-minded citizens of every creed, or of no creed in particular. Industrialism has been hampered by grave economic deficiencies which left a degraded sediment at the bottom of society. For centuries antiquated and corrupt methods of

[13] A. Seth Pringle-Pattison: "The Idea of God in the Light of Recent Philosophy," p. 411 f.

[14] "Theism and Humanism," p. 36.

[15] James Anthony Froude: "The Council of Trent," p. 294.

government prevented remedial legislation in behalf of manual toilers. Their countless hosts seem to have been outside the pale of social justice; to have had no connection with real citizenship. Ministers of State as wise as Pitt, Burke and Fox in Britain, practically ignored the economic revolution that began in their day. Casual references to it made by ardent sympathizers with political freedom were usually inspired by fear of the submerged masses. Of American Constitutionalists, only Hamilton, who had read to good purpose "The Wealth of Nations," foresaw the possibilities of an industrial uprising; but his masterly "Report on Manufactures" passed unheeded here. Later statesmen of intellectual brilliancy, of lucid understanding which permitted of no self-deception, and a political creed that stressed the fundamental equality of all citizens, did nothing more than improvise economic measures to stave off the day of reckoning. Those who now have to meet its demands apprehend the need of a social justice, the prolonged delay of which adds to the menace of its issues. Nor is it surprising that some propositions have been made for its attainment which are as impossible as the redistribution of the solar system. Endeavors to achieve the sudden transformation of a neglected industrial system by the utterance of second-hand platitudes have resulted in further disappointment. Reason and right are not permanently changed, however, by times of social yeast and fermentation; and these are sometimes useful to stir up the stagnant thinking of those by whom enthusiasm for social equity is seldom well received.

The laws of commerce no ruler and no system can break. They are despotic, changeless, as old as the act of barter between man and man. The economic circle describes its course through indifference and agitation, after which the world again returns to its own. Meanwhile there cannot be too many staunch advocates of the good will and fair play which are as requisite for industrialism as sunlight for the sprouting seed. The opposing tendencies of capital and labor are balanced by justice, not by almsgiving, which creates some of the miseries it relieves, but by no means relieves all the pauperization it creates. Yet the fury of their debate might be checked if both sides would practice amity and moderation. As it is, they often remind one of a caustic criticism of Landseer that he painted his men to look like dogs, and his dogs to look like men. The assumptions that capitalists are bloated "spiders of hell," and that workers are infamous conspirators against the public welfare, are almost criminal when injected in a highly inflamed quarrel. Why should these contestants become impersonal and non-moral under provocation, or act as though they were no longer human beings but symbols of their respective factions? Yet it is very probable that the majority are committed to what they deem equitable. And the more one knows of employers and employees as a body, the more one admires their social constancy. They carry on the gigantic and necessary tasks of nations and of the world, and since the last war, they have done additional wonders for reconstruction in many lands.

The maturer treatment of industrial problems will be found in a kindlier spirit, in give and take, in experiments not always insured against reversal. They will not be solved by men who deem themselves invariably right, and take their stand upon a fictitious rectitude, any more than by men who defend wrong positions with transparent casuistry. Ownership is not an unforgivable sin; profitable trading which serves the community does not necessarily brutalize society any more than suitable work degrades the worker. Commercial exchange, and the right to produce or to sell what is produced are inseparable from the health of a community.

One of the obstacles to the growth of social compunction and justice is the intrinsic caution of human nature. Men themselves are the intractable element in reform. They dislike change, and require something more than heated or even verifiable impeachments before they can be induced to act against the existing order. The late war set aside, for the time being, their innate conservatism. It increased the self-respect of the laboring classes, and gave their claims a place and presentation they had not known before 1914. Fences were broken down, industrial groups were fused, social ideals and methods were synthesized. Whatever may be the ultimate economic forms adopted by civilized States, many of them will date, in my judgment, from the first quarter of this century. One could predict their speedier settlement if the artisan were not so often estranged from his task, and the employer from his responsibilities. The age of industrial innocence, when the workman put his personality into his work, and insisted that it should excel all similar work, has given place to an age of mechanism, which often dehumanizes him.

The deliberate underestimation of capitalism has been offset by the failure of Marxian Socialism, which is now being rejected by many of its former intellectual adherents. The reaction is not confined to Marxian Socialism. The most severe censors of Socialism in general are disillusioned people who lately professed it. But though capitalism will not be abolished until some sufficient substitute has been provided, the defense of some of its worst practices should cease. The stand made against the twelve hour day by Bishop Francis J. McConnell and his associates of all the Churches, was a direct and irrefragable appeal to the public conscience which did succeed beyond a peradventure. The idea of wealth as mere wealth, and the fear of what it may do, no longer weigh unduly with enlightened leaders of the Church. Capital and labor should be recognized as copartners, not competitors. The wage-earner's proportion of the profits should be paid to him, and he should also be willing to bear his share of the losses. Agriculture requires a land-owning as well as a land-tilling yeomanry. The peasant classes in democratic nations should be merged into propertied classes and given an interest in the State. A home-owning proletariat through a more equitable distribution of industrial proceeds would be a strong and lasting fortress for society's general protection. These changes are either imminent or in process. The social order we know is as certain to disappear as mediæval feudalism or seventeenth century monarchism. But it would be a lasting reflection upon Church and State if its disappearance should be attended by the violence which retards everything for which men greatly hope.[16]

The laborer, skilled or unskilled, is the living material out of which a better social organism will have to be built. States, therefore, will have to provide for contingencies ahead, and widen their intelligence, their sympathies, and their policies to include those contingencies. It is also one of the responsibilities of capital to make labor attractive, to upraise and dignify its duties so that they shall not appear forbidding, and to do this with a regard for what is right, but without a suggestion of the detested odors of patronage or compulsion. The value of the humblest toiler as an honorable servant of the common weal has not been adequately signalized by society at large. His deferred promotion in public esteem to at least as high a level as that given to the man-at-arms cannot be brought about too soon for the sanity of social relationships. Nor should it be forgotten that in these discussions the last word belongs to the voice of humanity, and not of legislation.[17]

V

Aggressive war is universally conceded to be the worst diabolism that terrifies mankind. Its outrages and monstrosities exceed nearly all others combined. Its latest outbreak verified Milton's line:

> "Who overcomes by force hath overcome but half his foe."

[16] The program for Social Justice of the Federal Council of the Churches of Christ in America clearly states the essentials of that justice. It should be read by Christian ministers and laymen.

[17] Cf. "The Church and Industrial Reconstruction," by The Committee on the War and the Religious Outlook; "The Return of Christendom," by A Group of Churchmen, with an introduction by Bishop Gore; "The Christian in Social Relationships," by Dorr F. Diefendorf; "A More Christian Industrial Order," by Henry Sloane Coffin; "Citizenship and Moral Reform," by John W. Langdale.

It degraded the combatants who fought for a conspiracy against civilization, and it did not ennoble all who fought against that conspiracy. Human relationships were dissolved; friend and foe were hedged about on their better side by its ferocious abominations. Its irreparable material and spiritual injuries became manifest once the furious exaltation of battle was exhausted. Commercial derangement, financial chaos, political confusion and moral anarchy followed as its aftermath. Many millions of lives and nearly two hundred billion dollars' worth of material were flung into its maw within four years. Yet notwithstanding these unprecedented losses of soul and substance, recovery from them has scarcely set in before other wars and their more deadly engines are projected. The sword which has already stabbed the world with many wounds that have not healed still darts and gleams through persistent mists of hate. But why repeat these warnings and denunciations? Because men cannot easily be indoctrinated with a sufficient hatred of war. It is a parasitical pursuit, yet it absorbs all other pursuits. It is an avoidable wickedness, yet it obtains in all lands, on all seas, and in the skies above. Its futility as an arbitrative method is notorious, yet preparations for it persist. Nothing is exempt from its service which human ingenuity can devise. It is likely to continue until nations renounce the belief that other nations are to be regarded as either amicable or hostile. Amicability or hostility are not the last words of an international philosophy. Racial interests cannot forever endure the impositions they express. Many ask why wars are waged either for friends or against foes; why they should survive the far nobler imperatives of civilized beings? Forms of thought and sentiment, far above these pre-scientific primitivisms, press the question: must brave hearts and young lives remain at battle's cruel behest, leaving sterile man's love of life and woman's entreaties for compassion?

The madness of needless war is traceable to the antagonism of two historic principles—the one Pagan, the other Christian—and both exclusive of each other. Mr. Kidd has shown that the primal contention of Paganism was the right of physical prowess to conquer, and to keep what it had conquered. Fitness to survive was the fitness of the fighting male; faith in force was evolved out of his aboriginal pugnacity. Everyone and everything paid tribute to the known ability for war. Upon it were based the imitative obedience of children, the subjection of women, the security of domestic life, and later, of the State. It received unquestioning support from religion, moral ideas and social customs. Even Jehovah was a man of war. The bald assertion that it never was and never could be an agent of human progress is too extreme. Wars of an emancipating or defensive character should be carefully distinguished from those which are wantonly aggressive. Perhaps it may be said that those wars are moral in themselves which redeem conditions worse than themselves. The resistance to the rape of Belgium's neutrality is a capital instance of this kind of war, and our Civil War may also be included in the same category. But the impulse to combativeness has attained a perfection of ways and means which jeopardizes the actual existence of civilization. The former sport of kings has become a game far too costly for nations. Man's control over his natural environment has almost blotted out the survival values of war, or made them an eloquent propaganda for peace. We have to strive, not for the extermination of the combative instinct, but for its direction against the treacheries and passions that breed war, and in behalf of the righteousness without which a warless world would be a whitewashed world.

The voices of Faith and Fear are again heard here: one asking for moral and physical disarmament, the other for military strength to enforce the national will. Both must be rightly understood if the political State is to affect anything better than a temporary truce. By wise counsel upon established lines of guidance, it may support international lawfulness and order; and this will be its policy if its rulers view dispassionately the worst iniquity of our time. But the remedies at their disposal are at best empirical. No political organization can create in individuals or in society that surrender to the Eternal Will which is the source of earthly justice and tranquility. The reason for this is, as Viscount Morley remarked long ago, that "the political spirit is the great force in throwing love of truth and accurate reasoning into a secondary place. The evil does not stop there. This achievement has indirectly countenanced the postponement of intellectual methods, and the diminution of the sense of intellectual responsibility, by a school that is anything rather than political." [18] The proposals of the State are too often shaped by fortuitous circumstances. Behind their mirage which flatters fallacious hopes is an impotence that has been repeatedly laid bare in crucial hours. No administration can lift human nature above itself, or submit its rebellious qualities to the divine law. Backward nations raise more troubles than they settle, and are overborne by their sheer multiplicity. Where is there in the Europe of today the man or even the group of men equal to the solution of the problems which the recent war alone has created?

For the enforcement of that divine law and the solution of these problems mankind will have to turn to the Evangel of God, lodged for the past nearly two thousand years in the ageless citadel of armed conflict. A religion that condemns violence and substitutes for it race fellowship can be no other than the irreconcilable foe of physical supremacy. Christianity's dramatic challenge of Pagan militarism has not been fully realized by peoples accustomed to it as the oldest of despotisms. They are practically unaware of the incipient deliverance already accomplished for them. It seems too good to be true that war has encountered a power to which it must lower its crest. Yet from the day of Christ's birth the boasted might of the gods of battle began to wane. No period nor State, however bellicose, has been free from His

[18] "On Compromise," p. 136.

governance. Despite official Christianity's humiliating concessions to Paganism, the spirit and teaching of its Founder have slowly undermined war's frowning battlements, adorned though they are by the votive offerings of all nations. The antagonism of Christianity in this connection would have been far more pronounced but for the wretched complacency of professedly Christian States.[19]

The former semi-sacred invocations to battle which princes had to make or abdicate, are forever beyond the realm of unanimous approval. An utter loathing of war actuates many of the best minds of the age. They view it, not as a recurrent biological necessity, nor as a sort of Malthusian scheme for relieving the earth of its superfluous population, but as the worst entail of racial barbarism. Three impressive modern assemblies have voiced this growing feeling. The first was the Conference at Vienna in 1814, after the Napoleonic struggle had devastated Europe and Asia for eighteen years. It met as a college of monarchs and their ministers, who believed that God's mandate was on them to find the terminus for military measures in a holy brotherhood of kings reigning by divine right. The second Conference convened at Versailles with the mandate of the world upon it for much the same end. The third met in Washington at the call of President Harding and undertook the more modest but practical programme of restriction of naval armaments. Comparisons between these assemblies would be invidious here, but the one irrefutable conclusion from their respective deliberations is that nations will have to choose between legal or conciliar adjudications of their justiciable disputes, and their eventual displacement as civilized and civilizing States.

Few responsible persons plead for an internationalism which wipes out States in wiping out their armed differences. The idea of a super-State is not acceptable to the twentieth

[19] Cf. Neville S. Talbot: "The Modern Situation" in "Foundations," edited by B. H. Streeter, p. 19 ff.

century mind. It is patent that the Byzantine type of internationalism, without form and void, attached to no particular country, and with no specific duties and obligations, is a theoretical unity repugnant to the Western nations. Nor does the example of Mohammedanism, which makes some pretensions to internationalism, move those nations to suppress the patriotic instinct.[20] But it can be made the nucleus for more inclusive and benevolent associations. It is the first business of the Christian Church to transform it, as a nucleus, into an actual and living center for peace. Granting that the undertaking has risks, and that total disarmament might defeat its object, surely proportionate disarmament, according to the growth of comity among nations, increases the likelihood of peace as a power organized in justice.

If the arbitration principle underlying the three historic Conferences mentioned has done no more than puncture the sophistry that war is inevitable, this in itself would have been their sufficient compensation. Should statesmen, however, desist from the further advance of peace interests, the psychology of conflict will recover from its temporary set back, and reassert itself in future generations for which the horrors this generation has witnessed will be as a tale that is told. The sight of fresh means to do ill deeds is, as Sir William Harcourt was wont to say, all too likely to make ill deeds done. To avert this catastrophe, moral as well as material causes for war must be incessantly attacked. If offensive war is forced upon mankind by militant nations, the truly Christian Powers will have to combine against them. This duty devolves upon English-speaking States, whose natural and acquired resources have an incontestable superiority over those of any other civilized countries. Such resources in their advanced economic development are the first line of defense, yet the wars that needlessly destroy them break the States that wage them.

[20] Cf. Ameer Ali, Syed: "The Spirit of Islam," Chapter VII. "The Political Spirit of Islam," p. 268, ff.

The will to peace is with us, but it is a long way from paramountcy. The bickerings of competitive trade, or disputes about valuable natural products, spheres of influence, concessions, and territorial privileges have weakened that will. Recent events and utterances warn us that the fuel for another conflagration is being accumulated, which the torch of a solitary blunderer may ignite. Concerted action, such as was suggested by Dr. J. H. Jowett, and is now embodied in "The World Alliance for Promoting International Friendship through the Churches," must be increased in stringency and extent.[21] It should be completely organized and its policies made known if the unclean will to conquer is not again to defile Christendom. Zealous intentions against that will are entirely insufficient unless they are consolidated in strategic action. The right of the Christian Church to summon nations to a truce of God was splendidly exercised by the Medieval Pontiffs. It should not be allowed to lapse by Protestantism's default. At all times, and in all places, it is our bounden duty to leaven world-society with the knowledge that not insensible weapons, but corrupted hearts are the burden of the issue between war and peace. We understand that disarmament largely depends upon the sense of security. But to be told by a professional British soldier of reputation, that human nature will not change, and therefore wars will always be; that though the desire of man is for peace, the law of life is war; that life lives on life; and that we might as well attempt to damp down Erebus with a duster as attempt to control man's aboriginal instinct for blood-letting by either syllogism or agreement, leaves every Christian without the excuse that he does not clearly comprehend the gravamen of this whole matter. Here he listens to the two voices: the voice of reasoned righteousness pleading for justice and tranquility; and the voice of armed

[21] Cf. J. H. Jowett: "What Has the Church of Christ to Say?" and "What Will the Churches Do?" in "The British Weekly," September 7th and 21st, 1922.

violence insisting upon the naturalness and necessity of legalized homicide.

VI

Secularism is the pervasive temper which hardens in habits and customs that separate individuals and society from life's deepest meanings. Its concrete forms include whatever in religion, art, letters, trade and the totality of human affairs cannot be connected with spiritual ideals. The purer purposes of enlightened hearts are usually disparaged by the secular mind. The malady is virulent and widespread. A strange inability to appreciate the values of existence is symptomatic of its infection, which can be detected in some policies of the Church as well as of the State. Its flow is haphazard, following the fashion of the hour, with no *beata urba* of the saint's adorable vision to attract it. Western peoples are peculiarly susceptible to its contagion. Whereas in the East religion and life go together, and the Oriental dwells by himself in an inner world where truth is what he likes to think it is, the Occidental is usually enclosed from birth in a material fabric which imprisons him, as the men of the Cave were imprisoned in Plato's "Republic." The material progress of European and American nations has interfered with their consciousness of eternal things. One is often made sadly aware of the absence in them of a knowledge and a reality truer and more real than those of mammoth cities, cliff-like buildings, railroads that rib continents, and ships that navigate every ocean. These grandiose temporalities encumber as well as aid modern society; the self-realization of souls is sadly bewildered by their distractions.

It should be remembered that a great deal has happened for man's spiritual emancipation since Plato's "Republic" was written. Christianity has shed light upon the things of earth, and thrown their pretensions into bold relief. Gross customs have been refined; standards of human action made more conformable to divine ordinances. The sacred knowledge that nerves the spirit, dissolving life's sensuous bonds, and upraising it to a plane above that of the Greek philosopher's speculations, is now disseminated everywhere. Expressions of a loftier religious consciousness, ideals that outsoar thought, religious experiences too fugitive for full articulation, characterize man's best moods, inform his conviction of right, and elevate his worship. We should not underrate these allies of his higher selfhood, nor hesitate to employ them against the miasma of secularism. Yet the present plight of the world, without a poet, a philosopher or an acknowledged religious or political leader, shows us, in the words of President Nicholas Murray Butler, that "the fresh voices of the spirit are stilled, while the lust for gain and for power endeavors to gratify itself through the odd device of destroying what has been already gained or accomplished." Even those who resent these strictures are more or less aware that the mechanism of modern life has outrun its moral and intellectual capacity, that some brightness has gone out of it and left it drab, that some virtue has disappeared and left it feebly querulous. The incantations of professional joy-makers cannot hush the strident complaints voiced by an age which has reached the point of secular saturation.

How often its erroneous ideas and malicious customs have been put to shame. Yet nothing short of a cataclysm could persuade their devotees to abandon them. Much abortive thinking which is as prejudicial to progress as are the superstitions of non-Christian peoples is inspired by the secular habit. It stresses nationalism as the assessor of human effort, and individuality itself as so much available stuff for the apotheosis of the State. A country's riches, expansion, material benefit and pride are the articles of its creed, too often implicitly accepted by the mass. Rudolf Eucken, who afterwards became the dupe and tool of imperialistic frenzy, had previously confessed that nothing could save us from being the puppets of a soulless State, unless we discovered and exerted the power to maintain the life of the soul against all attempts at encroachments.[22] The iniquity he first pitied, then embraced, is also nurtured by Bolshevism. Both these social abnormalities, Imperialism and Sovietism, are conspicuous examples of the extremes of secularism: the one blasphemes Deity, the other renounces Him. Both are forged at opposite ends of the same heresy, which first withholds his elemental rights from the individual, and then pulverizes his independence under the pretext of promoting the good of its favorite group.

I shall not discuss any other manifestations of the secular malady, except those found in the political realm. Concurrently with democracy's development in lawfulness, its problems of first rate importance are before us. The Protestant Churches, which only recently gauged their magnitude, as yet offer little that is practical for their solution. Behind the carnival of unsafe pleasures and the dissolution of numerous social ties which antedated the war, is that blind belief in the State which refuses to admit its inherent limitations, and uses vivacious terms in asserting its omnipotence. Its trust in political organizations as God's instrumentalities for world reconstruction culminated at Versailles, where it also met its Waterloo. There the sanguine hopes and expectations stayed upon diplomatists were rudely dispelled, and those who had been exalted beyond measure were cast down to the depths. Whatever they could or could not have achieved, it is now evident that the torn ligaments of civilization's ideals will have to be healed by other hands than theirs. Until half a century ago secular politicians were overshadowed by poets, scientists and ecclesiastics. It was then an open question whether men of learning or men of faith should hold the center of the stage. But while they wrangled, politicians forged to the front, and under the impetus of a few very able statesmen, captured the popular

[22] Cf. "Life's Basis and Life's Ideals," p. 359, f.

imagination. Their slightest variations of personal conditions or their partisan shifts have hitherto formed the staple of the news.[23] There are present indications, however, that the public is somewhat weary of its misplaced adulation. The amazing disclosures during the last decade of the ineptitudes and misdemeanors of statecraft have had a sobering reaction upon nations. But some of its buoyant spirits survive every deluge, and though here and there one disappears in the turbid waters, a dozen successors bob up. They outbid bishops, missionaries, theologians, scientists, explorers and philosophers, when it comes to publicity and popular influence. We know full well that many of them are of the best quality; have stainless honor and a praiseworthy usefulness. We also know that some leaders of international reputation have only to be stripped of their togas to uncover their native mediocrity. Nevertheless, they represent what democratic sovereignty often prefers, and serve to supplant the ethical and intellectual superiority it is rather prone to suspect.[24]

Sensible people are never indifferent to the necessity for effective politics and politicians, but their recent attitude toward international affairs has often been little short of disastrous. So far from easing the travail of the world or of affording it some sort of moral control, they have seriously injured its higher interests. We should learn from these lamentable shortcomings of the State and its officials never again to render unto Cæsar the things which are God's. If you would not thresh grainless straw do not search in politics for what is not there. We are neither to censure faithful public servants because they are not thaumaturgists, nor repeat the offense of many churchmen by lowering the claims of Christianity to meet political requirements. The State can seldom, if ever, do anything better than support the

[23] Cf. Principal L. P. Jacks: "The Degradation of Policy," in "Realities and Shams," p. 74 ff.

[24] Cf. Viscount Bryce: "Modern Democracies," Vol. II. p. 112, ff.

Christian ethic. Political systems, whether autocratic, oligarchical or democratic, will be judged in history by their adherence to the Eternal Order which authorizes that ethic. The perpetuity of that Order is the secret of the rise and fall of empires and republics. Nor has it changed an iota since the morning of the race, when earth seemed nearer to heaven than now, and the lawgivers of the olden time somehow managed to obtain larger appropriations from its wisdom. Assuredly they defined the essentials of political morality in codes and discourses which after times have neglected at their peril. For whatever else a living and growing State takes on or leaves off, it cannot relinquish the principles of these ancient prophets and sages without a speedy reaction toward weakness and eventual decay.[25] Not only clergymen, but many politicans and statesmen are convinced that secularism has shot its bolt. Their acquaintance with human likes and dislikes and with the variations of society assures them that unless nations as well as individuals are re-schooled in spiritual ideals, the outlook for the white race is ominous. They need, as the late President Harding said, "the touch of the finger of God" existent behind all laws, before the good they have dreamed or willed, has even a semblance of reality. The voice of the Church has too often been stifled because "the high proved too high, the heroic for earth too hard." The voice of the State too often has been raucous with a secularism which proposes little that is not liable to deterioration and even to degeneracy.

If these two voices are to blend in the kingdom of the new humanity, the Christian clergyman, who should be the model patriot, must bestir himself. You wish that the New Testament's architecture of the social fabric could become and remain an actuality, as did the magical palace which Solomon caused the genii to build for the pleasure of Queen Balkis. You visualize the strength and loveliness of the Gospel's

[25] Cf. "The Legacy of Greece," edited by R. W. Livingstone. A volume of brilliant essays.

ideals, and how exquisitely they harmonize with those of Israel's seers and with human needs. Surely their appeal should have been heard above the clamor of hate and faction; they should have purified the human heart of its heathen antagonisms at home and abroad. Yet reflect that though forgotten by others, scarcely recalled at intervals by the preacher himself, the Gospel of God for the race is never temporal, always eternal. "The passion that left the ground to lose itself in the sky," becomes a fortress aflame because the Author and the Perfecter of our Faith forgets nothing. Life's purposes are in His grasp, and they will be attained when men make them their own.

SECOND LECTURE

PAST AND PRESENT

"Then in such an hour of need
Of your fainting, dispirited race,
Ye, like angels, appear,
Radiant with ardor divine!
Beacons of hope, ye appear!
Languor is not in your heart,
Weakness is not in your word,
Weariness not on your brow.
Ye alight in our van! at your voice,
Panic, despair, flee away.
Ye move through the ranks, recall
The stragglers, refresh the outworn,
Praise, re-inspire the brave!
Order, courage, return.
Eyes rekindling, and prayers,
Follow your steps as you go.
Ye fill up the gaps in our files,
Strengthen the wavering line,
Stablish, continue our march,
On, to the bound of the waste,
On, to the City of God."

MATTHEW ARNOLD: *Rugby Chapel.*

SECOND LECTURE

PAST AND PRESENT

Patriotism not enough to redeem the evils of the age—The need of greater devotion to Justice and Peace—The relation of the white race to other races—National prominence in history has perils of its own — Individual character the requisite of social progress — The demand for some modern equivalent of the Mediæval Church — Politicians are sometimes more responsive to religious ideas than intellectuals — The lack of sympathetic comprehension in literary and academic coteries — Churchmen's complaints against Institutional Religion — Orthodox devotees to arbitrary theories — The perspectives of history are an aid to correct appraisals of the present — Its annals as a part of the spiritual education of the race — Its lessons teach that nations are woven into one web — Historic examples of the survival of the fittest — Biography is the open door to history — Benefits of the study of State and Church in the light of their own past.

THE all-black and the all-white method of judging the past makes its periods either all wheat or all tares. Thus the War has caused many to speak as though it ended in an irreversible verdict for eternal wrong, and those who went into it with clean hands to end it were equally guilty with those who plotted and precipitated it. Others refer to the Victorian Age as one of self-seeking materialism projected upon calamitous lines. The politics of Central Europe, and, to a lesser degree, those of Britain and North America are described as agitated by greed, hatred and hypocrisy. It is also urged that the catastrophe which fell upon the age was at once its condemnation and penalty. So much for the artist who thinks in sepia and paints in unrelieved blackness "sweat-shops, conscienceless capitalists and human bondage." Those of the white school ask us to admire commanding figures of the period, aristocratic rulers in every realm, moving in the serenity of which Tennyson was the singer. An impartial historian, Lecky, gives it as his opinion that no country was ever better governed than Britain between 1832 and 1867. Most Americans would also say the same of Lincoln's America: an interval, be it observed, marked by our Civil War, and by the goading of Britain's manual workers into successful revolt against penury and starvation. Those who would live hopefully should not accept the black or the white interpretation of history. Half the charm of history, and far more of its truth, consists in its infinite shadings, contrasts, high or low lights, and paradoxical situations. When clothed in the blue distance it takes on a somewhat deceptive beauty, but microscopically scrutinized, its minor phases are misleading, and its repellant features exaggerated. True, its last decade has been disastrous, but need we always enlarge on that? Is not the defeat of the arch-criminals against civilization an alleviating consideration? If the Chauvinists won in 1914, and the long expected "Day" came, they are not now boasting of their victory.

It cannot be denied that nearly all nations were under a morbid tension before that year. What ensued may be praised or blamed, but much that preceded it puts any faith in diplomacy or statesmanship fiercely to the test. The "unreasoning progress of the world" was full of material successes, but its international problem was prodigal of their destruction. The British Premier said the other day that the nineteenth century held its head high and that our century is paying the price. Perhaps it would be as near the facts to say that the pre-war world masked very treacherous conduct behind its proprieties. Its heartless chase for power, territory, and commercial supremacy brought armaments to the front, and made war appear necessary and just, as the militarists desired it should. Affairs were handled in such a manner that under the crushing load of huge armies and navies, economic sacrifices, and recurrent political crises, the beginning of hostilities would be welcomed as a relief from continual suspense. In reading the statements and apologies of the men chiefly responsible for this grand delusion, one's main reaction is a feeling of their ignominy, and of the gullibility of those whom they delivered to desolation. Their portraits are drawn in the first chapter of the Book of Proverbs. They "hated knowledge, and did not choose the fear of Jehovah;" now they must "eat of the fruit of their own way, and be filled with their own devices." [1]

We are told that pious moralizings about these events and personalities get us nowhere. Nor does it serve the purpose to be always reminding nations of their selfishness and rage. Why are they thus distracted? The reply is because they have been deliberately over-stimulated upon their baser side. The practice of drugging a race horse for a burst of speed which leaves it the winner but foundered, illustrates the processes of a patriotism that instills ill-will and jealousy of other peoples. This is the revenge which the past takes on the present, and there are no nations that can plead entire innocence or immunity. When their guides and teachers are more willing to believe in peace than in war, I, for one, submit that the nations will gladly respond to the belief. Edith Cavell's patriotism cannot be questioned, but her dying words, "Patriotism is not enough," will outlive every other memory of her life except the way in which she left it. The ulterior motives of an unmoral love for one's country give rise to those popular sins that must be rebuked. For this cause the writers of the Bible suffered many things, and some of them witnessed for it with their blood. There will be no real betterment of international relations until the issue is clearly defined. Its definition and the defense of the right against patriotic impulses, require a far greater devotion to pure equity than has hitherto been shown when such impulses were aroused.

The enormous waste of life and treasure which has not solved these acute problems, nor resulted in any really con-

[1] Proverbs I. 29, ff.

structive policies, is not the whole story. Behind material losses, the collapse of currencies and the inflation of prices, is the collapse of credit. These in their turn are trivial when compared with the social disruptions and moral degradation in which they originate. Yet the folly and futility of war will never cease because of these losses, although it may be halted for a time when the world realizes deeply that the life of civilization depends on the continuity of peace. But the impulse to war will have to be exterminated by something more powerful than economic or social arguments. It has left a standing bequest of old feuds revived, new ones started, and the cupidity of nations excited afresh. The spiritual energy which should expel these complexes has not been experienced as yet, except in isolated individuals and groups. A truculent peace like that of Eastern and Central Europe, increasingly dark with antagonisms, restive, unwilling to disarm, and almost sure to end in conflict, agitates a Christendom half awake, disorganized, liable to a return of the thing which it dreads, and yet invites. Its diplomacy, notwithstanding the glamor which surrounds its trained exponents, is merely an expression of a single nation's opinions backed by force.

The changed attitude of Asiatic races and of the Orient as a whole, adds to the dangers sensed by students of world affairs. Personal observations made in China, Japan and India, the three principal countries of the farther East, convince the traveller from the West that the prestige of his race is at a very low ebb. The pacific character of the Chinese people, and the remarkable ascent to power in peace and war of the Japanese, are very contrasted phenomena, but they contribute to the increase of Oriental dominion. What may occur in the near future has ominous meanings for Christianity. Oriental dominion over Asia could not be established at this time without injuring the educational and evangelizing institutions which are the sources of a better life for that continent. Political or philanthropic measures which mitigate the peril not only of war between nations of our race, but of war with the countless millions of other races, cannot be advanced too rapidly, especially by Great Britain and the United States. Should such hostilities come, these two Powers would probably sustain the brunt of conflict. Hence, great as are the responsibilities of other Western nations in the Orient, those of the English-speaking nations are infinitely greater. Lord Grey's dictum that humanity must make peace or perish has but to be viewed, with Asia and Africa as its vast backgrounds, to give it very grave significance. Racial antipathies let loose on such a scale as they would supply, and armed with the material equipment of modern war, may outstrip the moral determinations of any age.

Professor John Burnet, in the last of the Romanes Lectures, is apprehensive that modern civilization is breeding barbarisms which will destroy it. Already, like the Greeks, many thinkers place the golden period in the past, and regard oscillation rather than progress as the law of history. There are, it is said, present portents of a nature similar to those which signified the downfall of the Roman State. Two cardinal differences, however, separate our Western world from its parent, the Græco-Roman world upon which the night descended eighteen centuries ago. First, the scientific mind makes it possible for small but well equipped bodies of men to control large numbers. This possibility, in its turn, renews despotism in Russia, and institutes the direct political action that has overthrown constitutionalism in Italy. Second, the territorial areas of ancient civilization, which were very much less than those of modern civilization, were largely confined to lands adjacent to the Mediterranean basin. It has also been pointed out that the frontiers of the Græco-Roman States were perhaps not sufficiently strong in their defenses against the invading hosts of Cimmerians and Scythians, Gauls and Teutons, Germans and Asiatic tribes, which periodically broke through the pale and finally captured Rome. But it was the inherent weakness at the heart of the Empire that betrayed it to its assailants. We have no such barbarian world to encounter, yet unquestionably there are races on the other side of the globe which could be very threatening to the Western peoples, if they took on the scientific learning that has made Japan a formidable international factor. We have only to probe a little more deeply into current events to see from what humiliation and impotence some of those races are slowly emerging.

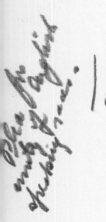

It behooves scholars and statesmen, therefore, freely to circulate the sound ideas that counteract the credulity of race prejudices, and to warn Americans who harbor them against their debilitating influence. Educators should select and train young men and women in the duty of dispelling patriotic ignorance, and of developing in Christian States that spirit toward non-Christian races which makes for unity and coöperation.[2] It would be the supreme satire of history if, after the Western nations had weakened themselves beyond recovery by their internal quarrels, they were vanquished by the Eastern nations which they have held in tutelage. But one course, in my opinion, can arrest the decay of their beneficial sway in the East. If the English-speaking peoples, separated though they are by geographical conditions and by some idiosyncrasies, shall prove capable of a mutual comprehension and sympathy at present unattainable elsewhere, they may find their lasting service and their own safety in protecting the world against the fate which I have suggested.[3]

We are informed that by common consent these nations have won a leading place in history, and so have drawn to themselves the attention of annalists and of mankind in general. But we are also informed that leading places are exposed to particular perils and that impartial students of

[2] Cf. D. J. Fleming: "Contacts with Non-Christian Cultures."

[3] Cf. C. H. Pearson: "National Life and Character," for a full discussion of the race problem.

humanity have no marked predilections for one nation or group of nations over others. "Mankind in general" is a vague allusion. The congested and helpless multitudes of Oriental lands know far less of us as we are, or of what we intend and accomplish, than we know of them, which is little enough. "Common consent" is also a misleading phrase. The success of Christian nations which have had duration of effort in non-Christian territories is produced by their ethical realities and by missionaries of the New Testament Evangel, whether lay or clerical, who engraft its teachings upon the native mind in practical ways. The plain tale of their doings puts down stupid objections to what has been a first class undertaking of good-will and pacification. They are the pioneers of deliverance from what has been described as one of the saddest tragedies of recorded time — the wide separation between the East and the West. They strive for brotherhood and amity, and what they quietly achieve, contemptible though it seems to some, may yet enable the historic centers of Christian culture to resume that place in world affairs, which is commensurate with their strength and their opportunities. To them we must look, and not to the steam-roller methods of goose-stepping, bemedalled militarists, or the exploitations of avid traders, for the freeing of men and nations from the disabilities that hinder the world's progress.[4]

It remains to be said that progress at home or abroad is impossible apart from individual character. Political, diplomatic and socially reformative efforts must rest upon the personal virtues which insure national and international rectitude. Those who ignore the divine regeneration of humanity cannot postpone the divine judgment, still less avert it. Religion, rightly interpreted as the original source of all liberty, as the freedom to do as men ought to do, as the soul of knowledge, as the fount of ideals which prevail over

[4] Cf. Edward C. Moore: "West and East," for a competent discussion of the missionary aspects of this question.

the sharpest separations of color and blood, has in it racial unities which can be made concrete in Christianity. "On the other hand," to quote the illuminating words of Dr. W. T. Davison, one of the clearest and most gifted exponents of the Christian Faith, "it is almost universally recognized that religion in the future must be broader, richer, and more comprehensive, if it is to command the allegiance of coming generations. It must be wide as life itself, taking as its province truth, beauty and goodness of all types, in all their manifestations. If religion is to sway all aspects and departments of human life — social, political, economical, national and international — as surely it ought, its message and guidance must be as wide and various as its claims. Ideas must be widened, channels of feeling and sympathy deepened and enriched, all forms of activity controlled and directed, purified and uplifted, man himself must become more of a man in every stage of development, through the indwelling power of the Highest of all, inspiring, inhabiting, and informing all." [5]

This is the religion that links the parent to the family, the family to the State, the State to the world, and the world to God. Whether men support it from conviction, or only from interest, it verifies the assertion of a Puritan patriot that, despite its formal divergencies, such religion is the first business of a free State and of States bent on freedom. Anglo-Catholics elucidate some principles upon which social reconstruction should be founded, and boldly insist that we unequivocally tell the world, civilization can only be reorganized on a definitely religious basis. They demand some modern equivalent for the powerful control of the Mediæval Papacy; they ask for a Church which embraces all the activities of life, and is hostile to nothing except the absolute rejection of Christian authority. An evident disquietude that many will appreciate prompts this request.

[5] "Hopes and Needs of a New Era" in "The London Quarterly Review," July, 1923, p. 14 f.

But surely those who make it forget that theocracies, whether monarchical or democratic, precipitated upon unwilling peoples, are all too seductive to ardent religionists of a type. Yet as we shall see, theocracies have planted Commonwealths and protected their liberties. For what is at one stage of human development a short cut to outward rule, may be at another stage the expression of a profoundly spiritual impulse. We should not summarily dismiss these proposals until we have attempted to provide an efficient method for Christianizing the modern State.

It is a truism that popular sovereignty has ceased to be a religion, since political and ecclesiastical governments are alike too often ruled by minorities. Its further reproach is that democracies are swept off their feet by oligarchies and also by demagogues, who have mastered the tactics of cajoling the people. Yet the system which is flexible enough to produce the demagogues, blocs, classes and groups that pose as its chosen embodiments, is also flexible enough to take what advantages they offer and then promptly get rid of them. Government by the people is still on probation, but it has the saving grace of belonging to the people, and when they choose to assert their rights, it becomes all sufficient on the spot. Its tenacity as a system is not a forced appearance, but a natural growth arising from the public will.[6] We must deal wisely with that will as it actually is, as well as urge that it be what it ought to be. The little gods of part truth and part convenience, and their prophets of straw, whom the people have worshipped, are laid low; albeit many worshippers grope in fear and darkness because their cher-

[6] There is a coronation of the President of the United States, which is as real and as impressive as that of a European King or Emperor. True, there are no costly robes or elaborate ritual connected with the ceremony; and yet the swearing in of Calvin Coolidge by his aged father, the light of a farmhouse oil lamp being the sole illuminant, was an occasion so reverently conceived by the American people that the emotions aroused are as deep and lasting as if the oath of office had been taken in Westminster Abbey, prefaced by the fanfare of trumpets, and associated with the glitter of the Court.

ished conventions have been ruthlessly assailed. If, as we are told in behalf of this disillusionizing process, reality prevails at last, and the hypocrisy which infected the Victorian period does not infect ours, perchance it is also true that we have not so many virtues to simulate. Unaccustomed independence is almost sure to err, yet it is better than a fettered social life. We must anticipate its excesses, in which each person figures as a separate entity, with separate habits and a separate end, without identical necessities or aims. Uncouth propensities for flirting with the impossible or the dangerous will distort public manners. The bizarre, the blatant, the questionable, will characterize the habits of knaves and fools. Grotesque developments in religion, morals and politics will flourish, comparable to the mythical tree Igdrasil, which drove its roots into Hades and spread its branches across the skies. Those for whom sorrow and death are negligible, provided they afflict others, will be oblivious to the "swollen stream of tears which is always falling darkly through the shadows of the world." Notwithstanding these abnormalities, history teaches that what Burke termed "the eloquence of eternal principles," cannot be silenced. Deep and formative influences, resembling those of Nature which have raised man out of the dust, he knows not how, are always at work. The secret river of God which brings to earth,

> "Authentic tidings of invisible things;
> Of ebb and flow, and ever-during power;
> And central peace, subsisting at the heart
> Of endless agitation,"

sweeps through the present as it has swept through the past. Its divine currents are always ready to break again into the world when men and women are ready to let them irrigate their hearts.

II

Evidently the theological student of this age has to choose between truth and ease, between love of reality and love of repose, between resolute search and the soft serenity that defeats it. Pious generalities which are the product of dizzy ideas, or consoling sentiments that evaporate at the crucial point, do not meet his requirements. He must blend in his preaching the intellectual qualities of the thinker with the vision of the seer, and remember that even the best good sense which rejects the inspirational values of the ideal will presently falter. There is nothing novel in this alternative between reality and repose. The thinkers of Greece and the prophets of Israel faced it fearlessly. They inquired beyond their actual knowledge for its transcendent sources with results beneficial to all.

But no sooner do we heed Goethe's familiar exhortation, "Choose well, the time is brief, yet endless," and push forward toward the unseen, than an earth-bound rationalism bids us stay where we are. Sensational psychology, not without its occasional glances at flesh worship, and a closet philosophy oblivious to the fact that life seldom, if ever, travels on pure reason alone, interpose their veto on our belief in the supernatural. They are not to be taken too seriously, since religion can rely upon man's native response to its appeal. Nor is there any actual waste of the spirit of the race in their interferences. But the modern world has not received from educated individuals who have the leisure and the capacity to think, the light and leadership which it had a right to expect. In this matter not a few intellectuals have fallen below the level of the much abused politician. He, at any rate, cannot be accused of supposing that politics has the trick of perpetual motion any more than mechanics. He has his faults and vices, as have those whom he represents, and of whom he is usually typical. But he is not besotted by theories which insist that regenerated politics can be manufactured like a suit of clothes. He thoroughly understands that the wicked who are slaves by their own compulsion rebel in vain. He would about as lief order a new flesh and blood body for a Hottentot as offer him a Hamiltonian Constitution for his tribe's adoption. He knows, as we know, sometimes better than we know, that it is only in the souls of men and women that a nation's strength and wisdom are woven, that the emancipated spirit is the citadel and palace of an enlightened State. When reformative or religious instincts are aroused, and move with gathering momentum, he is among the first to realize that a change is overdue. If these popular awakenings are bound up with conscience and morals, his alacrity to acquiesce in them is usually the more unmistakable. Moreover, his bearing toward the Church is nearly always respectful, and in most cases reverent. He esteems her spiritual traditions because he is conscious of their salutary control over the masses, and although he can seldom revive these traditions, he favors their revival. There have been capital examples of statesmen whose services to religion have imparted fresh dignity and honor to the State, to the nations and to mankind. In brief, few public men are unaware of the people's prevailing faith in a righteous God. Nor is their knowledge of this belief at all inconvenient for major politics. Without it the national fiber is relaxed, and political action is apt to be low-minded and circumscribed. In perilous times a godless State fed upon materialized notions becomes a hotbed of villainy, and is deprived of the moral certitudes that justify sacrificial exertions. These facts help to explain the dissolution of once powerful social organizations, and convey their solemn warning to those that are still intact.

If the politician may be said to steer his course by the inevitable, the intellectual whom we have in mind takes delight in opposing it. When he is asked to aid in extricating his fellows from the labyrinth in which they wander, he either assumes an air of anxious immobility, or continues to pursue his highly specialized and speculative tendencies. The lack of spiritual affinity between him and those whom he looks down upon as vulgarians is indicated by the slang word "highbrow," with which the latter have dubbed him. Notwithstanding that there is a larger audience for every variety of vice or virtue than there has ever been, he remains aloof from what he calls the mob, and thanks God, if there be a God, that the product of his brains is not intended for popular consumption. He seldom if ever sees the crowd, since his gaze is fixed on authors whose cynical appreciations and warped judgments are purely ephemeral, and have little or no perceptible relation to literature. He agrees that we should possess culture, ideas, and chosen spirits responsible for both. But these must be selected from the cults that scorn the multitudes. Whatever they generally disbelieve is true, whatever they generally believe is false. He might have been a Christian in the times of persecution, but he is almost certain to reject the Christianity that built the cathedrals. Now that the flood gates of democracy are wide open, the torrents of life pouring out from them are abhorrent to his view. He asserts that all knowledge worth distributing can only be realized in its fullness by the few.

Another species of this genus cultivates the will not to believe at all. He treats religion in an icy fashion, is reluctant to admit its good, refers to it with a supercilious accent or else in derogatory terms, and if pushed to a preference, chooses Epictetus or Marcus Aurelius as his mentors.[7] Professional academics and authors of this description are at zero in a time like ours, when sympathy and comprehension mount up in the scale of appreciation, and hospitality of mind is welcomed. "The London Spectator" insists that the ability to enter into our neighbor's moods and circumstances is respected as in itself a sort of talent, and some who

[7] I well recall visiting a church in London, noted for its advanced theology, where the minister who conducted the services said, in announcing the first lesson: "We shall read a selection from the second chapter of James Anthony Froude's 'Short Studies on Great Subjects,' volume one."

are incapable of it, are careful to pose as sympathetic. Ignorance of these pertinent ideas is bad enough, but ignorance of Christianity, as Christ taught it, is very much worse. When intellectuals abuse their opportunities by severing the spinal cord of religious belief, through which civic and moral welfare function for all, they are open to justifiable rebuke. Their spiritual negativism and intellectual snobbery are repudiated by the large majority of teachers, authors and essayists. The plain citizen also resents their procedure and is unmoved by reasonings which leave his higher being and its purposes in the air. He is not so hemmed about by philosophic doubts as to be oblivious to his spiritual lineage. He knows that no intelligence, however well proportioned; no breath of mentality, however cogent, can take over the sovereignties of the moral sense, or perform the tasks allotted to the soul's highest intuitions; and he also knows that the convictions by which men live do not come by speculative reason.[8] One can imagine a symposium of philosophers, scholars and physical scientists exchanging opinions and confidences before ordinary individuals. Perhaps their differences, which are legion, if not reconcilable, might be accommodated. Yet should the teacher of revealed religion, whom some intellectuals deprecate as unsuited to the needs of living men, intrude in that diversified parliament of talents, and ask; "What theory is in the saddle now, and where will it ride?", their deliberations would be lost upon outsiders unless the spiritual ideal was mounted. The rarest learning, the purest reasoning, the cleverest logic are but the elaborate triflings of a paganism at bay unless they are united to ethical and religious aims.[9] What is more, modern pagans gamble with treasures they are supposed to

[8] In a recent inquiry upon "Civilization in the United States," by thirty Americans of this type, no reference was made to religion.

[9] Wittenstein, whose "Tractatus Logico-Philosophicus," with a preface by Bertrand Russell, is one of the significant essays of the times, confesses that "ethics are transcendental": and that "the solution of the riddle of life in space and time lies *outside* space and time." We might not agree as to the meaning of the italicized word, but it suggests the failure of naturalism.

safeguard, if their conclusions are at odds with the common heart and the common conscience.

When those pontifical purveyors of original notions fall foul of each other, Christianity comes into its own. One among them, who has recently turned traitor to his literary coterie, charges its members with dullness and even hypocrisy. Their productions, he says, are shorn of tenderness, beauty and wisdom. The critic in question is a politico-social radical, who can be, as we know, a very serviceable person. But he hints that if his fellow radicals, who usually describe Christianity as an intellectually commonplace and morally exhausted creed, were only honest with their readers, they would confess themselves charlatans and pretenders. What is worse, he dares to insinuate that some of these progressive spirits secretly lean toward traditional beliefs, and that their denunciations of orthodoxy, as the scarlet sin of the mind, are no more than a gesture. They are to be regarded as literary adventurers who make or break their idols at the instigation of caprice or imitation. We are not concerned with the truth or falsity of this arraignment. But it suggests that religious ordinances which are obnoxious to such sceptical extremists do not of necessity stand or fall at their fiat; and that the problems before us are not to be solved by the pundits who would dispatch historic Christianity to the rear. Yet this statement should be protected against the growing tendency to substitute the narrowest creeds for the spirit and teachings they imperfectly express, or to elevate the limitations thus made to the rank of the spirit and teachings themselves.

To the closed door of every age there comes a knocking at judgment's midnight hour. Unless the household within has a better plea to submit than is given by those whom we have described, its prospects are not particularly bright. The real intellectual danger of today is not from religion, even when it is inert, controversial or barren, but from the emotional impulses or deranged states of mentality to which many writers are liable. Fixed ideas, suspicious or sentimental moods, judgments that become vendettas, outbursts of passion, and libels upon the historic Faith of love and righteousness are forms of moral insanity which are more detrimental to society than its physical diseases.

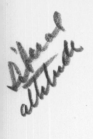

Some clerics, who consider it a crime to hide their light under a bushel, are disposed to find fault with Christianity and the Church. One of them inquires if the well intentioned and loyal constituencies which preachers have visualized are real or imaginary. He believes they are the latter, and that those who recommend Christianity to this generation will collide with an intrusive paganism which has neither the cultural nor the spiritual values of the classic type. The Church, he affirms, has been barely holding her own, but flattering herself that whenever she makes an affirmation in behalf of faith and morals, the people would at once respond. Demos was supposed to be on the Lord's side, and to such purpose that there was more religion outside the Church than inside. If the last statement yields scanty comfort to professed Christians, the explanation accompanying it is still less consolatory. Its author states that there has been a sudden subsidence in the ageless tradition the masses have held in respect to the Church, which has shaken her from top to bottom, and alienated them from their own past, making them too glaringly conscious of their present for her benefit. Do they not need to cherish what is contemporary, since no generation has been so entirely cut off from its predecessors? The notion that such a severance is impossible is derided as a parvenu among ideas. Another cleric tells us that there is very little popular demand for the ethic of Christianity, to say nothing of its theology. Its very sentiments, the dregs of which were once found in novels, ballads and melodrama, have been completely drained away. If so wholesale an abstraction of religion had actually taken place, the dominant moral ideals and inspirations of mankind would have been lost to it. The hope of progress, the possibility of progress, and the fact of progress, which are of the bone and sinew of the Christian Evangel would likewise have disappeared. But this is one of the imaginary catastrophes that never happen.[10]

Philosophers, historians, biologists, theologians of the traditional or liberal kind will have much to say about its probability or otherwise, yet the final appeal will not be to them. The latest accessions to the Protestant Churches in America and Great Britain, which are the largest they have enjoyed for some years, seem to indicate that they have a fighting chance which should induce their detractors not to report their end prematurely. A further indication that the race is plastic in the hands of its Maker is perceptible in the mystical possibilities derived from the doctrines of science itself. Something more than mere knowledge is involved in men's reactions to them. Not only philosophic but religious implications, which must be courageously explored, are evident in the recent discoveries of organized knowledge. Those who believe that humanity can be remoulded by God may be heartened or again dismayed by the findings of pessimism; but they will submit their hopes and fears alike to the test of life itself. They are conscious that the Church has not only outlived the late War, but a thousand wars before it. Despite the febrile condition attributed to her by her numerous opponents, she will outlive the passing world for which she is God's priestess. Faith, hope and charity have survived, as St. Paul assured us they would; they are resurgent in her and in mankind, and the Divine Will sustains their interaction.

Nevertheless, declamatory malcontents insist that though Christianity and to a lesser extent, the Church, may exercise some authority over individuals, they are weaker than a bruised reed in the world at large. This view is held by the

[10] We remember that in Russia the Bolshevists decided to kill the Church and bury it. Having accomplished this, as they thought, and paid the undertaker, the evidence goes to show that we shall see a resurrection there, not from the grave, but from a temporary obscurity.

advocates of super-orthodox beliefs, who, assuming for the Bible an infallibility which it never had, announce a cataclysmic ending for our age. Their attempts to compress the infinite philosophy of Christianity within a hard and fast literalism disfigure Evangelical doctrine and bring an undeserved reproach upon its adherents. They rely for their interpretations of the cosmos and of man upon Scriptures of an apocalyptic sort, the burden of which is mainly applicable to the conditions under which they were written. The Christian economy, as construed by them, is rent asunder by an immovable antagonism between the sovereignty of our Lord and that of Antichrist. In their treatment it becomes either all mercy or all vengeance, either a heaven precipitated into an impossible earthly state; or a hell too universal, materialistic, and useless to be credible to reverent adorers of the Divine Goodness. God's clemency and wisdom toward widely different ages and races are placed by them beneath the jurisdiction of an arbitrary power. Everything in creation is explained under the duress of a sixteenth century theory of Biblical perfectibility and in accordance with a few Scriptural announcements of contemporary disasters. In behalf of this theory, itself the dubious product of a stormy period, organized knowledge is excoriated, social progress is pronounced a sham, and the world is sentenced to an almost worse doom than that decreed either by scientific materialism or philosophic pessimism. Millions of devout but mistaken men and women who have found personal deliverance from sin in the Gospel, risk their religious sanity and wholesomeness in these speculations, and in grinding theological axes for the fray. Although history has poured contempt upon their theories, from Apostolic days until now, these persist as an output of that state of mind which is fervid but forever closed. They are liable to the taint of Pharisaism, and prone to reserve a sparsely populated Paradise for themselves. Such Judaizers of the modern Church exist feebly when she is prosperous, but usually revive in her sorrows. Like other and larger associations of the orthodox, they seem utterly unaware of the discredit which has come upon much creedal religion, since experimental science began to contribute to the progress of mankind.[11]

The discredit cannot be removed by threats and fulminations. Nor can the majority of the American people who are today unchurched, be brought to a sense of their Christian duty by the insistence upon fixed standards of belief that are no longer final. Those who propose to restore creedal religion should do so without fear of fundamentalists or of extreme liberals. It must be reëstablished by Christian thinkers who reject the opinion that theology is undermined: in whom the spirit and content of religion are set on finding clearer and more comprehensive formulations of the Faith; and for whom the requirements of the religious consciousness are guaranteed by the spirit and writings of the New Testament. The theology they derive from their research may be historical, psychological or humanistic, but it should at least be Christian theology. (Strictly defined, there is no Protestant nor Catholic truth in theology, labels that are erroneous and misleading, but simply truth, as Christ revealed it.) It should insist upon the purity of motive and of conduct, which is well pleasing to the God whom the prophets declared, and our Lord incarnated. It must beware of the alloy of excessive speculation found in the gold of much past and present theology. It must remember that while there is a difference between the religious and the philosophical standpoints, they always intersect, and are mutually helpful, and also that what their intersections produce is to be proved by its ability to develop higher ideals and more righteous living.

[11] Cf. S. J. Case: " The Millennial Hope "; Oscar L. Joseph: " The Coming Day "; H. F. Rall: " Modern Premillennialism and the Christian Hope."

III

Let us turn now to what Dryden calls,

> "The firm perspective of the past,"

where speculations are under bonds, and events have been followed by intervals sufficiently wide to verify their meaning. Another poet, Lucretius, one of the noblest in Roman literature, in a fine figure speaks of the detachment of view necessary for those who would rightly use that perspective. He depicts the marshalling of the warriors on the plain, the gleam of their burnished arms, the fiery charges of the horses that shake the ground. But on the far-off heights above, all the scouring legions seem motionless, and the confusions blend, as it were, in one steady sheet of flame.

This aloofness does not mean that we should treat the past as a refuge from duty, but as a storehouse of the ripest experience available for the discharge of duty. It prevents us from overrating the importance of the present, and teaches us that no outward show of movement is of much consequence when compared with the changeless principles behind it. The more thoroughly we explore the latitudes and longitudes of Time, in which the regenerating winds of the Spirit have blown as they listed, the more certain we shall be that those winds still blow. The records of Church and State are an unfenced expanse where, almost without exception, the relation and witness of Christianity to the Divine Order can be recognized to advantage. Bishop Mandell Creighton reminds us that the theological and philosophical phases of the Faith, its connections with nations and the world, and the creeds which have shaped its various policies, are part and parcel of the religious education of the race. The consequences of the Emperor Constantine's conversion, the significance of the controversy between Nicæan bishops and their adversaries, the outcome of the General Councils of Constance and Trent; Augustinianism as St Augustine evolved it, Lutheranism according to Luther, the Presbyterian and Puritan systems as Calvin and Cartwright conceived them, or Methodism as Wesley led its triumphant march, are subjects deserving our closest scrutiny. The judgments upon Church or State that persist are those founded upon the continuous experiences of their life in successive ages. Judgments upon them inspired by mere reaction from what is happening, often relax our hold on lasting realities, and are as ephemeral as other contemporary judgments from which they, in turn, react. Surely we have had our fill of both kinds.

Wherever we concentrate in history, whether it be upon the immemorial associations of Jerusalem, Constantinople, Rome or Geneva; as Christians, we should visualize the wealth of our religious heritage; as churchmen, we should feel at home; as citizens, we should observe the chequered progress of the State. The reasons for the present significance of all institutions embodying Christian truths, or for their varied but indestructible elements, can never be fully understood by those who refuse to study their origin and growth. Nor will the narrow and confusing dogmatism of sectarian opinion be displaced by a truly catholic doctrine unless men venture beyond the confines of their respective denominations. The Reformed Churches must learn that Rome always has stood for ideals far greater than Protestantism has ever appreciated; and Roman Catholics must learn that Protestantism has been the charter of the soul's freedom in Christ. No priesthoods or prophetical orders, no sacramental or theological teachings, no concepts of holiness or oneness, no movements of reform or returns to ancient ways have existed in the past that did not convey lasting benefits to humanity. The assertion of the thirteenth century Mediævalists that Christ was the Lord of lords, and the plea of the sixteenth century Reformers that man's approach to his Maker should be untrammelled, have issued in the furtherance of the Gospel. If there is to be in our day an abandonment of provincial religious structures in behalf of a larger, truer temple of God as the home of all nations, Christianity will be best applied to that end by those teachers who know its annals, and are baptized afresh in its spirit.

What in history, sacred or secular, so called, is to us vague and formless, should be vivified. For, valuable as are the records of the Church because they tell us of God's manifestation to men, and of their rejection or acceptance of Him, the history of the State is scarcely less valuable. It emphasizes those human and natural elements of life which have a sacredness all their own. The scholar who toils diligently in both realms will frequently find them without frontiers. He will be amply rewarded if only by his increasing consciousness that Church and State shall eventually be united in the Kingdom of God here on earth. The priestly systems of Asia, the intellectual glories of Greece, the military and legal imperialisms of Rome, the spiritual authority of the early Christian Church, the Papal government of Catholicism, the development of modern States under Protestantism, and the industries, policies, philosophical or religious developments that characterize these States, Churches and periods, are at your disposal. The ground is well prepared, the materials are more than plentiful, the ages containing them are veined with life. They need but the harmony and unity which the student should bring to them, to show him the wonderful activity and variety of the entire evolution.

If we do not have to exclude from our sympathetic interest any department of history, neither do we have to consort with degrading memories of lives that were never really lived, or of deeds which should never have been done. Of course we shall encounter the worthless and the immemorable; the gifted minds that were recreant; the liars and the cowards whose infamies blister human records. But neither these, nor the parasites, the bullies, the sharpers and the scoundrels of bygone days need trouble us. We are not to be too much engaged with princes who betrayed the State, with prelates who betrayed the Church, or with politicians who fawned for place and power. They are intended for our warning, not for our intimacy, and should be left in the quarantine to which they belong.[12] In the words of Frederic Harrison: "If history has any lessons, any unity, any plan, let us turn to it for this. Let this be our test of what is history and what is not, that it teaches us something of the advance of human progress, that it tells us of some of those mighty spirits who have left their mark on all time, that it shows us the nations of the earth, woven together in one purpose, or is lit up with those great ideas and those great purposes which have kindled the conscience of mankind." [13]

These evidences of a common design governing the whole historic structure add to the attractions of the subject. The economic or constitutional aspects of the State, and the teachings that have endowed the Church with her rightful claims upon humanity, are almost without exception a consistent development. To take a further example, the numerous alignments and sects of modern Christianity did not drop out of space, but emerged, each in its own succession, from one preëxistent Divine Society. Most of them did not imagine themselves to be leaving the Church, but preserving her against her enemies or cleansing her of her evils. Their breaches have widened or narrowed during the lapse of centuries, yet neither the Roman nor the Greek Catholic, the Anglican nor the Protestant Communions, have escaped the original Church which promulgated the Faith and produced the Bible, to which they alike appeal. [14] Plainly, few things, if any, that have been cease to be; they

[12] The penchant for large tomes dealing with "Bad Men" and "Bad Women" is more marked in Europe than in America, but both continents can do without the product. To get at the facts contained in these biographies it is necessary for authors to breathe the air of moral cesspools: and only readers with morbid tastes could possibly endure narrations which are made up of intrigue, adultery and murder.

[13] "The Meaning of History," p. 11.

[14] Cf. W. G. Peck: "The Values of the Sacrament. An Essay in Reconstruction."

only undergo changes. There will be no new world in the sense of sudden and immediate novelty. Foolish animadversions of things past, foolish exaltations of things present, foolish expectations of things future, are ever with us; the last, perhaps the most pathetic of the three. All, as George Saintsbury reflects, have been encouraged by the omnipresent reaction of a great war. But none could domineer over men's ideas so easily were they more deeply versed in what has been.

History reminds us at every stage of the shining virtues which are often found with distressing vices in the same human character. It shows us that some of its priceless values have been obtained in desperate conditions. Thus ancient Greece, from a fairly inclusive viewpoint, has been compared to "a giant dreaming of freedom while locked in the arms of a courtesan slave." An intellectual and ethical eminence, entirely foreign to her surroundings, unknown to previous or after ages, gave her during the fifth century B. C. an unequalled drama, poetry, philosophy, political ethic, and art. Out of the Greek mind at its climax came the creative light without which heat is useless; to which men like Socrates, Plato, Aristotle, and other Greek masters contributed their full quota. It seems impossible, as "The London Spectator" comments, that a nation so justly celebrated was degraded by savagery, unbridled lust and slavery. Yet its underworld was a Saturnalia of hideous depravities, and the wickedness now uncovered in it challenges belief. The social order rested upon human bondage; the City-States violated the tenets of their philosophers by making ceaseless war upon each other. Unnatural vices were practised; even human sacrifice was suggested as the best "medicine" for an ailing commonwealth. Citizens who met to hear and discuss the sublime tragedies which still echo in men's ears were themselves a sort of corporate tragedy.[15] The curious self-

[15] Cf. W. Warde Fowler: "The City-State of the Greeks and Romans," Chapters IX and X on the internal and external causes of decay.

sufficient groups which listened to the greatest thinkers of the race, or watched the building of the Parthenon as the crown of Attic splendor, were only one remove from the heathen tribes they despised. What could be more remote from classic Greece than naked primitivism? Nevertheless they lived side by side. Evils and infamies best left undescribed were in proximity to the allegiance to reason, the reflective breadth and clearness of statement of the Greek mind at its best. One is almost driven to the conclusion that it was an extraordinary episode, preparatory for the Great Teacher who spoke a dialectal form of the Greek language, and for the deliverance of His message in those cultural forms which insured its acceptance beyond the boundaries of Judaism. In Christ and in Johannine Christianity, a purified, ennobled Greece lived again, and distributed her gifts to mankind in the Faith that owes much to her.[16]

IV

If it seems to you that the flagrancies of our age almost excuse every former period of wrong doing, look back, not to antiquity, but to the Europe and America of your nearer ancestors, when history was made in iniquitous as well as in righteous ways. The eighteenth century is the immediate precursor, save one, of our own. Because of great revolutions in politics and social theories, the world of today makes the world of yesterday unreal and remote. The student feels that it is as distant as the Renaissance, and in numerous aspects, not nearly so attractive. Philanthropy had an infrequency which made it singular. The Decalogue went out of fashion. The social virtues fell into abeyance. Mark Pattison describes the era as "one of decay of religion, licentiousness of morals, public corruption, profaneness of language, — a day of rebuke and blasphemy . . . an age destitute of depth and earnestness; an age whose poetry was without romance, whose philosophy was without insight,

[16] Cf. C. Ackermann: "The Christian Element in Plato."

and whose public men were without character; an age of 'light without love,' whose very merits were of the earth, earthy." [17] Since this sweeping verdict was pronounced in 1862, we have learned to understand the eighteenth century better. We know that despite its sordidness, it was not and could not have been wholly corrupt. Agents and forces of purification are always present in every society, however debased and degenerate that society may be, though often too far below the surface for their presence to be detected by the superficial observer.

18th cent.

Yet beyond question the disorders of civilization during the years included in Pattison's survey were far-reaching and obstinate. National character was such as to make belief in a constitutional government impossible. The wise political instincts now attributed to English-speaking peoples, and their actual establishment of civic stability are much more recent than is usually supposed. Levity, selfishness and turbulence were prevalent. The reign of the Puritan saints was succeeded by the revels of the Stuart and Hanoverian sinners. The profligates of the Restoration produced a progeny almost worse than themselves, whose refined but cynical brutalities it would be difficult to exaggerate. The highest elements in human existence were frittered away; conduct ran in wrong channels; conscience was prostituted; then indeed was

> "Time a maniac scattering dust,
> And life a fury slinging flame." [18]

Monarchs and nobles of the Continent displayed a callousness which took no account of the occasional famine prices of food, of the starvation of the plain folk, or of the high rate of infantile mortality. Land owning barons and gentlemen of quality regarded the nameless hordes on whom they

[17] Mark Pattison: "Essays," Vol. II. p. 42.

[18] Cf. The Author's "Three Religious Leaders of Oxford," pp. 240 ff.

relied for everything as their servile creatures. Religious zeal was denounced as a species of madness. The skepticism which infected universal society became skeptical even of itself. Lewdness and debauchery corroded the social dependability of the peasantries who imitated their superiors. Pompous bishops and pluralist parsons, who seldom fed their flocks, lingered in places and followed pursuits forbidden to the cloth. Victimized by poverty, disease and drunkenness, the people resorted to lawlessness. The severity of criminal codes, which in Britain alone made more than one hundred offenses punishable with death, and used sign posts for gibbets, could not repress theft and murder, nor maintain public order and safety. Society became a melancholy wreck: the despair of the moralist and the legislator. Carlyle thundered against the century, and said its one decent act was to blow out its own brains in the French Revolution. Yet from this degraded period emerged those spiritual forces that revived the Church, and set up representative democracies in Great Britain, France and the United States of America. It shows that the growth of civilization, the spread of knowledge, the habitual reverence for law and order, and for all social essentials, have usually sprung from great individuals. They transformed this era, they ended its anarchies, they upheld the State, they breathed new life into an expiring Faith, they lifted the curse which had fallen on a hapless age. For it was the age of Wesley, of Washington, of Johnson, of Jefferson, of Burke, of Hamilton, of Pitt, of Marshall, of Fox, and of Franklin: men who were magistrates of God in their respective realms.

Christianity itself is the foremost example of this habit of the past to bring forth meat out of the eater. Nor was it ever so conclusively demonstrated as in the most important movement of Time. It would be difficult to reduce the human beginnings of our religion below their actual levels of helplessness and insignificance. As a supernatural Faith it was repudiated by the Jews among whom it originated.

Rise of democracy

The death of its Founder was entirely too casual to excite any comment from the Romans or the Greeks. His teachings were not known by contemporary scholars and thinkers, and by only a few of the poor and the lowly to whom He communicated them. What followed on this non-apprehension of the world's supreme Figure is to be discussed in later lectures. But the discussion will be valueless unless we learn from it that these strange admixtures of utmost evil and utmost good, of veritable feebleness and omnipotence, are not excluded from our own or from any other time. It is erroneous to suppose that the ages of faith which produced saints and heroes are closed to us, or that those saints and heroes belonged to a more divine type, living in a far less oppressively human environment than ours. From the philosophic standpoint such conceptions are void of historic content, arbitrary, and mischievous. As a matter of fact, the world of the Apostles was an infinitely viler world than the one we know. Yet it sufficed for them as ours ought to suffice for us. St. Paul's letter to the Romans testified that they knew the worst and believed the best about it; they saw its damning iniquities, but they also foresaw its dawning glories. Their contemplation of those immutable principles which sustain society convinced them that the Creator's Love and Wisdom had invested too heavily in man to forsake him.[19]

Can we not conform our outlook and approximate to theirs? According to our trust in them and in Him Whom they obeyed, be it unto us! That trust will at least get an even chance if we keep an eye upon the comedy of men's indiscriminate condemnation of this half-way house which they inhabit. Of course the race will outgrow it, but it will not do so by demolishing it. Fox said of Burke that he was an exceedingly wise man, but wise *too soon.* If so great an intellect as Burke's was sometimes at the behest of his imagination, truly we have need to watch against the in-

[19] Cf. S. Angus: "The Environment of Early Christianity," Chapter III.

solence of our ill founded fears or hopes. I am not of those who contend that the open expression of truth is seldom practicable. On the contrary, its suppression deadens life. The brave avowal of sincere beliefs is our indefeasible obligation. But they should be well meditated, rightly stated, constantly revised, and compared with the consentient beliefs of an authoritative nature. He who avows them should always be able to detect the needs of the hour and the signs of the times. After these precautions have been taken, it is often the case that what is loosely phrased, "the spirit of progress," is an imponderable which eludes the shrewdest efforts to discern it.

An open door to history is in the biography inseparable from it, since if persons rather than events attract us, we cannot get at them without knowing their surroundings. What is more, there is a meaning in which those persons are the past we really know. Its temper, its tendencies, and its aims are incarnated in them. Nothing is more Hellenic than Plato and his "Republic," or more mediæval than Hildebrand and his theocratic autocracy. If the Renaissance found its diplomatic voice in Machiavelli and its cultured voice in Erasmus, it also found its religious voice in Luther and Calvin. The England of the New Learning lived in Shakespeare, in Jonson and in Marlowe. The England of the Reformation reached its military climax in Cromwell, its poetical climax in Milton, and its political climax in Lord Somers and John Locke. Revolutionary France was prefigured in the Encyclopædists — in Voltaire, Diderot and Rousseau. The constitutionalism of our Republic is best understood by mastering the leading conceptions of Washington and those of the statesmen who served with him; and Lincoln remains, as he is likely to remain, the ideal personalization of representative democracy.

The general course of nations as well as their outstanding personalities, and what they have loved or hated, lost or won, their peculiar bent, or specific contributions to mankind, appear in the history of Church and State. Their importance for the theological student surpasses that of ephemeral volumes of sermons, or of sectarian discussions that are not based on primal realities. Although these two organizations have long monopolized the social structure, their harmonious coöperation is still an indefinite prospect in all Christian lands. Numerous and weighty reasons support the contention of scholars and statesmen that their true balance has not been struck, and not a few maintain that its adjustment is the problem of problems to which competent thinkers should address themselves afresh.

The State with which the Apostolic Church had relations was the most efficient social organization known to mankind before the Christian era, and it was then at the high point of its efficiency. When our Lord was accused of endeavoring to make Himself a King, His judge, Pontius Pilate, Procurator of Cæsar in Judæa, represented the Chief Magistrate of a nominal Republic which ruled the western world. The conflict begun by that trial, and by the creation of the Divine Ecclesia in the midst of that Republic, has by no means subsided. The relaxation of religious and domestic discipline, the tyrannies of scientific, literary or ecclesiastical hierarchies, the exactions of temporal power, the illicit developments of individualism, and the excessive claims of social groups lend weight to the conclusion that restraint is still a necessary art of government. The majority of nations needs a more enlightened guidance than their traditional methods afford, better protection from selfish greed within and without their jurisdiction, and a steadier help toward practical betterment.

The study of the State in the light of its own past, is reinforced in democracies by the argument that they do not give men and women that equality of economic opportunity which is the logical sequence of political equality. Their social development falls short of the goal here named. Earlier ideas that all persons were equal in character, intelligence and ambition are negatived by the evidence of humanity itself. There is an irremovable distinction between an impossible natural equality, and an attainable political equality. The theory that men are created free and equal is relegated to the lumber room of decrepit notions which flourished in an agitated time. It is exceedingly doubtful if the leaders of the American Revolution ever held the theory in the sense often attributed to them.[20] Be this as it may, when strictly interpreted, its inevitable outcome is a Socialism which violates the best political instincts of freedom-loving States. Their choicest products are leadership, and the conceptions and policies of leadership. These alone insure social progress, and they are usually found, not in the majority, but in the one or the few. The wise words of Sir Henry Jones are worth recalling in this connection: "The road to ruin for an ignorant and selfish democracy is far shorter than for any other kind of misgovernment; the fall is greater and the ruin more complete. There is no builder of the common good who builds so nobly and securely as a wise democracy, and there are no hands which destroy so hopelessly as the hands of the many." [21]

Yet democratic States evince a growing belief that the industrial movements which have revolutionized modern life, require the extension of the principles of right and justice, to include equality of economic opportunity. How far that extension can be made by secular governments without a regeneration in the moral and religious habits of the people, is a matter we shall have to notice later. Unquestionably, the modern limitation of government to political affairs has removed formidable obstacles from the path of popular rights and duties. But will its expansion to cover industrial and kindred affairs maintain or abolish the individualism upon which nations, and most of all, democracies, very much depend? Experience teaches that the moral control of the

[20] Cf. Viscount Bryce: " Modern Democracies," Vol. I. pp. 48, 60. ff.
[21] "The Principles of Citizenship," p. 73.

people's work and pleasure is a hazardous and difficult task for the political State to assume. Though the present revolt against the frightful increment of veritable heathenism which disgraces professedly Christian nations is widespread and clamant, the contention as to whether the temporal or the spiritual powers, or both conjointly, shall purge the general situation of its social abnormalities is now before us daily. Those who insist upon the absorption of Church and State in the Kingdom of God have little support from the modern State. The Church and the nation are no longer coextensive, and the theocratic identification that once prevailed in them does not obtain in law. The Jewish ideal that there is no severance between the divine and civil rule, is set aside today by legal precedents derived from the Roman Empire and from the Reformation. These precedents are strengthened by memories of the hardships and humiliations inflicted upon the State by the once powerful Mediæval Church.

There was no comprehensive religious organization similar to that of Israel in the Roman world. Even single cities such as Rome, Athens, or Ephesus, were religiously separate. Nevertheless, a strong minority of Christians and non-Christians in civilized States favor their recognition of religion, because they have lost faith in the theory of society's inherent progress. Man's conquest of his natural environment, his enactment of better laws, and his execution of equal and speedy justice, will not, in the opinion of numbers of thoughtful people, satisfy his aspirations for reform. These, as they view the situation, are seriously impeded by political and national barriers against which the religious temper of Europe and America is vehemently moved. A great deal that is offered in defense of those barriers by publicists and statesmen is looked upon as archaic and mischievous sentimentalism. Psychologists and biologists, who ridicule what they describe as the empty platitudes of a shortsighted patriotism, have their own specifics. Yet their scientific estimates of social betterment are no more acceptable to theocratically disposed men and women than are those of the political empirics.[22]

Christians who believe that the Kingdom of God must be built here and now by His omnipotent and saving grace, vouchsafed in response to human sin and human faith, are inclined to ask for the spiritualization of all politics. But the far larger number who believe that Christianity is more true than practicable, cling to the scepter of secularism, and reject the Cross of sacrificial renunciation. It is abhorrent to them that the State should be in the dust, even to serve the God of all nations. Enough has been said to vindicate the attempt of honest-minded Churchmen to penetrate behind Protestantism and Catholicism, and find in their common origin the things that shall make for their peace and their effective human service. Should the Churches prefer the non-communicative isolation which has hitherto been their fetish, the charge of these vital human interests which I have named may be taken over by destructive forces with lamentable consequences. There are indications that the struggle for their control is between a Socialism of varying degrees of religious belief or non-belief, on the one hand, and Christian fraternity on the other. Those who are pledged to the latter should remember that the moral values of society emerge, not by preachment and debate, but by squarely meeting their conditions. If the Church is to meet them, she must not only proclaim good will, but augment her social control in behalf of its diffusion. Society, as we find it, is infinitely distant either from an abandoned depravity or a spotless holiness. It is composed of human beings such as we are ourselves, who are in the process of becoming, either for better or for worse. They are susceptible to religious overtures; they have primary, secondary, and even tertiary requirements that call for that manifold wisdom of God which

[22] Cf. Albert Schweitzer: "The Decay and the Restoration of Civilization," chapter IV; and, "Civilization and Ethics," chapters XXI and XXII.

His Ecclesia is supposed to have and to administer. Their spiritual and social movements, past and present, are revealed in the unfoldings of Church and State. And since the latter is the senior of these two all-inclusive human associations, to it we turn first for our instruction in well-doing.

THIRD LECTURE

THE GROWTH AND PURPOSE OF THE STATE

"Like the baseless fabric of this vision,
The cloud-capp'd towers, the gorgeous palaces,
The solemn temples, the great globe itself,
Yea, all which it inherit, shall dissolve,
And, like this insubstantial pageant faded,
Leave not a rack behind."

SHAKESPEARE: *The Tempest,*
Act IV. Scene I. 151 ff

THIRD LECTURE

THE GROWTH AND PURPOSE OF THE STATE

The genesis of the State — Its evanescent forms — A perfect State is imaginary — The Home as the source of the State — The formation of the Clan and the Tribe — Their traits as organizations — Tribalism and nationalism in Oriental Empires — The City-States of Greece — Their great service to human associations — Rome's constructive political genius — The autocracy of the Classic State — Plato's Ideal State — There is no break between ancient, mediæval and modern States — The Greek period akin to our own — Mediævalism's fascination due to a reaction from modern Intellectualism — The social organisms subordinate to the Church — Charles the Great and his imperial system — The Feudal States — Chivalry as a Christian cult — The golden Thirteenth Century — The beginnings of Parliamentary rule — The prevalence of the national State in ecclesiastical internationalism — The sources of American democracy.

THE genesis of the State is hidden in the dim prehistoric voids of the past. Its development has been compared to that of a vast primeval forest. It looks like a thing unsown, always living, always dying and renewing its life from age to age. "No one has planned and no one has planted it. But it has its laws of growth all the same, and its own grave grandeur. Every individual within it, struggling for his own life, and reaching up towards the sunlight, contributes not only to the variety but to the vast unity of the whole. The statesman, the philosopher, the preacher, the legislator, the judge, the soldier, the maker of tools, the tiller of the soil; the wise and good in every degree, nay, the foolish and wicked, by their negative experiments have for successive generations shed their lives like forest leaves to make the black soil on which our social institutions grow." [1] It awaits every human creature at his birth and commandeers the resources of his

[1] Sir Henry Jones: "The Working Faith of a Social Reformer," p. 17.

conscious life. Its summary process excites protests from individualists who assert that State control cannot be wisely adapted to personal rights. Its annals show that there has been no theory of such control that did not have conspicuous limitations. Hopeful experiments were comparatively short lived; the best constitutional provisions proved to be but temporary conveniences. The problems of political rule are renewed in every fresh development of civilization; many have withstood all previous efforts for their solution. Yet without the State men cannot cultivate their intellectual and spiritual faculties. Their habits, occupations and desires are not well qualified unless they are subordinated to its authority. They did not choose it, but it chose them, decreed their outward manner of being, and laid its burdens upon them. Their welfare is inconceivable apart from its training and partnership in mutual coöperation and loyalty.

What the relation of the politics of the State is to those of the Eternal Order is frequently debated. Without doubt it arouses an absorbing devotion almost comparable with those offered to the historic religions of the race. Yet patriotic passion is by no means invariably associated with the laws of supreme righteousness, and its separation from them has been the source of evils which impartial historians feel bound to condemn. The disparity between patriotism and justice has given rise to much moral and religious literature. It can only be lessened by the increasing realization in advanced States of a world commonwealth that has to be gradually evolved out of a purified and exalted race-consciousness which is now steadily advancing. Visioned spirits who foresee a universal State in which the Highest Will shall reign and prosper, are not to be chided for their want of patriotism. Far otherwise; their conviction that the State is an emanation of one supreme ordination for mankind is preservative of its life and power.

Portrayals of the perfect Commonwealth are found in Hellenic and Hebraic writings, which, in turn, have exercised a lasting influence upon later idealistic authors. Their optimistic tone pleases the majority; even those who regard them as dreamers delight in their dreams.[2] Nor can we afford to dispense with many ideals of the State which are at present inoperative, since some which were formerly regarded as impossible of realization have forced their way into general acceptance. Yet society is so constituted that it quickly resents the interference of ideals with its inherited proclivities. The strenuous opposition to the Eighteenth Amendment of the American Constitution is an example of this resentment. It has no validity in reason. Science, education and good morals have outlawed the use of intoxicating liquors as unnecessary even in moderation, and dangerous in excess. Nevertheless, the element of theoretical excellence which the amendment presupposes traverses some very human inclinations. Proposed Utopias will have to encounter these inclinations which will not be put down without resistance. No system of the doctrinaire that is so far ahead of the average citizen as to be out of his sight can do much more than challenge his lethargy. The majority of them, vague though benevolent, have hitherto failed to hasten the tardy growth of the State in moral character and resolution.

For many centuries, however, it was reverenced as the arbiter of ethics and religion. Its social and political principles included those of a loftier kind, and governed all alike. This domination surpasses in duration that of all other corporate bodies of mankind. The venerable guilds of trade, intercourse, art; even the brotherhoods of ecclesiastical beliefs and usages, are juveniles before the age of the State. They have had a prolonged tenure and a wide range in society, and determined much of its thought and action. But their antiquity and strength appear recent and subordinate in the light of those possessed by the State.

[2] Cf. "More's Utopia," translated into Modern English by G. C. Richards, where the value of such idealizations is discussed at length.

Notwithstanding its immemorial alliance with humanity, another existing institution is prior to the State in point of time, and superior to it in sacredness. The household was the first association of individuals; within this original unit, as Aristotle said, social order, affection and obedience were first generated. Its members were made one by the ties of consanguinity, which held them in an unbreakable bond. Implicit submission to parental authority was the first nexus, not only of dwellers under the domestic roof, but of the various organizations subsequently derived therefrom. In the stern school of the aboriginal home, made imperative by the need of food and shelter, were taught the lessons of social conservation that underlay the general welfare. Its occupants shared their gains and losses. Its religions instructed them in self-sacrifice for the sake of the family. Those persons alone were virtuous and honorable who best fulfilled their domestic duties. Their gods were the divinities of the hearth, the fold, the field, the forest, and the chase. They guarded the home, led the clan or the tribe in war, and protected them in peace. Nothing within the narrow range of primitive ideas was free from patriarchal supremacy, and the recognition of rights and their obligations which it enforced has since been verified by experience. So closely were responsibilities related under this primal jurisdiction that the sin of Achan was viewed as a family offense; its guilt and its punishment fell not only upon Achan himself, but upon his immediate relatives.[3]

When several families coalesced in the clan, its allegiance was given to the eldest male descendant, whose seniority in some instances had to be qualified by ability for leadership. Chieftainship required skill in battle, shrewdness in debate, and tactfulness in the settlement of internal disputes. Right choice of hunting grounds, successful sowing and harvesting of crops, clever manipulation of superstitious beliefs and customs, were the principal demands of the position.

[3] Joshua VII. 16 ff.

When two or more clans united the tribe was formed. No one tribe admitted that another was its superior except under compulsion; all asserted their independence, if necessary, by force of arms. The traits of family life, interdependence, helpfulness, heroism, antipathy to outsiders, persisted in tribal life, and eventually became the characteristics of the embryonic State. They prevail now in civilized as well as uncivilized nations; their vestiges are discernible throughout human society. What little we know of the prehistoric races is greatly to their credit. In a world of glaciers, moraines, morasses, jungles, impassable deserts, seas and mountains, where monstrous creatures swarmed, these earlier men and women waged and won a desperate struggle for existence against almost insuperable odds. Were our knowledge of their achievements as complete as that which we have of those of leaders of after ages, possibly the latter would have to give place to these brave primeval heroes who gained a precarious foothold on the planet. The more facile world in which we live was begotten by their exertions. To their indomitable perseverance, their courage, their alertness against imminent and deadly perils, the modern man owes not a few of his salient virtues, as well as the basis for his conquest of Nature.[4]

II

There are numerous hypotheses concerning the connection between tribalism and the nationalism, such as it was, of Oriental empires. But the systematic arrangement of facts which establish or seem to establish that connection has yet to be made. It is fairly certain that City-States existed in the Tigris-Euphrates valley. The earliest known kings of that region were not the rulers of countries, but of cities; of Kish, of Asshur, of Lagash, of Nippur, of Ur, and of

[4] Cf. W. Goodsell: "A History of the Family as a Social and Educational Institution"; Mathilde and Mathias Vaerting: "The Dominant Sex"; A. R. Wadia: "The Ethics of Feminism"; W. F. Lofthouse: "Ethics and the Family."

Babylon. The City-States of Greece were probably an inheritance from these localized kingships. Yet to demonstrate that they were is beyond our present knowledge. Indications also prevail that Greece borrowed her mythological cults from the Orient, but to prove this is, again, a very difficult matter. Scholars who can deal directly with the widely different literatures of the Orient, and at the same time command the infinite resources of Greek history and letters, are exceedingly rare. Those who are busy recovering the scattered remnants of Oriental life have had little time for tracing the movements of life and thought in the Hellenic peninsula. Whatever migrated from Orientalism and found a more hospitable home among the Greeks was transformed to suit their ideas and conditions, and therefore is not readily recognized. Take as a concrete instance the relative positions of sun and moon in mythology and religion. Among the Eastern Semites the moon outranked the sun, but it is just the opposite in Greece. The value of the moon's more tranquil light to dwellers in tropical climate is obvious. It gave them opportunities to resume activity in toil, and especially for travel. But in temperate climates the sun's heat ceased to be an enemy and the moon became by so much less a friend. The truth is that we are only at the beginning of a better understanding of the relation between the Orient and Greece, and an extended period of research awaits the learning which shall correlate them.

Considered as dynastic despotisms, the empires of Egypt, Assyria and Babylon make a notable exhibit in man's advance beyond tribal affiliations. But they magnified his idea of patriarchal absolutism in a monarchy which had few restraints, and his idea of the defense of the clan in military States that lived and died by the sword. Knowing much more than was formerly ascribed to them, they accomplished far less politically than could be reasonably expected of them. One of their fruitful reactions was an indirect stimulus of those prophecies of Israel, which showed that

have since occupied the political, philosophical, or artistic mind that were not Greek in their origin. The thinkers, builders, sculptors and statesmen of that nation bequeathed to posterity not only its parent metaphysic, its most moving drama, its permanent examples of architecture, but also some of its best political ideas. By the last bequest civilization has been enriched beyond comparison. The Greek mind made swift and true reactions to human organizations and struck their balance equitably. Nor were they left suspended in a metaphysical trance. The Greek language lent itself to every practical political measure. Its simplicity, conciseness and expressiveness in a certain sense created, almost as much as they connoted, some leading concepts of human rule and governance. It was impatient of twistings and embellishments; compact with a vitality of meaning that made excesses abhorrent to the Greek. The suavity and moderation of speech which suit the direction of visible institutions were its native qualities. It had the appositeness and pertinency befitting the most intrepid and cogent political reasoners of any age. Gravity and distinction belonged to it. It gave utterance to civic instincts and arguments which hitherto had been devoid of expression. It was the speech of freedom and of right.[7]

Rome's statesmen inherited from those of Greece. Cicero and Seneca alike emphasized the natural equality of the human family. For them the Commonwealth was the affair of all the people who composed it: a gathering of the people associated under a common law and enjoying a common weal. They urged that the bond of justice must be maintained between rulers and ruled, and Seneca anticipated Christian teaching by insisting that the slave was of the same nature as his master, and even capable of conferring benefits upon him. But these enlightened ideas, which go far beyond those of some Greek political philosophers, could not avail against the Oriental despotisms which infected

[7] Cf. "The Legacy of Greece." Essays edited by R. W. Livingstone.

Rome after her conquest of the Eastern Empire. Her chief strength lay, not in the enlightened principles of solitary thinkers, but in her solidarity and practical sagacity. She subdued and long held inviolate what Gibbon describes as "the fairest portion of the earth, and the most civilized portion of mankind." Her constructive genius in jurisprudence and in colonization, in the founding of cities and the rule of alien peoples, is still before us in every reputable court of law of every well administered modern State. Not only the broken pillars of the Forum, but the deserted fortresses on the Empire's farthest frontiers; the arch at Treves, the Temple of Claudius at Colchester, "the White City" beneath the Wrekin in Shropshire, Hadrian's Wall on the Scottish border, and innumerable other memorials perpetuate the valor blended with wisdom of Rome's imperialism. The peace she imposed by its dominion, though constantly interrupted by the wars imposed on her by her great domains, was a spacious interlude in which modern civilization, law and citizenship began to be. They were never afterwards entirely forfeited. But the dignity and elevation Rome bestowed on them, once obscured, were not restored until after the lapse of centuries. Neither her legal nor her military monuments are so likely to dominate the future intelligent mind as are the political concepts of Greece. They admonish us that if States would live in the after developments of society, they must subordinate their temporalities to their ideals. These have to be restated, attached to actual conditions, and involved in the flow of human life which survives the nations that originated them. It is a hard saying for the patriot, and yet a true one, that great Commonwealths, like great characters, find their lastingness, not in themselves, but in what they contribute to the aggregate of human good. They will perish, but their contribution will remain, and by its values they will ultimately be judged.

Orientals, Greeks and Romans alike agreed that the entire

field of human thought and action was the property of the State. Greek colonies, however, were completely independent from the first.[8] No other ties save those of sentiment and interest existed between them and their planters. Yet what strong ties these can be was exemplified by the cohesion of the British Empire under the strain of the World War. The one exception was Athens, whose colonies, like those of Rome, were replicas of the mother State. Domestic, economic, social and religious concerns were altogether at the will of the State. Roman law allowed no unlimited right of association and its violation was regarded as equivalent to treason. One of the chief causes of the persecution of Christianity was not, as is so often supposed, religious intolerance, but imperialism's jealousy and its suppressive instinct for all possible rivals.[9]

Dean Inge asserts that in the modern State we find only the corporate existence of *ἰδιώτης*, but that the classic State laid claims to the rights and offices of the modern *ἐκκλησία*. He also shows how the better side of Greek life suffered under Plato's successors, who did not even follow the best light obtainable from physical knowledge. Their luxuriant mythology was the raw material of both poetry and science; but it became, for the most part, non-moral, and could not instil in the citizens the virtues resulting from faith in a universal moral sovereign. For ethical guidance they looked not to priests and temples, but to senates and legislators. Their flexible conception of State supremacy, unmoderated by any exclusively religious beliefs, was furthered by these leaders of classic antiquity, who left nothing to the discretion of the individual. His existence was declared valueless in itself; only as it served the might of the

[8] The typical Greek colony was neither in origin nor development a mere trading post. It was or it became a "polis," a City-State, in which was reproduced the life of the parent State. Cf. Encyclopædia Britannica; Vol. XII. Eleventh Edition, Article: "Greek History."

[9] Cf. Herbert B. Workman: "Persecution in the Early Church," Chapter III, "The Causes of Hatred," p. 105, ff.

State was it worthy of attention. Politics was the sole and the indivisible authority; citizenship the sacred calling and the seat of all prerogative. None could contend against a semi-omnipotent organization which assumed that the passengers were made for the ship and not the ship for the passengers. No opening was left from which any rebel could defy the enclosures of the State or draw a line across its activities. The spiritual education of the people, the relief of the helpless, the freeing of the slave, the cravings of man's higher nature, obtained nothing from an institution which regarded humanity as mere material for the sustentation of its life and authority. What the bondsman was in the grasp of his owner, the owner was in the grasp of the State. Two closely related elements are perceptible in this theory. First, the State was viewed as an end in itself, to which the individual was an accessory; and, second, since the State was co-extensive with human life, it followed that sooner or later it would regard its own regnancy as far more important than the welfare of the citizen. This theory has been sufficiently tenacious to withstand every subsequent attack upon it, and many millions of men and women have died within the last few years to impress upon the world its fatal consequences.

What has been stigmatized as Prussianism is the scarred and battered descendant of the far past, with numerous indorsements from rulers and legalists of widely separated times and nations. They insisted that the highest social developments could only be reached by making the State supreme, and the individual the acolyte of its supremacy. In ancient as in modern days the theory survived all changes. Monarchy, oligarchy, aristocracy, democracy are familiar forms equivalent to the rule of the one, the few, the select, or the whole body of citizenship. But though these forms appear and disappear, they do not materially affect the absolutism of the State. The nations, then as now, were composed of those who inherited the same traditions, spoke the same language, and adhered to the same laws and customs. But the State, omnicompetent in human life and affairs, like Tennyson's brook, "goes on forever." [10]

Its greatest exponent of antiquity was Socrates, whose name is still worth an armed host in its behalf. He contended that one's country was higher and nobler than the individual, his parents, or any other of his ancestors. The reverence of men of understanding and the approval of the gods were fixed upon the State, which the Greek philosopher personalized and addressed in the speech of entire acquiescence and of homage. Her punishments should be suffered in silence, and her commands as implicitly obeyed as though they proceeded from a divine source. If they seemed to be unjust, the citizen should endeavor to change the mind of the State, failing which he was bound to execute her policies and endure her penalties without murmur or protest. Socrates, however, voiced the sentiments of an exclusive caste of male slave-owners, whose ideas of social order assumed the natural inequality of human society. Their theory was supported by Aristotle, who regarded slavery as a necessity for the higher forms of civilization; an opinion echoed by John C. Calhoun and his party in the middle period of the nineteenth century. When Aristotle inveighed against democracy as an evil form of government, the type he visualized was that of an incensed and disorderly mob assembled for mischief, without the directing reason essential to wise measures, or to their calm deliberation. He often suggests but never solves the problems arising from the relations of individuals and groups to the State. "And even if we reckon greatness by numbers," he says, "we ought not to include everybody, for there must always be in cities a multitude of slaves and sojourners and foreigners; but we should include those only who are

[10] "The People," a later term elevated by ethical usage, and brought in to signify the aggregate of population living under one political organization, was originated by the wider sympathies of genuine commonwealths. It shows correspondence with the psychical entity of nations, and foreshadows a world fraternity which advanced political thinkers desire.

members of the State, and who form an essential part of it." [11]

These aristocratic views were opposed by the Stoics and Epicureans, who regarded them as a scandal upon human nature, and leaned towards the assertion of man's personal rights. The moral teaching of the Stoics that there were in every individual certain spiritual realities which should be respected; that his intellect, his freedom, and his equality were birthrights beyond the jurisdiction of the State, partook of a religious character, and supplied one of the classic proofs of the folly of framing an indictment against human nature. They advanced enlightened social ideas, altogether absent from the Socratic theory, that have since been confirmed by the verdicts of civilization. But thinkers like the Stoics and the Epicureans are a small minority in this world. Thought works too slowly and while it grows the people perish for lack of knowledge. Further, it must be conceded that Socrates expressed the gist of Greek beliefs, and that these beliefs were vital to the continuance of the State as it was then constituted. He argued that since none could be an end in himself in a ruling society made up of a minority of slave owners, all must be its contributory agents. For once the unity of the structure was impaired, it was exposed to the fanaticism of demagogues, who, beneath the guise of patriotism, were intent on promoting their selfish contrivances. These conclusions have large meanings for modern nations. To us, with our ideas, no right seems clearer than the right of men to think and speak as they please about political matters. But the extreme interpretation which Socrates and Aristotle placed upon the State's control over the individual was at least rational. They averred that what men of character and ability doubted about would be held as doubtful. Dogmatic formulas would be disbelieved or disregarded. Politics, which was for them the rule of life, and

[11] "The Politics of Aristotle," translated by Benjamin Jowett. Book VII. Chs. IV–V, p. 214 ff.

the sanction of law and authority, would dwindle into a set of variant opinions. Practice would be made dependent upon expediency, and the State would be left jettisoned, without certainty about its nature or its obligations. It exists, as we know it, to conserve the individual's rights, to encourage his initiative, and to aid him in the discharge of his responsibilities. Though some contradictory forms of modern communism are, to a given degree, a revival of the Socratic doctrine, the idea of individuality is very differently construed now, and placed in more striking contexts. Yet its independence is never to be looked upon as synonymous with license. Personal choice and the will to do as one pleases are restrained on every side by the requirements of the social order, and are subsidiary to the welfare of that order.

I have said nothing about Plato's vision of the Ideal State, which properly belongs to the literature of lost Utopias. Nor is it probable that he believed his ideal could be realized in human society. The ethic which always exceeded religion in the concepts of Greek philosophers prevailed in Plato's dream. It is more valuable for its gravity and loveliness than for its practicability. In the ultimate, man's intellectual and moral development is the decisive factor in the character and benefit of the State, and this development is impossible without a reasonable religious faith. For want of it the authority of Greek and Roman States waned and then vanished. Yet what peoples they were! What a sense of the beautiful, the serene and the just was their's! What laws and literatures they bestowed upon us! If modern inquiry shows that heredity, environment, climate, diffused intelligence, the spread of commerce, and personal gifts or attainments directly affect the well-being of the State, do not ancient nations remind us that its soul is religion? One wonders if they could have perished had this truth been known and heeded by their great leaders.

III

The differences between the provinces upon which Greece or Rome set their seal, and those that lay beyond their boundaries, are plainly perceptible in mediæval and modern States, and forbid those divisions of history which are usually artificial in proportion as they are precise. There has been no actual break between classic and mediæval civilization, nor between Mediævalism and Modernism, but only intervals of depression varied by occasional revivals. Race continuity persisted; even a certain continuity of culture made itself felt, and the fact of these continuities should mould our conceptions of the Middle Ages. When we speak of them as "purblind," as pagan eras, or as "the dark cavern," we but pamper a prejudice incapable of correct historic estimates. Granted that the mediæval writers know no Greek, yet they established a literature of their own. The poetry of Chaucer, "The Book of Divine Doctrine" by St. Catherine of Siena, St. Francis' "Canticle of the Sun," the translations of the venerable Bede, the Chronicles of Matthew of Paris, the learning and instructions of Abelard, the story of "Sir Gawain and the Green Knight," have nothing particularly purblind in them.

Succeeding eras are nearly always severe in their verdicts upon those immediately preceding them. The attitude of some contemporary intellectuals toward the Victorian authors and publicists is a case in point.[12] There is a strong probability that those of the Renaissance were as grossly unfair to the mediæval artists and scholars. Assuredly they were not lacking in moral or spiritual insight. Clairvaux and Cluny, Paris and Oxford, did not send out the radiant light of Greece, but they sent out the divine light of Christianity. The mediævalists are charged with not being classical or

[12] Fashions in things intellectual are as real and as potent as they are in women's dress. A few years ago Neitzsche was all the rage. He was a terrible fellow! Today he is remembered only in snatches.

The light from within
medieval

artistic, yet they built Chartres and Lincoln. Giotto showed what the period could do in painting, and Dante was its august interpreter in poetry. Its saints and mystics read after a greater Teacher than Plato, and its seers were nearer to His Spirit and power than were some of the savants of the New Learning. Doubtless mediæval teachings were often intellectually poverty-stricken; and, as a consequence, the ancient ways of civic life became degenerate in due time. It was a period of extremes, of humility and pride; of love and hate; the ideal and the actual were often far removed from each other. Yet its climacteric in St. Francis and in St. Bernard, whose fame has been somewhat dimmed by that of St. Francis, showed that in religion, at any rate, it was no longer in a state of transition from the antique, but had attained a spirituality wholly its own and one reflected by after times.[13]

the fate of state finally determined

This kind of spirituality finally determines the fate of States. Thoughtful people may be thankful for their relation with Greek and Roman ancestries. Statesmen and historians may obtain from them in the critical moments of society those examples and precedents, rules and methods, that serve the present age. Yet in men's highest moods they confess that the needed guidance for individuals and for nations is not to be had from classic thinkers and rulers. The torch of knowledge can be rekindled in Athens, as can that of human justice in Rome. But for the light within that comes from beyond, inquiring minds repair to the Hebrew prophets and the Christian Apostles:

"As men divinely taught, and better teaching
The solid rules of Civil Government
In their majestic unaffected style,
Than all the oratory of Greece and Rome.
In them is plainest taught, and easiest learnt,
What makes a nation happy, and keeps it so,
What ruins kingdoms and lays cities flat." (*Paradise Regained*)

[13] Cf. H. O. Taylor: "The Mediæval Mind," Vol. I. Chapters XVIII and XIX on Saint Bernard and Saint Francis, p. 408, ff; Chapter XXI, "The Spotted Actuality," p. 487, ff.

The hold which Mediævalism has gained upon some artistic and religious groups today is not to be ascribed to the fascinations of Gothic architecture, or of Sir Walter Scott's novels. Nor is it rightly explained as a recrudescence of superstitions and symbolisms repudiated by scientific intelligence. Its strength lies where it always lay, in the craving of men and women for authoritative certainty about religion and their own souls. Life is soon over, death is impatient, some fixed beliefs seem essential as to their meanings here and hereafter. Such beliefs, Mediævalism, despite its errors and faults, professed to give, whereas much Modernism bids us have courage in our darkness, or faintly glimpse the larger hope. However unthought or unstudied any system of a social or religious character may be which ends this suspense, it will make a powerful appeal to certain temperaments. Again, the recurrent life forces that ebb but to flow again bring with them reversions to the past. Intellectual wisdom emanates from Greece; political wisdom from Rome; faith in the unseen is vibrant everywhere in the Middle Ages. Why should not they draw men and women back at crucial moments? Nothing in them addressed mentality alone. The consciousness of Church and State related itself in every way to religion and to Deity. Spiritual belief and duty seemed more simple then than they seem now. Certain childlike qualities making him unaware of that vastness of the universe which has burned the modern man's sense of nothingness into his very soul, never fell away from the mediæval man. Conscious communion with God often took on the semblance of sense perception. The apparent testimonies of an invisible realm which have become shadowy to myriads of our time were then intensely realistic.

Modern unfamiliarity with mediæval life exaggerates its charm, just as the archaisms of an older poet's verse give it a prestige it does not wholly deserve. Yet for those who are not absorbed by outward things excursions into its tranquil regions have their reward. The dearth of modern religious life in certain directions causes many to feel that, though the people of the Middle Ages doubtless were dirty, ignorant and miserable, they made trial of their times as we have not done of ours, and possessed some gifts and graces which this age could use to advantage. The mysteries that stirred their souls are no longer mysteries to us; some indeed are infantile puerilities. But the verities they steadfastly believed are not entombed, as too many imagine, in the cathedrals and monasteries of continental Europe, Great Britain and Ireland. Not even Dante's poetry, retrospective though it was, gave complete expression to the mediæval mind. Behind his epic, as behind lordly minsters and sacerdotal observances, there was a theology, a philosophy, a ritual, a polity, which subordinated the social organism in Church and State to the Christian doctrine. Perhaps this surrender to a religion so backward in learning was unwise; assuredly it was unconditional. But though we affirm our possession of that religion in purer forms, it has not triumphed in Modernism as it did in Mediævalism. The intellectual ugliness, political dishonesty and international malpractice of some modern and demoralized nations arise in large measure from their revolt against changeless spiritual laws. This revolt in turn is due to that lack of religious authority, the want of which destroyed an ancient civilization in some respects superior to our own.

It is therefore requisite in dealing with Mediævalism's grotesque admixtures, its virtues and its vices, that we should recognize in it the ever present spirit which dedicated outward things to religious purposes. Nor did its leaders invariably suppose, as some modern thinkers have stated, that religious formulas solve religious problems — an assumption contradicted by the difficulties which multiply in the face of its superficial treatment. They knew that those problems originated, not in doctrines and theories, but in life's factors, and that they could be solved only by dealing directly with those factors. The statement applies to the theocratic State of Mediævalism. Had it not enforced its dictates upon all and sundry, it could hardly have survived its hostile environment. This enforcement is not discounted by railings against its legitimacy. Its large-hearted and level-headed consideration better becomes us than heated assertions of our own superiority. The Mediæval State, as a part of the Church Universal, can hardly fail to have interest for every lover of State and Church. Let us study it unembarrassed by present shibboleths, or by catchwords of the part enlisted against the whole, or by the sentiments of provincialism.

IV

The first obstacle the Middle Ages had to encounter was the social submergence and anarchy which followed the Fall of Rome. Not only normal and human, but abnormal and inhuman elements permeated the results of that event. How far the victorious Teuton was better than the defeated Latin is not a settled question. But it is a settled question that the European peoples who had been ruled by Rome have been the progenitors of modern civilization. There is no space to discuss here in detail the clans and kingdoms that emerged from the debris of her destruction. Visigoths, Ostrogoths, Saxons, Alemanni, Bavarians, Lombards and Vandals — each group had its place and part in the gradual evolution of the Mediæval State.[14] But the solitary and dominating figure arising out of the chaos of society was that of Charles the Great, who was a Christian king before he became the belated successor of pagan Emperors. His grandfather, Charles Martel, had already lessened the power of territorial bishops, by assuming sovereign rights over their appointment and deposition. The second son of Charles Martel's son Pepin, Charles, fell heir to domains

[14] Cf. R. W. Church: " Beginning of the Middle Ages"; H. B. Workman: " The Foundation of Modern Religion"; André Lagarde: " The Latin Church in the Middle Ages"; F. J. Foakes Jackson: " An Introduction to the History of Christianity, A. D. 590–1314."

extending from the Bohemian frontier to the Atlantic ocean, and from the North Sea to the Alps and the Pyrenees. His compact with the Papacy sanctioned its canon law, and surrendered the administration of the Church to the hierarchy, reserving to him the temporal power. This he held as its over-lord; the benefices of the bishoprics remained at his discretion, and his capitularies regulated much of the rule of the Church.[15]

But far more important than these arrangements was his self-elevation to the primacy of Christendom, in which the Pope was spiritual Emperor, and Charles a secular Pope. Europe then became a Papacy in religious matters, and a feudalistic State in civil affairs. Lord of the ecclesiastical hierarchy whose ideal was a Christian Republic, patron of the Holy See, master of mighty armies, Charles, despite his want of education, combined love of law and a deep regard for justice with a superb gift of organization. He was at once a conservative and a reformer, a soldier and a philanthropist, a loyal churchman and a resolute foe of clerical usurpations. The Christmas Eve of the year 800 is the date of the death of the old world and of the birth of the new. During High Mass in the Basilica of St. Peter's on that historic night, the Pontiff placed on the Emperor's head the diadem of the Cæsars, and saluted him as "Charles, the most pious Augustus, crowned of God, great and peace giving Emperor." After the interruption of centuries of comparative barbarism, the Church again found herself in possession of a world-wide power.[16]

[15] Cf. "The Cambridge Mediæval History." Vol. II. Chs. XIX and XXI.

[16] In number the men who promoted the scholarly interests of the Carlovingian period were few, and fewer were the places where they throve. There was the central group of open-minded laymen and churchmen about the palace school, or following the court in its journeyings, which were far and swift. Then there were monastic or episcopal centers of education as at Tours, or Rheims, or Fulda. The scholars carried from the schools their precious modicum of knowledge, and passed on through life as educated men living in the world, or dwelt as learned compilers, reading in the cloister. But the rays of their enlightening influence were scanty enough in that period's encompassing ignorance.

Since the nations of Europe did not then exist, the imperialism of Charles was the buttress of the rights of the State. How necessary its protection was became manifest after his death in 814, an event which let loose endless confusions that ran amuck for two hundred years. National sentiment was incipient in the crop of kinglets which sprang up in every province, and somewhat active in the higher clergy who undermined the authority of the Frankish Empire for the sake of their ecclesiastical privileges. Eventually, the follies of rulers, the gradual dismemberment of the system which Charles had established, and the decline of Papal authority left the great barons and prince-bishops free to do as they would. Some ruled well, others ill, but all ruled arbitrarily. Feudalism arose to pillage merchants, freeholders and peasants, to domineer over helpless monarchs, and to clash with the episcopacy. The elevation of the nobility in the State degraded every other rank and condition. It seldom forgot its internal strifes, except when its members united to harass the Church or to oppress the populace. Self-constituted conquerors and military adventurers prevented national expansion and prosperity throughout Europe. The Norsemen invaded and plundered Great Britain and the eastern coasts of France and Ireland. The Hungarians harried the Rhine Valley and camped under the walls of Capua. Saracenic armies garrisoned the seaport towns of Italy. Robber colonies infested the border lands of every State. The outcome of this turbulence was the setting up of royal dynasties as the symbol of State unity, and the restoration of the Empire under the House of Hohenstaufen. Monarchs who were nothing more than meek patrons could not keep the peace of Europe. A species of nationalism which had proved disastrous to political and religious unity, was now to be subordinated to the Holy Roman Empire in its renewed form. But the subsequent controversy between the Empire and the Papacy, to be presently related, ended a compact which had unified religion, federalized Europe, given kingship a sacred character, embodied beneficial theories of the State and of the obligations of nations.

Those who complain of this alliance of Church and State should consider that the spirit of ageless paganism which dwelt in society, could not be expelled except by their united power. Theologians and priests insisted that the Church was not in the State, but the State in the Church, because she threw her influence into the scale of lawful authority against that of cut-throats and bandits. Men attached themselves to clerics whose minds were stored with the knowledge of the Scriptures and of the Latin Fathers. In the poverty of their own ideas, to whom else could they go? It was the Church which furnished rulers, statesmen, scholars, and supplied governmental methods that appear reactionary to the uninformed, but were a marked advance on anything else of the kind existing then.[17] Between the time of the first appearance of Christianity within the Roman Empire and that of its spread far beyond the Empire's frontiers, its teachings had been dogmatically formulated in a Church which had inherited the organizing genius of Rome. This finished system, which claimed divine approval, was endowed with the surviving culture of a former civilization, and thus presented to the unsophisticated and unlettered peoples of Europe. It offered them supernatural aid, and a better knowledge and control of life than they had, or could obtain elsewhere. The manner of its presentation hastened its acceptance. Its missionary activities brought it numberless converts, whose loyalty to the Holy See, like that of generations to come, was assured and contented. Their's was the attitude of felt ignorance before recognized wisdom; of obedient and affectionate children who worshipped the Church as the Mother of the State and of their individual and collective good. The social development of Europe was hastened by this imperial propagation of Christianity. For centuries the Northern as

[17] Cf. Lord Acton: " The History of Freedom," p. 33, ff.

well as the Southern peoples were to be held in willing submission to the constitution and forms of Mediævalism, which they had thus received. They continued to revere the Roman source of Christian teachings, and to look with awe upon the sanctity and knowledge that encompassed them.

During the twelfth and thirteenth centuries Feudalism was the corner stone of the State, the social system *par excellence* which maintained government, enacted legislation and administered justice. The only power capable of resisting its control was that of the ecclesiastical hierarchy, and they collided when the progress of Feudalism in Teutonic States threatened the independence of the Church by subjecting her prelates to the secular princes. A word describing so remarkable a system is necessary at this point. The monarch was the sole land-owner; and dukes, counts, barons, knights, bishops or abbots took their title to the land, either directly or mediately from him. In return for their holdings they were pledged to render military service, and under certain contingencies, monetary aid to the king as head of the State. His tenants had sub-tenants of their own, some of whom were freemen, but the majority bondsmen. Even the free cities of the Middle Ages, which were antagonistic to Feudalism, both in spirit and organization, were forced to compromise with it.[18]

Like all social systems it is to be considered not only for its evil but for its good; for the difficulties it overcame, and the dangers it avoided. Its exactions were often softened by the introduction of Chivalry, which was grafted upon Feudalism by the Church. Although the ethic of Chivalry was intrinsically militaristic it had its ameliorative side. Its influence has been exaggerated by romanticists who depict it as asking that flowers should always spring in its path to birth. It is to be understood as a beneficial, and for a time, a

[18] Cf. "Foundations of Society" by P. Vinogradoff in "The Cambridge Mediæval History," Vol. II. Chapter XX; and "Feudalism" by P. Vinogradoff in *id*, Vol. III. Chapter XVIII.

vigorous attempt to apply some Christian precepts and typical masculine virtues to human conduct. It also brought into social relationships an ideal quality which still pervades them. Its precepts were no more universally obeyed than are those of the best kind today; but it rediscovered not a few gracious fellowships, and gave woman a moral status unknown to antiquity. Under its impulse, rough untutored warriors became urbane and gallant gentlemen who modified the turbulence that threatened the first feeble motions of nationalism. The story of Sir Lancelot idealizes the process. His geniality of soul, the shining qualities of his knighthood, the worshipful affection he bore for the advancement of right, and for the defense of his dearest one, are mirrored in the tale. Adventures in which other knights had found their undoing ended well for him, because of the love that shone high and clear over his quest. But for Chivalry, we probably should never have heard of Sir Lancelot, nor of the Beatrice of Dante, nor of the Laura of Petrarch, nor of Shakespeare's Miranda, nor of Goethe's Marguerite. Its adoration of the Virgin, although not equally helpful all round, was a religious source of its moral resolves; and its professed reverence for purity in woman was a protest against the pagan ideas which insisted on her static inferiority.[19]

Between the years 1100 and 1500, the State gradually attained stability and power. Its vested interests and social efficiency increased apace. Religious and political progress was unhindered by the chaos that had ensued after the ruin of the Roman and Frankish Empires. It has been suggested that this was the constitutional period of English-speaking nations, and that the parliamentarians of the seventeenth century who reduced the royal prerogative, were reclaiming their former rights rather than asserting new ones. Some historians indorse the view that the Lancastrian dynasty

[19] Cf. G. G. Coulton: "Five Centuries of Religion," Vol. I, Chapters IX–XI on "The Mother of God," "The Gospel of Mary," and "Women and the Faith," p. 138, ff.

conceded precedents valuable to future democratic States. Others contend that these concessions have been overestimated, and that Coke, Pym, Eliot, Hampden and their fellow patriots went beyond all Lancastrian precedents.

We return from this digression to observe that for four hundred years, Europe enjoyed a comparative peace which the black magic of no Attila, Napoleon or Hohenzollern disturbed. For once in a millennium the dynasties, raised to power by statecraft or the sword, gave a respite to war-torn humanity. The political sciences outran those of armed violence, and consequent moral and religious advantages were gained during the late twelfth and the thirteenth centuries. The age of Aquinas, Roger Bacon, St. Francis, St. Louis, Giotto and Dante can be safely regarded as the most purely spiritual, most really constructive and most truly philosophical period of Mediævalism.

V

In every way it is borne in upon us that its society conformed to no one type. The character and attainments of Englishmen, Germans, Frenchmen, Italians and other nations exhibited their usual diversities, which also differed from those of their Teutonic, Celtic, Gallican and Latin ancestors. Yet, as we have seen, they had some things in common, which have not been approved by all modernists. They are accused of a dry theology, of a useless metaphysic, and of monastic selfishness. But it is very doubtful if mediæval progress was at any time paralyzed by two of the strongest and basest of human motives — greed and fear — as modern progress has been paralyzed by them. The practices of the period, like those of our own, were never so good and seldom as bad as appearances indicated. When it drew near its end it gave birth in the great thirteenth century to Modernism. A phenomenal outbreak of religious devotion relieved the hearts made sick by hopes deferred. Behind its vitalizing advance came the inventive fertility, imaginative wealth, and spiritualized ideas, upon which Frederic Harrison pours fervent praise. In statesmanship, he tells us, it can only be matched by comparing the age with that of Pitt and Burke, of Washington and Marshall. There was no discord in its development; kings, priests, prophets, poets, teachers, evangelists, artists and artisans were of one mind and purpose; and could knit together, according to one design, the symmetrical social fabric which was their chief ambition. Mr. Harrison's statement that it cannot be called in any special sense the material, the devotional, the political or the poetical age, since it was equally and all of these combined, should perhaps be qualified. But doubtless its united belief and worship, its single code of manners, its uniform social discipline and education conferred upon the thirteenth century an honorable distinction far beyond that usually attributed to Mediævalism at any time.

Those who deprecate the idea of solidarity in Church and State are not sustained by references to that age. It was blessed with unities that for a brief moment overcame men's divisive tendencies. One Church, one sacred language, one accepted type of beauty, gave to the European peoples their current ideals of the good, the true and the æsthetic. Albert and Aquinas had no peers in philosophic range till Descartes came. Roger Bacon was far more worthy of fame's tribute than the Chancellor who bore his surname. These thinkers were not afraid of life. They could visualize its meanings and coördinate its knowledge in some subjective systems which did not die till their work was done. The Universities, headed by Paris, were the centers of an eager culture, and the "schools" of the nations gave full stature to the Universities.[20] Besides Paris, there were those of Oxford, Orleans, Toulouse, Montpelier, Cordova, Seville, Toledo and Bologna. Great cathedrals arose which still reveal to us more religion,

[20] Cf. Hastings Rashdall: "The Universities of Europe in the Middle Ages."

more humanity, more individual and collective aspiration than the reading of many books about the century.[21] Macaulay, in spite of his utilitarian outlook, waxes eloquent, even for him, over its achievements. He likens them to mountain fastnesses out of which the largest rivers flow to fertilize the plains below. Its annals, he tells us, may seem sterile and obscure to the unobservant, yet in them are contained the secrets of present freedom and democracy. Then and there, Christian Europe began to exhibit those saving merits which it has since in part retained, and which enabled it to colonize America and transmit civilizing forces to Asiatic and African lands. The political doctrines of the English State, which have preserved their identity through all successive changes, were for the first time clearly ascertained and stated. "Then first appeared with distinctness that Constitution of which all the other free Constitutions in the world are copies, and which, in spite of some defects, deserves to be regarded as the best under which any great society has ever yet existed during many ages. Then it was that the House of Commons, the archetype of all the representative assemblies which now meet, either in the Old or in the New World, held its first sittings. Then it was that the common law rose to the dignity of a science, and rapidly became a not unworthy rival of the imperial jurisprudence. . . . Then it was that the most ancient colleges which still exist at both the great nation's seats of learning were founded. Then was formed that language, less musical, indeed, than the languages of the south, but in force, in richness, in aptitude for all the highest purposes of the poet, the philosopher, and the orator, inferior to the tongue of Greece alone. Then, too, appeared the first dawn of that noble literature, the most splendid and the most durable of the many glories of England." [22]

Not only in Britain, but also in the principal countries of

[21] Cf. Frederic Harrison: "A Survey of the Thirteenth Century," in "The Meaning of History," p. 145, ff. Also James J. Walsh: "The Thirteenth: Greatest of Centuries," pp. 1–17.

[22] "History of England," Everyman's Library Edition. Vol. I. p. 21.

Europe the idea that culture and not race is the foundation of a second Statehood was advocated by scholars and teachers. It was a time of fusion, when the last traces of conquest temporarily disappeared beneath the rising tides of human consciousness. Even its sculptures are separated from those of the twelfth century by a wider gap than any that divides the two periods in law or in language. At the root of the matter, as touching law and constitution, those changes were made at that time which left future ages little to do but improve in their details. The political and social institutions of England, France and Germany gradually assumed those forms that characterize European and American nations today. The last six hundred years of their story were here marked off from the six hundred years that had gone before.

No generalizations, however broad, can include the totality of world forces that operated in the thirteenth century. Nor are we to suppose that it was a solely creative period. During its years the Eastern Empire fell beneath the arms of the Frank, and the Eastern Caliphate before the arms of the Mogul. The Western Empire suffered defeat by the Papacy, and the soldiers of the Cross were driven from the Holy Land. Nevertheless, whatever happened in "this age of wonder" or afterwards — when wave after wave of change pounded over Europe, while Venice became the mistress of the Eastern seas and Florence stood out as the new type of democratic freedom, when the nominal kingship of the lords of Laon and Paris expanded into the broad realm of Philip Augustus and Philip the Fair — the temporal and spiritual gains of the thirteenth century enumerated here remained to its honor and for the lasting good of humanity.[23]

13th cent a creative one

Those who enter the Mediæval State through the gateway of Chaucer's joyous poetry or of Gothic architecture, may find it difficult to reconcile their gladness, grace and power with the physical and moral wretchedness of the European peasants and artisans. The uprisings of the Jacquerie in

[23] Cf. E. A. Freeman: "The Norman Conquest," Vol. V. p. 439.

France and of the rebels of England's south-eastern shires, apparently confute the eulogies the historians quoted bestowed upon Mediævalism. The explanation is that the revival of life and progress of the thirteenth century was followed in the fourteenth by an orgy of feudal misrule and violence. The Hundred Years War between France and England, the dismemberment of France, the Wars of the Roses, the distractions of Spain and the decadence of the Empire destroyed many of the fairest prospects of Europe. Until monarchs like Louis XI, Ferdinand V, Charles V, and the English Tudors suppressed Feudalism, it terrorized the State and kept the middle classes in subjection. Like the expiring Imperialism of our day, it took a heavy toll before it finally disappeared.[24]

VI

The love of liberty as part of the universal good, which even the poorest serf felt, and the hate of liberty as a detestable innovation which animated his oppressors, were then as now, polar instincts in Church and State. For princes and prelates who were intent on their unity, and on that preservation of loyalty to both which, as they conceived, determined the welfare of men and women in this world and the next, obedience was the first lesson of social progress. For those who were forced to obey, freedom was the first condition of any progress. Yet obedience was well worth learning, even though it required ages to make it an instinctive motor reaction. By the steady pressure of its authority the Mediæval Church-State modified the very brain tissues of Christendom, inculcating habits of thought and psychic qualities which will endure as long as European and American civilization lasts. But the revolts of the longsuffering populace against the relentless discipline betokened its approaching end.

[24] Cf. F. Melian Stawell and F. S. Marvin: "The Making of the Western Mind," Chapters XVII to XX.

Further, the changing geographical situation, and its resultant economic conditions, were inexorably stronger than the once all-powerful union of Papacy and Empire. Natural rights overturned monarchical, ecclesiastical and feudal supremacy. The reaction against unlicensed power began in the reign of Henry the Third of England, reached its high water mark in the fourteenth century, and did not recede until it had increased the independence of nations, and made wide openings for their existence as separate States. Not only the Jacquerie of France and the peasants who followed Wat Tyler to Smithfield, London, but the Albigenses of Languedoc and the Hussites of Bohemia were restive under a conservatism which had been too dearly purchased to be wisely catholic. "Poor men," cried Wyclif, "have naked sides and dead walls have great plenty of waste gold": a bitter cry indeed, and one into which, as Principal Workman comments, "half the Reformer's social writings could be compressed."

In 1381 it looked as though the ardent hopes of the thirteenth century had been extinguished in blood and fire. England and France were under the spell of militarism. Their governments were weakened by anarchy from below and by despotism from above. Religion sank into a decline which the break down of the monastic orders aggravated. Yet public order survived, and feudal princes and lords were taught to beware of their hitherto despised underlings. After the visitations of the Black Death, agrarian problems multiplied, and the rural populations showed an unwonted self-assertion. Serfdom began to die by general consent. Barons moved more cautiously among their dwindling prerogatives and claims, because they recalled the possibilities for reprisal that slumbered in the proletariat. The constitutional changes already discussed brought into the English State the Parliament, which was recruited from county families that had long been active in local affairs. The embarrassments of the Crown were the opportunities of more liberal minded citizens. They remembered as Englishmen the prestige of the Saxon Witenagemot, and of the great Charter which had been wrung from King John, the ablest and least scrupulous of the Norman princes. Before the Parliament, of which they were the original members, had been in existence two hundred years as an institution, it had asserted its authority in a memorable manner. In spite of its then extremely limited representation, it deposed four monarchs, and conferred a legal title upon three new dynasties.

Upon the Continent the quarrels of Pontiffs and Emperors which persisted intermittently for four centuries, resulted in the humiliation of both antagonists. Papalists and Imperialists strove for absolute authority only to invalidate it. Both were at last compelled to appeal to the peoples of Europe as the final court for its assignment, and they began to believe it would be a good thing to reserve it for themselves. In the distresses of spiritual and temporal overlords who had brooked no rival, the civil and religious liberties of modern States were born. Guelfs who fought for the Papacy and Ghibellines who fought for the Empire, alike acknowledged a third estate destined to eclipse these ancient sovereignties. Once the appeal was taken, it released a flood of elucidations and propositions. The large hearted giant of Scholasticism, St. Thomas Aquinas, showed with his accustomed penetration that laws derive their sanction from the nation, and are not binding without its consent. Marsiglio of Padua, whom we shall meet again as by far the ablest writer and apologist for the Imperialists, agreed in substance with the declaration of St. Thomas.

Luther's dramatic entry at the Diet of Worms in 1520, did not avert his condemnation by Charles the Fifth. But the Emperor's edict was a temporizing measure of political exigencies which he could not overcome. Nor should it be forgotten that the Diet over which he presided also indicted the Holy See for its notorious evils. Since the Reformation, the State has repeatedly deposed the Church in Catholic as well as in Protestant countries. Various reasons were given for her deposition, but the essence of all was that she trespassed upon an ever growing State authority essential to nationalism. So the building of the modern State became the task of patriots and the goal of history. Even the doctrine of the "Divine Right" of monarchy was little more than an impersonalization of State supremacy against the claim of international ecclesiasticism to rule the world. In England, France and Germany it wrought good as well as evil. Americans should deal gently with it, since the colonial settlements out of which their Republic originated, would have been humanly impossible had not the island kingdom of the Tudors set up housekeeping for itself. Always isolated, independent, and stubborn when aroused, England had never been as docile as Continental Catholicism desired, nor felt the need of Continental life for a federal rule. One of Henry the Eighth's subservient parliaments proclaimed that monarch Head of the Church, not only to satisfy his degraded lusts, but also to insure the integrity of the State. He deserves no consideration, and his relation with Anglicanism has been a historic reproach that was widely misunderstood then as it is now. Sir Thomas More and Bishop Fisher, who denied the royal supremacy, which numerous other English churchmen only accepted under duress, went to the scaffold for their convictions. But the Crown and the Nation which the Crown represented were at last free to follow their own course. In France the legal authorities increased the absolutism of kingship in Church and State, establishing the Concordat of 1516 as their instrument for that purpose. Under the Houses of the Valois and the Bourbons the Gallicanism of royalty supplanted that of the parliaments and the universities, practically placing the Church at the disposal of the monarchy. The framework of the parliamentary system of Spain which links together the fortunes of Church and State, is now the oldest in Europe.

In Germany and Geneva, Lutheranism and Calvinism based their theory of the State upon a natural rather than a political analogy, to which further reference will be made. All rule being derived from God, the State was the medium of the Church, and the Church the source of those ideals that are vital to the State. While civil in form, the laws of nations were sacred in origin. Protestantism gained princely adherents because their rights and claims throve upon that diminution of ecclesiastical prerogatives, which was hastened by the secularization of the Pontificate.

In this rapid review it should be noted that the constitutional history of England, which directly affects that of all other English-speaking peoples, has been revised and corrected during the last fifty years. The idea of the Victorian historians that nearly everything equitable in political institutions is traceable to the primitive democracy of Teutonic ancestors, has been very much modified. The Barons at Runnymede and the Parliament convened by Simon de Montfort, were not endeavoring to regain the lost liberties which England owed to Hengist and Horsa. They were endeavoring to transform the absolutism of monarchy into a limited rule. This they succeeded in doing, and though the constitutionalism of the fourteenth and following centuries was at first feeble, and at after intervals almost non-existent, it paved the way for the Puritan Revolution which ended the Tudor type of Crown governance. From the accession of the Stuarts onward, the struggle between the royal prerogatives and those of Parliament was compromised by the arrangement which gave the Crown the forms of power but reserved its realities for the Parliament.

Some American conceptions of popular sovereignty were evolved out of the Puritan Revolution, others were obtained from the contact of the Pilgrims with Continental Protestantism in Holland. The French Encyclopædists played their part in the process, giving to Jefferson and the patriots who agreed with him not a few basic ideas of democracy. But the inescapable atmosphere and traditions of a thousand years of Anglo-Saxon life and law are discernible in the leading ideas of our constitutionalists, especially of Washington, Franklin, Hamilton, Madison and Marshall. Other streams of thought and influence flowed into the life of this Republic, and not all have been of equal purity.[25] Vapid talkers, men of mere words, wind-bags, have too large a vogue just now. The hopes placed upon them are destined to be disappointed. Their interpretations of the voice of the people makes it resemble the bleating of the sheep. The nation which has helped to lead the way of the world's progress has come to the margin where other powerful States preceded her. Some of these, like Spain, chose wrongly and decreased; others, like Britain, chose wisely and increased. Upon America's choice, and that of kindred peoples, depend, so far as one can foresee, the character and fortunes of the future State. "When half gods go the gods arrive," and we can rest firmly in the faith that our well-intentioned citizens shall not want for a leadership worthy of the mission of this Republic.

U.S. danger line

[25] Cf. Nicholas Murray Butler: "Building the American Nation."

His efforts -
To locate seat of authority
Determine rel. bet ch & State

FOURTH LECTURE

THE MODERN STATE

Let us now praise famous men,
And our fathers that begat us.
The Lord manifested in them great glory,
Even his mighty power from the beginning.
Such as did bear rule in their kingdoms,
And were men renowned for their power,
Giving counsel by their understanding,
Such as have brought tidings in prophecies:
Leaders of the people by their counsels,
And by their understanding men of learning for the people;
Wise were their words in their instruction:
Such as sought out musical tunes,
And set forth verses in writing:
Rich men furnished with ability,
Living peaceably in their habitations:
All these were honored in their generations,
And were a glory in their days.

. . . .

Their seed shall remain for ever,
And their glory shall not be blotted out.
Their bodies were buried in peace,
And their name liveth to all generations.
Peoples will declare their wisdom,
And the congregation telleth out their praise.

Ecclesiasticus XLIV. 1 ff.

FOURTH LECTURE

THE MODERN STATE

The Renaissance and the Reformation produced radical results in every walk of life — Erasmus and the Humanists need to be impartially appraised — The leaders of the sixteenth century were men of extraordinary caliber, peculiarly fitted for their tasks in that period of religious, social and political transition — Luther and Calvin — Lutheranism and Calvinism compared — The spacious days of Queen Elizabeth — The Puritan and Pilgrim testimony and the settlements in the New World — The misrule of George III, the American Revolution and Clive's conquest of India — The uprising of European democracy, the industrial revolution and the rise of the modern State.

The Reformation period, like the Victorian, was so crowded with major events and personalities, that the numerous volumes written upon it have ill-sufficed to do it justice. The ceaseless revolution of the world was then attended by a political and religious upheaval, the results of which still agitate our time. Many cherished habits of Mediævalism disappeared in the sixteenth century, while the phenomenal developments of thought and action which succeeded them, ushered in the Modern State and with it, scientific progress. Confined as we are to generalizations, it should at once be said that the secession of European States from Papal control, was the last and most notable phase in the gradual decline of the majestic Church of the Middle Ages. Inherent causes would probably have brought about a disruption, even without leaders. The lessening empire of the Church continued after the Reformation, not only in Protestant countries, but also in Catholic Austria, Spain, France and Italy. With the one exception of John Calvin, the reformers who rejected Rome's spiritual jurisdiction were not unusually daring innovators in thought or action. We do not associate with them the intellectual scope and depth of philosophers like Descartes and Spinoza, nor attribute to them the intrepid courage of the founders of the Dutch Republic. They remained orthordox in the Faith, and some among them modified their zeal for individual freedom when other Protestants whom they opposed, applied its principles for themselves.

Neither the creators nor the allies of the New Learning which preceded the Reformation, have always received the sympathetic treatment they deserved for their efforts to maintain an unbroken social organization. Firmly persuaded as they were that nothing which had ever interested the human mind could wholly lose its vitality, they looked long, meditated deeply and acted cautiously before consenting to changes.[1] In the ferment of a revolutionary time when parties and interests were hostile to one another, and ancient institutions and opinions were fiercely attacked or obstinately defended, the quiet reasonableness and equable flow of Desiderius Erasmus (1466–1536) and his disciples were sure to be heavily discounted. Yet among these were judicious and dispassionate men whose neutrality was better fitted than heated partisanship to rightly determine the issues of the age. They felt that not a few ambitious schemes for the removal of notorious evils contained, in their excess, the possibility of even worse evils. At once reactionary and reformative, conservative and iconoclastic, fervid haters of superstition and fervid lovers of the verities it polluted, the Renaissance scholars could not outride the storm they had helped to arouse. Theosophists tell us that Atlantis and Lemuria perished, because the immense magical forces which their inhabitants called up escaped their control. The Renaissance could not be thus destroyed. It "liberated the human intelligence and set men free to dwell in a world of beauty and of humane studies." The Reformation which

[1] Cf. Walter Pater: "The Renaissance," p. 37; also, "The Cambridge Modern History," Vol. I. Chapters XVI to XIX.

followed it, "liberated the human conscience and set men free to act according to their own inward promptings and convictions." [2] Each of the two processes of liberation, rightly viewed, assisted and supplemented the other. But the less fastidious Luther and the more logical Calvin outdid the sons of the Renaissance in the making of the modern State. Nevertheless, to say that the latter individuals were without wide influence; to deny their great value to society; to assert as some do that they were not inspired by laudable motives, is mere critical sansculottism.

Erasmus and his fellow Humanists were worthy of their classic lineage as scholars and thinkers. They rendered permanent service to their own and after times; and may be even more beneficial in the eirenic days to come. With nearly every one of their translations and books some error was banished to the shades, some baseless claim muttered its anathema and fled. They replenished in many realms men's scanty stores of truth, and evinced the merits of less biased minds in a whirl of reckless propaganda. We are drawn to them principally through Erasmus, especially during his visits to Holland and to England, and his residence in Basel. To him gathered the wits, scholars, teachers and university celebrities of Europe; some already famous, others candidates for fame.[3] His "Encomium Moriæ," "Adagia" and "Colloquia Familiaria," had charmed every college and court with their amusing but telling allusions to grave subjects, their genial wisdom and piercing yet painless satire. Goethe insists that the improvement of the Church should have been left to men like Erasmus. Perhaps so, but how was he to get

A. E. Zimmern: "Personality in National Progress," in "The Coming Renaissance," Essays edited by Sir James Marchant, p. 225.

[3] Cf. Henry Osborn Taylor: "Thought and Expression in the Sixteenth Century," Vol. I. Bk. I, "The Humanism of Italy," Bk. II, "Erasmus and Luther." Also "Humanists," by Hugh Watt in "Encyclopædia of Religion and Ethics," Vol. VI. p. 158, ff; E. M. Hulme: "The Renaisance and Reformation," ch. XI, "Humanism and Heresy"; L. Elliott Binns: "Erasmus the Reformer, A Study in Restatement"; Preserved Smith: "Erasmus, a Study of his Life, Ideals and Place in History."

the power to which he was not born? The forces behind the impending revolution were too swift for his literary leisure. "While the grass grows, the steed starves." His interests were divided; he had friends in every party; Clement VII made him a donation; the nuns of Cologne tempted his jaded appetite with sweetmeats; Archbishop Warham presented him with the living of Aldington; and Bishop Fisher gave him a professorship at Cambridge. The favorite scholar of Europe, the brilliant but magnanimous foe of dying Mediævalism, he refused to take a stand like that of Sir Thomas More, with whom he had lodged, conversed and prayed at his suburban home in Chelsea. He was not built for a fray which meant the axe and the flame; nor could he any more consent to the overthrow of the Papacy than he could be silent about its sins. He hesitated to identify himself with either faction, and admitted his hesitancy. "I seek truth," he said, "and find it at times in Catholic propositions, and at times in those of the Protestants."

It is not surprising that Protestants denounced him as a defaulter on the questions he had agitated, or that Catholics deplored him as a satirical rationalist whose learned jestings perverted faith and discipline. Nevertheless, the great fight for the intellectualism which saves faith from superstition, was fought and won before his death. Without men of his make up, though not of his quality, the protests of Luther and Calvin would have fallen short of their mark. The source of the humanities which he expounded was never apart from religion; always of its very essence. The loyal bond of "good letters" united him to the choicest spirits of the age. He was more than a consummate scholar, more than the friend and gossip of every select circle in Europe, more than the educator of a continent, more than a chastened mediævalist; he was the high minded, sincere Christian who could not abide the beggarly traditions that had profaned the reasonableness of the New Testament Faith. His contribution to that Faith through his scholarship is mentioned later in these pages. He aided by its means the saner developments of Christianity in a time of rabid controversies.

Nor were his contributions to politics less conspicuous. His conception of the ideal ruler when compared with "The Prince" of Machiavelli, reveals the mettle of the man, and also the gulf between the Latin and the Teutonic Renaissance. The intrigues and assassinations recommended in cold blood by the Florentine as statecraft, had no place in the mind of Erasmus. He advocated a constitutional monarchy as infinitely better than absolutism, declaring that kings as the servants of their people should make the general welfare their chief concern. Taxes and imposts, he urged, should be as light as possible, and levied on luxuries instead of necessities. No war should be undertaken without good and sufficient reasons which commended themselves to wise and patriotic citizens. We have still to wait for a fuller realization of the excellent principles which Erasmus advanced under the most difficult circumstances, and which remain to his praise as one of the founders of an adequate domestic and international science of politics. His temper and message are admirably expressed in the following poem:

"When he protested, not too solemnly,
That for a world's achieving maintenance
The crust of overdone divinity
Lacked aliment, they called it recreance;
And when he chose through his own glass to scan
Sick Europe, and reduced, unyieldingly,
The monk within the cassock to the man
Within the monk, they called it heresy.

And when he made so perilously bold
As to be scattered forth in black and white,
Good fathers looked askance at him and rolled
Their inward eyes in anguish and affright;
There were some of them did shake at what was told,
And they shook best who knew that he was right." [4]

[4] Edwin Arlington Robinson: "Collected Poems," p. 193.

After Luther's first brave stand against the Papacy, he economized his later reflections for practical or political ends, and by so doing became one of the chief personal sources of the complex Protestantism which includes within itself many various tendencies. These tendencies exist together regardless of consistency. We are instinctively aware of them in those older factors of Church and State which prevail in contemporary society. It is in its struggle with those factors that what we call the modern world becomes conscious of its differences from the world of antiquity. Observe, in passing, a few of the differences as evidences both of the similarity and dissimilarity existing between those two worlds. It is a recognized axiom of democratic States that the civil and ecclesiastical powers shall exist separately. The State no longer entreats the spiritual sanction of the Church. Yet its theory that religion is the living source of civic life and duty is a tribute to the fact that part of the past always survives in the present. The supremacy of the State is no longer regarded as denoting a collection of more or less unimpeachable qualities, but as an entity consisting of the highest possible conceptions of political wisdom and of the general welfare. Reason and justice limit that supremacy, and when they are violated it is jeopardized. In the absolutism of ancient States natural rights were unknown, and what liberty men had was identified with their citizenship. The Greeks could not conceive of a distinction between natural and civic rights; hence they knew nothing of private as contrasted with public law. The Romans separated these rights and laws in principle, but ignored them in practice. Man, as man, is now sacrosanct to a high degree; and his claim to fair treatment by the State makes humanity the starting point of its laws. These pregnant changes have ennobled human existence on every side. Its higher vocations flourish without any particular concern for political or ecclesiastical imbroglios. Men of letters, artists, scientists, investigators, social reformers and intellectual radicals or conservatives pursue the tenor of their way, as Erasmus formerly but vainly wished them to do, immune to the tumult of political factions.

As I have said, the pivotal fact of the Reformation, not wholly novel yet quite decisive, was the disengagement of the modern State from the federalizing internationalism of the Papacy.[5] This is the verity of verities behind the expansion and freedom of life which is being discussed: the one great gain that must be stressed in any account of the modern State. A more enlightened attitude toward all classes of society signifies its comprehensive character. Nor can they be rightly reckoned lesser men who, although sometimes lacking gentleness, moderation and sobriety, were too constant in their love for reality to consent to the peace of the desert; to the negative peace which spells evasion, stagnation and death. The sixteenth century produced such characters beyond the ordinary, and it was their lot to abolish the last form of the ancient State in dissolving the Mediæval State. The reconstruction of the modern State was necessarily left unfinished by them and is still in progress.

Within a few years after the burning by Luther of the "godless books of the papal decrees," the provinces of Northern Germany, Scandinavia, England, Scotland, the Dutch Netherlands and portions of Switzerland had each seceded from the Papal overlordship. Poland's defection lasted for several years, after which she was restored to Rome by the enterprise of the Jesuits. The sovereignty of the Holy See was assailed in the hereditary provinces of the Hapsburgs; but the reigning dynasty and the landed aristocracy defeated the attack, and these provinces retained their fealty to Rome. Hungary's characteristic independence kept the Genevan theology alive to divide the nation. In Italy and Spain the loyalty of their monarchs to the Papacy was assured from the first, and they quickly extinguished spasmodic efforts to end its rule. Hereafter, in Protestant States, the personnel, the revenues, the ritual, the administration, and even the creeds

[5] Cf. Preserved Smith: "The Age of the Reformation," p. 743, ff.

of the Church were subordinated to the Civil Power, with which no super-State, ecclesiastical or imperial, was allowed to interfere. In this epoch-making transfer lies not only the gain of civil and religious liberty, but also the loss of Christian catholicity. The complete separation of European and American society into temporal and spiritual associations followed; and as a further sequence their constant bickerings and wars.

II

The remoter causes of this transition period carry us back to the Wars of the Roses in England, to the repeated plagues of the Black Death in Europe, and to the decay of monasticism throughout Christendom. Yet one name must be mentioned at some length, since it suggests all that was at once most formidable and victorious in Protestantism as the parent of the modern State. Far exceeding the names of such monarchs as Charles VIII and Louis XII of France, Ferdinand and Isabella of Spain, or Alexander VI, Julius II and Leo X in the Roman Pontificate, is the great name of John Calvin. Upon this solitary Frenchman of Picardy rested the gigantic burdens of intellectual Protestantism and of developing nationalism. In a controversy that drove even sensible men to the last extremity, he had to uphold and forward the inspiring but more emotional onset of Luther. Throughout the negotiations and battlings which resulted in the genesis of the modern State, one perceives the courage, the strategy, the psychic force of the Genevan giant. Like Napoleon, he seemed to be, not a man, but a system. Yet he touched the hearts and captured the minds of the sternest, strongest race of colonizers and conquerors in the modern age, and shaped in them the one

> ". . . . . . tyrannic thought that made
> All other thoughts its slave."

Nor could he have been the oracle of princes and their ministers, had not his endowments furnished a further proof of the doctrine that the extraordinary individual is the solution of problems otherwise insoluble.

The civilization preceding that of the sixteenth century was based on a belief in a Divine Revelation, for which the Church was both the embodiment and the organ of its discipline. Troeltsch observes that nothing can overcome the influence of such a belief when it is a real and unquestioned social factor. Implicitly to accept the teaching that the Divine Will is everywhere present and exactly defined, and that it has an infallible institution as its authorized agent, is to sever the Gordian knot at a single stroke. This entrance into human life of the laws, forces and aims of Deity determines everything. Supreme over all is the *Lex Dei*, composed of the *Lex Moysi*, the *Lex Christi*, the *Lex Ecclesiæ;* and including within its scope and meaning the *Lex Naturæ*. At their source these laws are an eternal unity, and it is only in sinful humanity that they diverge. Under the guidance of the Church their equivalence is to be restored, though conditioned by the continuance of original sin. The faultless logic and careful elaboration of this dogma were among the last efforts of Christian antiquity. In theory it lifted the authority of the Church to superlative heights, and invested it with an invulnerable defense in the common obedience to the State.[6] Calvin's thorough intimacy with the theory was equalled by his belief that it could be demolished; and he marshalled his energies for that sole purpose. If the initial opposition to the Mediæval Church came from a single monk in one of the smaller provinces of the Empire, the campaign which vanquished it in the northwestern States of Europe, was waged by one imperial mind from the city of Geneva. Calvin could hardly have dreamed of the triumph which awaited him as a young man of twenty-four, when he read an apology for evangelical views which so enraged the doctors of the Sorbonne that he had to flee from Paris. His "Institutes of the Christian Religion," the first text book of Prot-

[6] Cf. Ernst Troeltsch: "Protestantism and Progress," p. 9, ff.

estant theology, was published in 1536, and translated by the author into French in 1541. The final edition which appeared in 1559, was five times as large as the first issue. In the year 1541, however, he had already relinquished the hope of literary leisure, and during September of the same year, established his home in Geneva, where he spent the remaining twenty-three years of his laborious life. There he became the personal focus of otherwise widely separated civil and religious interests. From his brain sprang the germinal ideas that were afterward developed in the political character of the leading nations of the West. His emissaries went from Geneva into England, Scotland, the Netherlands and across the border into France. The conceptual strength of his adamantine creed, as they taught it, was expressed in the Augustinian doctrine of Predestination, which supplied the answer of original Protestantism to the vital question: How can a soul be assured of its acceptance of God? It does not fall to me to discuss in its particular articles the theology of Calvin, or that of Luther and Zwingli, to all three of whom Augustinian Predestination, as they adopted it, was equally original and equally necessary. But Calvin went beyond the other two Reformers in making it the life blood of his religious thinking. He drew upon its assurance of the eternal salvation of the elect, for their support in his conflict with the Roman hierarchy and its powerful constituencies. Lutheranism, on the other hand, shrank from the relentlessness of Calvin's reasonings, and rebounded to those ideals of universal wisdom and love which antagonized his main doctrine.

One's sympathies are strongly engaged with the more humane teachings of German theology about this issue. It seems an inexplicable mystery of the history of Christian thought that the revival of Augustinianism in Calvin's theory of Predestination, should have overthrown mediæval ecclesiasticism. The mystery is deepened for those who pay little regard to the work of theology in the making of States, by the fact that it was with the utmost reluctance the laity assumed an antagonistic attitude toward the old régime. Had not its scandals been too gross, its oppressions too unbearable, probably neither Luther nor even Calvin could have overthrown it. A single doctrine abolished that reluctance, not in heady and impetuous men, but in the immobile self-contained races of the North and the West. It also produced pioneers, statesmen, scholars, divines, soldiers, who colonized the new world and transferred the scepter of political influence to the Thames and the Potomac. [7]

Those who agree with Professor Ellwood's contention that Christianity must be "non-theological, because theology remains a realm of speculation and of disputation and divides rather than unites men," find scanty support for this opinion in the origin of the modern State.[8] Seldom, indeed, has there been a more widespread or formative response than that made to the doctrine of election, which unified and equipped the strongest modern nations. The mystery is solved in the words of Troeltsch: "The consciously elect man feels himself to be the destined lord of the world, who in the power of God and for the honor of God has it laid on him to grasp and shape the world. The man who is simply saved by grace, also, of course, receives his salvation direct from God, but in his dread of acting on the assumptions of predestinarianism avoids any strict delimitation and relation of the spheres of God and the world, and takes refuge rather in a purely religious sphere, out of the world." [9] No such dread troubled Calvin. He went far beyond the original proposals of Lutheranism, in which, to be frank, the Catholic formula-

[7] Cf. T. M. Lindsay: "A History of the Reformation," Vol. II. Bk. III, "The Reformed Churches," Bk. IV, "The Reformation in England"; H. O. Taylor: "Thought and Expression in the Sixteenth Century," Vol. I. p. 384, ff; Preserved Smith: "The Age of the Reformation," chapters III, V, VI, VII; Hugh Y. Reyburn: "John Calvin, His Life, Letters and Work"; "Calvin and the Reformed Church" by A. M. Fairbairn in "The Cambridge Modern History," Vol. II. Chapter XI.

[8] Cf. Charles A. Ellwood: "The Reconstruction of Religion," p. 11.

[9] Cf. "Protestantism and Progress," p. 63.

Effect of Calvin's doctrine upon chu. State

tion of religious problems was retained, though a different solution was offered for them. By excluding all human effort and making salvation solely dependent upon the Divine Will, he rendered the Roman system negligible for those who believed his dogma. Many did so believe it and to great effect. Faith in Predestination revolutionized Scotland, broke the grip of Philip II on the Low Provinces, planted the New England colonies, diminished the authority of the English Crown, and had much to do with wresting the North American continent from the Spaniard and the Frenchman. It was for Calvin's strangely inspiring creed that Knox opposed the faction of the Guises in Edinburgh, and that Cromwell's Ironsides trampled down the Stuart Cavaliers at Marston Moor and Naseby. Macaulay in his well known "Essay on Milton" speaks thus of the Englishmen who were recreated by this theory: "The Puritans were men whose minds had derived a peculiar character from the daily contemplation of superior beings and eternal interests. Not content with acknowledging in general terms an overruling Providence, they habitually ascribed every event to the will of the Great Being, for whose power nothing was too vast, for whose inspection nothing was too minute. To know him, to serve him, to enjoy him, was with them the great end of existence. They rejected with contempt the ceremonious homage which other sects substituted for the pure worship of the soul. Instead of catching occasional glimpses of the Deity through an obscuring veil, they aspired to gaze full on the intolerable brightness, and to commune with him face to face. Hence originated their contempt for terrestrial distinctions. The difference between the greatest and the meanest of mankind seemed to vanish when compared with the boundless interval which separated the whole race from him on whom their own eyes were constantly fixed. They recognized no title to superiority but his favor; and, confident of that favor, they despised all the accomplishments and all the dignities of the world. . . . Thus the Puritan

Two Protestantisms — see below
Luther
Calvin.

was made up of two different men: the one all self-abasement, penitence, gratitude, passion; the other proud, calm, inflexible, sagacious. He prostrated himself in the dust before His Maker; but he set his foot on the neck of his king." [10]

III

Calvinism, however, while democratic in theory and as such, the progenitor of much modern democracy, was aristocratic and even autocratic in practice. Its efforts to restore primitive Christianity, and to transfer its authority from an infallible Pontificate to an infallible Bible, were largely formative of the State as it now exists. Here were two Protestantisms which must be taken into account. Lutheranism, as the source of Germany's religious culture and influence, should be distinguished from Calvinism, as the main political creator of English-speaking nations. It would require a very acute psychological process to trace their evolution for the past four hundred years, and to discern the reasons why Lutheranism has remained comparatively stationary, while Calvinism has expended its enormous forces in the ethics, social ideals and political organizations of Holland and of the English-speaking peoples. Both systems united at their sources, which were the personalization of religion and the establishment of the Holy Scriptures as the sole standard for matters of faith and conduct. But though these two concepts formed their common origin, the methods of their development have widely varied, and its chief controlling factor was Nationalism. In countries where political or patriotic stimuli were feeble, the responses to religious reforms were also feeble. Holland, Scotland and England reacted to Calvinism as *nations*. The reaction of Germany and Switzerland to Protestantism was far less complete; that of Italy and Spain, fitful and ineffective. In France,

[10] Cf. "Macaulay's Critical and Historical Essays," Everyman's Library, Vol. I. p. 186.

where the Crown finally incarnated the State, royalty played fast and loose with Catholics and Huguenots. At one time it seemed probable that Gallican independence and its traditional jealousy of papal usurpation would open the way for the Reformation in France. The probability was heightened by Calvin's expositions and discourses, which were so lucid, logical and pertinent as to constitute a classic expression of the French mind. But the Protestant contingent never numbered more than a tenth of the population of France. She thus never conceded as a nation, the theological premises of one of her most illustrious sons. Yet some of the great men and many of the great women of the world have been produced by France, and the Huguenots can claim their quota of such men and women: most clever and capable, the stay and refuge of a State which now excites both hope and fear.

Although Calvin took his theory of Predestination from Zwingli and Luther, both of whom denied the freedom of the will, and all three were indebted to St. Augustine, its historic import and results are rightly associated with Calvin's works. These have none of the spiritual charm and humaneness of Luther's noble treatise, "The Liberty of a Christian Man," which should be prized by all readers of genuinely religious literature. The love that is life; that

> ". . . . gives to every power a double power
> Above their functions and their offices,"

does not predominate in the "Institutes." No trace of poetic feeling, no touch of imaginative color, no symptom of the recognition of human weakness, reward the patient reader. Man is but the chaff and dust in a colossal experiment which sacrifices every instinct of justice and mercy to scholastic reasonings. Yet Lord Acton pronounces the book the finest literary achievement of the Reformed Faith, and one which, by its thoroughness, definiteness and comprehensive range, transplanted that Faith to flourish in many lands where Lutheranism could not obtain entrance.[11] Dr. Alfred Plummer compares Luther and Calvin, the two religious progenitors of the modern State, as first-rate intellects who were equally confident but not equally dogmatic. The German saw in Rome a system which cheated man of his salvation; the Frenchman, a system which cheated God of His honor. But Calvin also perceived that the hitherto matchless organization of the Papacy could only be penetrated by one even more compact and consistent. He knew no fears and entertained no doubts. As Luther had left Erasmus behind, so Calvin left Luther behind. He would not retract and he could not retreat. The Mediævalists had made man feel inferior; he made the elect man feel that he was God's viceregent. In this real sense, exclusively papal privileges were transferred to the Calvinistic saints, who proceeded to rule their portion of the earth. Luther, on the other hand, often confessed his errors, and that some of his undertakings were not well informed, some of his measures improvident. It is probable that Calvin had the greater mind, and Luther had the greater nature. The latter during his lifetime exercised the larger sway; the former has exercised the larger influence upon subsequent generations. Both laid down rules and required statements of belief which necessitated the abrogation of some of their own principles. As knowledge grew and experience widened, other leaders appeared who, though less conspicuous and less able, were quite as sturdy, and they refused to submit to the dictates of the two Pontiffs of Protestantism.[12]

The changes which followed were very evident in England, where Rome's antagonists were ensconced in an island Kingdom and Church, enjoying their ancient rights and peculiar privileges. From the reign of William the Conqueror, who brusquely refused to do fealty for his throne to the Pope, to that of Henry VIII, whose disgusting marital escapades have

[11] Cf. "Lectures on Modern History," p. 131, ff.
[12] Cf. Alfred Plummer: "The Continental Reformation," p. 164, ff.

been indicated, there had been a rising tide of indignation against papal assumptions and encroachments. Doctrine, ritual and discipline were not so seriously disputed, since their revision could be left to the constitutional liberty of the Church. On the Continent, however, these issues were dominant, and the differences they kindled led to the rejection of papal supremacy. The English Reformers began where the Continental Reformers ended, yet neither group originally intended to take the steps which had been taken by the other. Nor was there in England or in northern Europe a revival of pagan immorality with pagan learning. The Court of the Tudors and of the Stuarts was often lecherous; but the æsthetic sensuality of the Latin Renaissance was largely unknown to Teutonic peoples. Neither the arts nor the vices prospered in Holland, Germany or England as they did in Italy and France. The Humanists of the former nations preferred sacred to classic learning, and used the latter to translate and expound the former.[13] The values of the individual, his right of access to his Maker, his increased power over his surroundings, were the favorite themes of contemporaries as different as Erasmus, Luther, Melanchthon, Zwingli, Sir Thomas More and Dean Colet. National temperament and ethical traits wrought further changes in English Calvinism. It has never been feasible to wind up an Englishman to the level of a logically perfect dogma. As a congenital pragmatist long before Pragmatism, he is prone to avow that nothing absolute can be affirmed in the speculative realm. He applies his ideas and emotions to strictly practical ends; his first query about a hypothesis is not, "Does it hold together?", but, "Will it work?"

The Scot at heart is far more romantic than the Englishman, but in the main, especially since the eighteenth century, both have belonged to the same civilization; and one which is very distinct from that of Ireland or of the Con-

[13] Cf. T. R. Glover: "Poets and Puritans," especially the essays on "Spenser" and "Milton," p. 1, ff.

tinent. The happier issue of England's affairs at the time in question was largely due to the personality of Queen Elizabeth, and to her astute ministers of State, her explorers and sea captains. She had the tigerish temper of the Tudors, moderated by her pride in her realm and her love for its people. Their tendency to insular prejudice was offset in her by a wide acquaintance with Continental politics. Her indifference toward religious reform was held in check by the fact that she was fighting a host of unscrupulous foes belonging to the older Church. The Catholics of Scotland, Ireland, Spain and France were arrayed against her. She well understood that her personal safety and that of the English nation depended upon Protestant integrity and Protestant good will. These she was at pains to conserve and cultivate, especially in the merchants and yeomen of the Kingdom. All its classes, including Catholics and Protestants, united in her support, attributing to her person and reign some marvelous but fictitious qualities. Toleration was disregarded when the throne was at stake. The Marian martyrs do not stand alone in the persecutions of the period. Many Catholics also suffered for conspiring against Elizabeth, or for denying the royal supremacy. Her better qualities were happily combined with those of the aristocratic and middle class families which had arisen to serve the State after the death of the older nobility in the Wars of the Roses. This unity of gifts in the Crown, the peerage and the commonalty, kept the nation on an even keel, and laid the corner-stone of Britain's Empire in the four quarters of the globe.[14]

The destruction of the Spanish Armada released the glories of the Shakespearean era, which became and remained forever independent of political controversies. What they have added to English influence in the world cannot be computed. The Stuarts who inherited Elizabeth's seat but did not retain her authority, could not dim the literary splendors

[14] Cf. F. J. C. Hearnshaw: "Democracy and the British Empire," pp. 3–68.

associated with her name. Inwardly dense, though outwardly alert, they were unable to perceive that the decline of the monarchical estate had set in with them while it was still at its height in the France of Louis XIV.[15] Extreme Puritans, who were sometimes disposed to replace the common law with the Pentateuch, were more astute politicians, judged by the outcome, than any Stuart who occupied the British throne.

Statesmen of large nature and efficient training, conscious that administration was upon their shoulders, were hard to find in the seventeenth century, during which the wise and cautious procedure of Cecil and Walsingham was lost in the shufflings and plottings of autocracy's dupes or agents. The execution of Strafford, the one strong character who served the Stuart dynasty, sealed the doom of Charles the First who deserted him. The plain people supplied the felt want of national guidance in Puritan parliamentarians like Pym and Hampden, and in Puritan commanders like Cromwell and Ireton. These men, so far from being the demagogues and charlatans which ignorance or prejudice has depicted, were at once the masters and the servants of the State. They identified themselves and their measures with a high and austere sect, devoted to the science of politics, and capable of those great achievements in peace and war that held an unwilling world in awe. Constitutionalism, as the essence of that science meant to them, was to keep in touch with public opinion, and to be ready to sacrifice class interest, unlicensed power, or monopoly to the general good.[16]

IV

The Pilgrims of the Mayflower were an offshoot of the Puritan movement which pushed Protestantism far beyond

[15] Cf. "The Cambridge Modern History," Vol. III. Chapters IX, X.

[16] Cf. Lord Rosebery: "Miscellanies Literary and Historical." Vol. I. p. 77, ff; Viscount Morley: "Cromwell"; Thomas Carlyle: "Oliver Cromwell's Letters and Speeches."

the first intentions of its founders. They were not Puritans in the ordinary sense, for the Puritan detested separation; but they owed the substance of their religious beliefs to the Puritanism begun by Thomas Cartwright and his fellow-refugees at Frankfort-on-the-Main. They made a historic plea for separation because they held that formal conformity in religious beliefs was reprehensible. All were pious, discreet, industrious, grave, and rigidly governed by their sense of right, cost what it may. With the colonists who had preceded them in Virginia they were content to remain subjects of that abject specimen of the divine right of kings, James Stuart the First of England. But it is permissible to suppose that they knew him sufficiently well to be far more at ease when the Atlantic rolled between him and them. Harried in the homeland, these sectarians whom Sir Francis Bacon, the shrewdest man of his age, excoriated as mischievous fanatics, took refuge in Holland, where they were hospitably received by their brethren of continental Protestantism. Their residence at Leyden and in the adjacent cities and towns soon convinced these Independents, however, that they should not sever themselves from their own country. Englishmen they were and Englishmen they would remain. Bred to husbandry, the majority of them resented the confinement and the low wages of Dutch cities. Strangers in a friendly but foreign land, its speech unknown to them; settled in their religious opinions, they took little interest in the envenomed controversies of Calvinists and Arminians, which then divided the Dutch in State and Church. Furthermore, their English persecutors used the avenues of diplomacy against them and made their tenure in Holland uncertain. For these reasons, and also because a fine strain of conscientiousness ran in them, the Pilgrims, as they were afterwards called, undertook an adventure that turned some currents of the modern State into new channels.[17]

[17] The term "Pilgrim Fathers" was first specifically applied to them in 1799.

The account of their voyage across the North Atlantic in the Mayflower, of their heroical endurance and faith, and their undesigned landing on the shores of Cape Cod in New England, need not be recited here. The epic courage and devotion to principle shown by them is not likely to lose its hold upon the popular mind. They accelerated in an unexpected manner the racial expansion which has made Britain the mother of free commonwealths. Their character as a sect and the influence they have had upon the United States and all other English-speaking lands, furnish fruitful lessons for the statesman to moralize upon, and for the plain people to recall.

American historians have been accused of bestowing indiscriminate eulogy upon the Pilgrims, and some writers assert that they have been mentioned too frequently and too flatteringly. Truly, in the view of their descendants, their excellencies seem to have had little or no admixture. But when the concessions due to their earthliness have been made, these East Anglian yeomen enable us to visualize afresh the strength and simplicity of that religious faith which drove them so far afield, in order that they might live, as they quaintly urged, "in a distant body by themselves." Beyond hereditary predisposition or educational development; beyond the pressure of circumstances, the unadorned tale of the Pilgrims manifests the resistless effect of human emotions when transformed by a spiritual ideal. Whatever the nature of that ideal may be, neither temporal consideration nor scientific argument can compare with its authority in the realm of actual progress. In their case it consisted in a profound belief that there is a Divine Order in the world, to which Church and State are alike subordinate, from which those institutions derive their rightful power, and in obedience to which lie welfare and perpetuity. For the sake of this belief they tore themselves away from their native land, and became as strangers and wanderers on the earth; setting out after the Abrahamic manner, not knowing whither they went.[18]

No informed person supposes that freedom was their discovery. On the contrary, what we term freedom, which is as often defined as relativity and with as little satisfaction, was the objective of other colonists in North America besides the Pilgrims. The first of the groups which came to these shores in the seventeenth century that declared for absolute liberty in matters of conscience, was the Roman Catholic Colony planted by Lord Baltimore in what is now called Maryland. It numbered in its ranks pioneers of progress and interpreters of man's larger selfhood. So did the settlers from Holland who founded New Amsterdam, the present New York, and occupied the Hudson Valley. Likewise the Virginian planters and the followers of William Penn, held strenuously to the main principles of social welfare and gave public recognition to their belief in the Divine Order for human society. The history of Penn's settlement is free from Indian troubles and religious disputes, because of his calm and peaceful spirit, and the wisdom of his plans for the colony.[19]

What freedom the modern State possesses is the result not alone of these migrations, but of those ageless processes and experiments to which many dissimilar individuals and communities have contributed. But the obedience which the Pilgrims and other American colonists rendered to conscience eventuated in a larger freedom, and this was the net result of their memorable enterprises. These stand out the more impressively because, though the Renaissance liberated intellectualism, it did far less for political liberty than it might otherwise have done. Erasmus, who was, as we have seen, the Humanist *par excellence,* was anxious to restrain

[18] Cf. Walter H. Burgess: " The Pastor of the Pilgrims, A Biography of John Robinson"; " The Pilgrim's Motive and Contribution," by Charles F. Thwing in " The Hibbert Journal," October 1920, p. 77, ff; Roland G. Usher: " The Pilgrims and Their History."

[19] Cf. Isaac Sharpless: " Political Leaders of Provincial Pennsylvania," p. 20, ff.

Luther's attacks upon the imperial sacerdotalism which he himself had so sorely wounded by his mordant humor. Nor were the Reformers accustomed to freedom's bracing air. Calvin invoked the sword of the State for the suppression of heresy, and even the gentle Melanchthon prayed for some brave assassin to murder Henry VIII. Knox had a law enacted by the Scotch Parliament, which inflicted the capital penalty upon attendants of the Roman Mass. Anglicans and Puritans of pious reputation spent their dying breath to fan the flames of religious feuds. At this melancholy juncture, when toleration was renounced by Protestants as well as Catholics, by doctors and prelates as well as princes and politicians, a few feeble bands of small social consequence discerned and unfalteringly applied the now accepted principle that religious liberty is the source of civil liberty, and that civil liberty is the requisite of religious liberty. Years before Cromwell asserted this broader view for the benefit of his Ironsides; before Milton and Taylor, or Baxter and Locke became notable for their arraignments of intolerance, the Pilgrims, to quote Lord Acton, "grasped with vigor and sincerity the principle that it is only by abridging the authority of States that the liberty of Churches can be assured." Thousands of Puritans, distressed and persecuted, or attracted by the commercial opportunities of the colony, followed them to New England. Few bore an unblemished testimony to this new freedom; some strove to limit its scope. But these drawbacks should not diminish their claim upon our regard. Critics who complain of their bigotry and dourness can reflect that man's martyrdom has not been alleviated by the perfect moralities which the cultured few desiderate, but by those active combinations of good with evil that so frequently cause justice and truth to take an oblique direction.

The heritage ensuing in liberty of conscience bequeathed to us by the Protestantism of John Robinson and his flock, by the Dutch Republic, by the settlers under Lord Baltimore, and by the Virginians, is more vital to the modern State than any one prevalent religious system. To the Pilgrims, as to the Cromwellian Protectorate, and also to the advanced legislation of the Maryland Colony,[20] belongs the distinction of having enforced a single ideal which, but for their initiative, might have been indefinitely deferred. With that ideal the well-being of freedom-loving States has since been closely identified. It survived the *ancien régime* which nourished decayed clericalism and feudalistic remnants in the national structures of the eighteenth century. To it Burke appealed; and he was the one English statesman whose lofty aspirations and splendid diction entitle him to rank with Milton. His innate conservatism did not recognize all the political doctrines which constitute an estimable State, but he revived and amplified, as the great Lord Somers had done before him, the principle confirmed by the Pilgrim Exodus, by the Maryland Plantation, and by the Puritan Revolution. The gravity blended with imagination which signalized Burke's public utterances, could not have been his; nor could his speeches have become the meat and drink of enlightened political minds on both sides of the Atlantic, had not the right to believe freely, to be open and candid without dread of tyranny, and to speak the thing as it is without compromise or deference, been advanced by the English sectarians and emigrants of the seventeenth century.

Their work as well as the land from which they drew is of first rate consequence for us, since the State in Great Britain was in many ways the progenitor of our own Republic. Mother and daughter nations were founded upon that faith in the Divine Order which also enthralled alike the Mediæval Papacy and the Calvinistic Theocracy. The succession of English sovereigns, from Alfred the Great through "the fierce Norman, the proud Plantagenet, the grasping

[20] The motives of this legislation have been questioned but I do not propose to go behind the returns.

Tudor, the fickle Stuart, the independent Oliver, the Dutch William, and the Hanoverian Georges," was maintained by the belief that in some way they represented that Order. This succession is paralleled by the gradual growth of the constitutional liberty of the citizen. During the changes wrought by the Norman Conquest, and the still greater changes wrought by the Reformation, that liberty survived successive shocks and advanced vigorously. It enrolled among its defenders and administrators men shrewd in debate, eloquent in speech, honored in their generation. Roman, Anglican and Puritan; Continental, Briton and American, contributed to its steady growth. Every true need of man, every provision for the requirements of his better nature, was held in solution by this patrimony of freedom. It was the State rather than parties and dynasties; its honor and its interest rather than the high politics of princes and cabinets, which fired the imagination and actuated the deeds of its best sons. The nation became the school in which they were trained. Its traditions were increasingly associated with those privileges of citizenship, which Americans of all lines of descent have been taught to value and uphold. Ever and anon, a single resolute patriot, loving truth and right alone, has brought the English-speaking and like-minded nations to his point of view, and rendered impossible the practices which once were universal. But rulers or statesmen like John the Norman, Charles I, James II, George III and the corrupted counsellors of the Stuart monarchy, who endeavored to thwart the will of nascent or actual democracy, were eventually swept aside.

V

The bold attempt of George III to obtain personal rule is a landmark in the process. His effort to recover the prestige and power of the Crown, which had been reduced to lawful limits by the parliamentarians of the preceding century, was prompted by his jealous dislike of the great Whig nobles. Their ancestors had dethroned James II, and brought in William of Orange and his wife, Queen Mary, to take her father's place. The third Hanoverian king, who resented their political and social power, boasted his unadulterated Englishry. Really, he was a German prince with the paternal ideals peculiar to that sort of ruler. He would govern as his predecessor James I had said, not according to the public will but according to the public weal. Nor could he at any time be convinced that he should not exercise unlawful control, so long as he used those parliamentary means which he obtained by his open corruption of a non-representative legislature. If dukes and lords of the Whig party distributed the favors of the State in the sovereign's name, but contrary to his wishes, he proposed to follow his mother's advice, and "be a king." For twenty years he systematized bribery by trafficking in honors, emoluments and publicly-purchased votes. The House of Commons obeyed his will, sustained his choice and dismissal of ministers, and allowed him to originate and carry out Britain's foreign and domestic policies.

Then came the American war, ended by the surrender of Cornwallis to General Washington at Yorktown, when the degraded system which had aroused the indignation and scorn of Pitt, Fox and Burke at last utterly broke down, and involved in its fall the dismemberment of a great Empire. Its principal author afterwards sank into madness and died in that condition. "All the world," says Thackeray, "knows the story of his malady: all history presents no sadder figure than that of the old man, blind and deprived of reason, wandering through the rooms of his palace, addressing imaginary parliaments, reviewing fancied troops, holding ghostly courts." [21] English-speaking peoples everywhere were now free to pursue another prosperous era of political development. The Republic of the United States had been estab-

[21] Cf. "New Century Library," Vol. XI. p. 385.

lished under the Presidency of Washington himself, of whom Gladstone wrote to George W. Smalley on October 4, 1884: "If among all the pedestals supplied by history, for public characters of extraordinary purity and nobility, I saw one higher than all the rest; and if I were required at a moment's notice to name the fittest occupant for it, I think my choice, at any time during the last forty-five years, would have lighted, as it would now light, upon Washington."

The British Empire, though shorn of its greatest possession, was compensated by Clive's conquest of India for much that had been lost in the West. Incidentally, the extent of that country, or series of countries, makes it an Empire in itself: a sub-continent stretching from the snows of the Himalayas in the north to near the equator in the south, with thousands of miles of coastline east and west, and a total area of 1,802,657 square miles. In this magnificent territory, an infinitely greater India than was ever imagined by any of its former rulers, or by Clive himself, the principles and laws of Anglo-Saxon rule have received what is, perhaps, on the whole, their most heroical test. Consider the population of India in its density, multiplicity of races and religious beliefs. Consider, again, the social customs and political condition of its ancient peoples, whose civilization in many instances long preceded our own. You will agree, I think, that the administration of nearly 700 native States and, in addition, British India, which comprises 267 districts, is a task only comparable in all history with that of the Roman Empire of antiquity. Here are over 217 million Hindus, 66 million Moslems, 10 million Buddhists, 10 million Animists, 3 million Sikhs, nearly 4 million Christians, and scores of other sects, governed by one hundred thousand Britons, with one hundred and fifty thousand Anglo-Indians, or Eurasians, as they refuse to be called, mediating between the Europeans and Asiatics. Whatever may be the future of India, there can be no question that the mere fact of Great Britain's prolonged tenure there and its consequent benefits, invest her incomparable service in the political evolution of mankind with further and honorable usefulness. Should India achieve self-government in the future, and her present disturbances subside and be forgotten, it may then be seen that not only at Westminster, but almost more at Calcutta, the British nation gained its true renown as a modern State.

The beginnings of its rule in India carry us back to similar beginnings in Canada, which was saved from the Bourbons by the statesmanship of Pitt and of Carleton, and by Wolfe's victory at Quebec. Rodney also thwarted the aspirations of the French monarchy by his naval triumphs, and Eliott by his successful defense of Gibraltar. The first Earl of Chatham, after whom Americans named the city of Pittsburgh, excelled as an incorruptible Minister of War, who pushed back the frontiers of British dominion, and bore down opposition to his measures by his dauntless courage and declamatory eloquence. His last public utterance was an unforgettable protest against the separation of the English-speaking race whose interests had been so dear to him, and whose future beyond the Atlantic he so vividly foresaw. His son, the younger Pitt, "the heaven-born minister of State," a pupil of Adam Smith in economics, resuscitated Britain's credit, repaired her finances, encouraged her trade, and placed her taxation upon a more equitable basis. He spent the ten years of tranquility between the American and the French Revolutions in restoring the strength of a still sadly shaken Empire. When the storm broke, and the world order which Dr. Johnson imagined to be static in its perfectness, fell into the gulf riven by the revolt of France, Pitt's shortcomings became palpable, and enabled Fox and Burke to assail his plans. He surpassed his father in peace, but he was inferior to him in the waging of war. Nevertheless, the Pitt genius was revealed in his calm demeanor before repeated disappointments and reversals, and in his determination to maintain, by force if necessary, the doctrine of Burke as against that of Rousseau. The military gifts of Napoleon, which procured him the First Consulate, the Emperorship of France, and also made monarchs look ridiculous, never dismayed Pitt. It may have been unfortunate that, by refusing to recognize the French Republic and to treat with it officially, he lent color to the charge that he was bent on war. And it is beyond cavil that his defense of "the public law of Europe" made him the ally and the paymaster of the thieving Central Powers, which were busy in successive partitions of Poland. But, in the large, his resistance to Napoleon's boundless sway, which Ugo Foscolo described as "like a July day in Egypt — all clear, brilliant and blazing; but all silent, not a voice heard, the stillness of the grave," has been justified by history. After Waterloo, when British influence was at its zenith throughout the world, his countrymen remembered with thankfulness that the great Minister who died with the triumph of Austerlitz weighing heavily upon his heart, had, to paraphase his own words, saved their nation by his energy, and Europe by his example.[22]

The uprising of European democracy against the privileges of aristocracy and feudalism followed the Napoleonic Wars. Its industrial revolution, precipitated by the condition of manufacturing centers, and by the rapid increase of the toiling classes, grew apace in England, France and America, and in other countries where the nation has since become the State, and "the people," a term expressing the public will and the public right to act powerfully and directly in political affairs. In Russia, Prussia and Austria despotic predominance proved fatal to constitutional freedom. The rudiments of liberalism were sternly suppressed, with the fatal outcome which, after minor eruptions, culminated in the tragedy of 1914. Into the chaos thus created we now gaze, wondering what will emerge therefrom.

It is impossible to compress into the space of a single lecture

[22] Cf. Lord Rosebery: "William Pitt"; J. H. Rose: "William Pitt and the National Revival," id. "William Pitt and the Great War."

an adequate portrayal of the modern State. Holland's important part as a factor in its evolution has only been barely mentioned. There the leadership of William the Silent, who would have his merry quips and jests when in the midst of the greatest struggle for a free State which the modern world has seen, was successfully pitted against the fanatical cruelties of Alva. William's northern stubborness, prescient statesmanship and deep diplomacy, were the accessories of a serene religious faith and a lofty patriotism which have had few superiors in any age, and were unequalled in his own. From him and his brave fellow-citizens all modern States have received a large measure of their lasting good.

The further neglect of Holland or of other participating nations in the process discussed may be forgiven, when we recall that the British Constitution alone is the growth of a thousand years, assuming ever-varying forms in obedience to chance and wisdom. The statesmen of 1688, who have scarcely been referred to here, moulded it into the form we now know. Since their time, the stupidity of the first Hanoverians gave it some advantages. Its provision for a Cabinet, independent of the Crown and subordinate to the Prime Minister, was enacted because George I. could not speak English. The Reform Bill of Lord Grey saved it from destruction in 1832. Our own Constitution was rescued from extreme peril by the Civil War of 1861 to 1865. The contribution of the French Revolution to the modern State was in many ways considerable, and European nations benefitted by its reactions. But though the theme is prolific of instruction upon the historic side, in the last resort its issues pass into the realm of morals, where we must now follow them.

FIFTH LECTURE

THE CITIZEN AND THE STATE

"Man's little house of days will hold enough,
Sometimes, to make him wish it were not his,
But it will not hold all. Things that are dead
Are best without it, and they own their death
By virtue of their dying. Let them go,—
But think you not the world is ashes yet,
And you have all the fire. The world is here
To-day, and it may not be gone tomorrow;
For there are millions, and there may be more,
To make in turn a various estimation
Of its old ills and ashes, and the traps
Of its apparent wrath. Many with ears
That hear not yet, shall have ears given to them,
And then they shall hear strangely. Many with eyes
That are incredulous of the Mystery
Shall yet be driven to feel, and then to read
Where language has an end and is a veil,
Not woven of our words. Many that hate
Their kind are soon to know that without love
Their faith is but the perjured name of nothing."

EDWIN ARLINGTON ROBINSON: *The Three Taverns* in *Collected Poems*, p. 470.

FIFTH LECTURE

THE CITIZEN AND THE STATE

The influence of education and religion upon the State — What is the common good? — Aristocratic, autocratic and democratic conceptions of the State — Ethical and political obligations should be reconciled if the common good of all is to be conserved and advanced — Causes of religious persecution — Freedom of the individual must be regulated by the good of many — The fallacious contentions of Hegel, Rousseau and other moderns — Two ideals of the State contend for acceptance: that of the Germanic-Teuton of world-empire with virtual slavery, and that of the Anglo-Saxon with actual freedom for mankind — Biblical teaching in regard to citizenship.

THE individual citizen is the responsible agent of the State's progress. He must foster its intellectual, ethical and religious resources. By him alone its collective good is maintained; upon him the general welfare depends. These statements are verified and enforced in the State's industry, its commerce, its laws, its liberties, and its religion. Hence the question is always before us: how can human nature attain a higher level, and so elevate the State and its pursuits? For if the values of its government are mainly determined by the moral qualities of its citizens, surely every gift and acquirement of citizenship should be devoted to the cultivation of those qualities. No sentimentalism, however profuse; no patriotism, however fervent, can avoid this inquisition, which searches the souls of politicians and churchmen. Hitherto, many of them have believed that education is the holy fire which keeps the melting-pot from congealing. They attribute nearly all improvement in the citizen and the State to the steady spread of useful knowledge. Tons of tracts, pamphlets and books have been written to advance this proposition. But though education has had big innings in some quarters, and no sensible person will underrate its gains in many quarters, its results are not entirely satisfactory. Knowledge is not wisdom, any more than some wisdom is necessarily goodness. Today the white race, despite its scientific advantages over other races, gropes in semi-darkness. Several of its most cultured nations have been justly reprobated for their crimes against civilization. Intellectual groups are not agreed among themselves upon what is the best policy for education, leave alone for the State. Secularists at last have mooted their suspicions that all is not as it should be with education: that it needs not only a far more complete acceptance by the people, but even some sort of spiritual direction. Heredity is invoked, and perhaps, at a pinch, religion might be brought in to aid the difficulty. The loyalty which citizens accord to the State, they tell us, should be reasonable and humane as well as emotional.

Few will disagree with them, but selfish ambitions and interests are too deeply embedded to be dislodged by rational or altruistic ideas. Those ambitions and interests require for their excision a surgery which neither systematic knowledge nor the State possesses. Nor is the State, viewed as a purely political organization, intended to possess it. Its functions are limited to external conditions, and those functions usually end where motives begin. There is no instrumentality of the State which can produce ethical aims, or govern the conduct they dictate, except as conduct relates to outward behavior. The State is not indifferent to such motives and aims: it simply exists outside their realm.[1] Here the dilemma arises that an organization common to all, and in which the universal welfare is directly involved, is itself dependent for its beneficial control upon hidden intentions entirely beyond its jurisdiction. Take a specific instance. You hear on all sides today pleas for the conciliatory temper which is necessary for the coherence and unity of the nation;

[1] Cf. L. T. Hobhouse: "The Metaphysical Theory of the State," p. 120, ff.

yet everywhere you perceive the presence of feuds and bigotries that divide the nation. Its separative forces are fostered by interests that have no legal barriers. Only voluntary dedication to a purer ethic; to love, justice, and brotherhood, can remedy the situation. But how this dedication is to be brought about, and to be made lasting and universal, is a question for which politics has no sufficient answer.

We are further told that men and women must act for the common good. But what the common good is and what it is not, should first be carefully ascertained and then definitely stated, after which it must be generally approved. Some clamant groups may be for it as certainly as others are against it. But when its essentials are rightly understood, they will be found to include not only the individual's temporal, but his spiritual existence; the whole being of the citizen. The State can help his access to those essentials by providing freedom for all political and religious beliefs which are not injurious to the body politic. It can afford equal opportunities in contract and trade. It can and it should enlarge educational facilities, and whatever else pertains to civilized communities. It can and it should take steps to relieve those communities of the present chaos in internationalism. But it is impotent to thrust these patent benefits, leave alone their idealized forms, upon those who are opposed to them. And when it has enacted laws such as conduce to their pursuit its duty is largely done.[2]

Enlightened political rule recognizes the many varieties of humanity with which it has to deal, and so far as possible, adapts its measures to their complexity. It gives sufficient room for the attainment of civic honesty and righteousness by all classes. Its legislation is flexible enough to comprehend many different cases under the few approved general princi-

[2] Cf. Sir Henry Jones: "The Principles of Citizenship," p. 117, ff; id.: "Idealism as a Practical Creed," p. 105, ff; B. Bossanquet: "The Philosophical Theory of the State," p. 295, ff.

ples that cover those cases. But what States correspond to this description or rule after this manner? If you are disposed to blame them for not doing so, recall that perhaps the majority of minds have small power to apply to the conduct of life even the best laws of the State. They are prone to accept as personally serviceable only what comes to them from actual experience. Even in the most advanced States festering evils exist, while some that have been abolished left scars on the nation's memory which no after events have erased. These evils furnish excuses for resistance to law, and also reasons for lawful agitation against them. Until they are removed, the State must remain open to social maladies that weaken it.

It is infinitely less difficult, however, to remove admitted evils than it is to eradicate their roots in human greed and selfishness. They may disappear for the moment, but they reappear, take more subtle shapes or more clever combinations which the endless grinding out of prohibitory laws does not suppress.[3] Self-interest is the sworn foe of public welfare; it has countless disguises and pretexts. Legal smoke-screens to conceal its nefarious designs are seldom wanting. It thoroughly understands that while men are equal before the law, they are unequal in ability. It is alert to seize the advantage offered by this inequality, and to obey that instinct of the jungle by which the strong prey upon the defenseless. Hundreds of millions of dollars are fraudulently obtained annually in this country alone from the victims of predatory individuals or corporations. Three billions of dollars more are lost or expended annually for the crime bill of the nation. But trafficking in the souls and bodies of men, women and children is far more deadly to the State's existence than all these financial depredations and expenses put together. This trafficking is done by non-social individuals and groups; they practice personal and sexual perfidy; they gloat

[3] There are nearly 100,000 statutes upon the legislative codes of the United States.

over dishonor and cruelty; they have prescribed courses of action which are not so much immoral as non-moral, and hiding places where the State cannot always demand an entrance. To what lengths they proceed let the daily press bear testimony. Secret or extra-legal iniquities which must proceed to a higher tribunal than those of earth for judgment, probably create more havoc in nations than open and punishable violations of their laws.

The democratic State which acts consistently will, so far as it can, take cognizance of anything morally wrong, not to organize or regulate it, but to repress it. It will protect the defenseless and the weak, permit no hardened criminal to go unwhipped of justice, and preserve the peace and order of the Commonwealth. But it can neither purvey good consciences nor purified hearts, nor can it supply its credulous citizens with a fool-proof universe. A further comment upon the problem is that nearly all democratic States presuppose for their very existence a morality in their human make-up that may, or again, may not get beyond the realm of supposition.

Occasions have arisen in the development of the modern State when protection had to be given to injured classes. Here the law forsook its strictly constitutional position, regardless of the objection that it was discriminating or paternal. It has already travelled far beyond some of its original definitions, not because thoughtful people desire it to do so, but because "necessity knows no law." If the common good or that of any particular group is threatened with injury which cannot be prevented by the State's ordinary use of its powers, it is justified if it uses them in extraordinary ways. For example, the Land Acts of Ireland were denounced by some economists as confiscatory. Doubtless from the viewpoint of the original owners they were confiscatory, but they restored the land to the people of Ireland, and thus accomplished "the greatest happiness of the greatest number."

Two conclusions may be drawn from these conditions:

first, that the State is conditioned by morality; second, that its morality is that of its average citizenship. The materialistic theories of the State which reject these conclusions are often clothed in high-sounding words of worldly wisdom, but they are deceptive. To concentrate upon the purely legal, economic or physical factors of the nation; upon its laws and their administration; upon its crops, tariffs, or trade regulations, should not exhaust the possibilities or the obligations of a forward-looking State. Although what it cannot do is quite as extensive and more important than what it can do, the intensive developments of society demand of it those ethical developments that safeguard society. Yet these, as we have seen, in the last resort, are no more and no less than the collective ethic of its citizenship. We must not tolerate the delusion, however, that man lives by bread alone; that his physical appetites or pleasures, his monetary gains or losses absorb his attention and fix his politics. By that delusion heartless competition without restraint makes a mockery of our boasted freedom; it even uses the historic language of that freedom to apologize for its misdeeds.

Biology, from which the student of the past gets occasional side-lights, corroborates the assertion of moralized politics that the struggle for existence not only cultivates self-interest in the individual, but also mutual sympathy and helpfulness in society. It is a blunder to identify that struggle with every repulsive aspect of selfish and sordid conduct. The purely self-seeking animal is a fiction; the self-sacrificing animal is no less primordial than its opposite type. From life's dawn altruism has been as conspicuous as egoism, and has saved Nature from being the blood-stained cockpit which some scientists once insisted it was. Life will be served, whatever may oppose, and its service is never for the dead, but always for the living. Its organisms have a priority which reacts against every menace and usually overcomes it. "They thrust and parry, passively experiment, or actively evade for one end: the conscious or unconscious attainment of better being." [4] What are these biological facts but the reflections in Nature of the eternal laws of truth and justice, which have origins familiar to believing men and women. If those laws make peremptory demands upon the lower phases of existence, how much the more do they exact from humanity as the apex of its pyramid? Neither the individual, the family, the community, nor the State can dethrone their supremacy. They are above earthly authority, and the nation which attempts to repudiate them strikes at the heart of its own life and freedom. Remote and recent events point the moral of an insolent egoism in the State no less than in the individual. When it undermines idealism, disavows social and religious responsibilities, yields to the idea that a nation must either devour other nations or be devoured by them, such a State digs its own grave. Bloated by spurious notions of its grandeur or invincibility, it falls beneath the condemnation of world society, or becomes the prey of internal dissensions and foreign hostility. History shows by a long list of examples that political sovereignty of any sort must respect its limitations or perish. It may not be able to coerce morality in the citizen, but it has a moral coercion laid upon it by "the Power not ourselves, which makes for righteousness;" and that coercion is absolute and final.

II

Democratic nations accept popular government, not solely to gratify the individual's desire for a share in government, but because they believe it contains the authoritative source of political power. This belief has produced a twofold obligation: first, that of an ethical kind devolving upon the individual; second, that of a political kind devolving upon individuals and society. A person is free, not only when he asserts his rights, but also when he obeys the demands made

[4] Cf. Ernest E. Unwin: "Religion and Biology," p. 66, ff; J. Arthur Thompson: "The System of Animate Nature," Vol. I. p. 293, ff.

upon him by the State. His good is involved in the good of his fellow citizens, and what is good for him alone cannot be advanced by endangering the common welfare. If the chief purpose of the State is to secure the largest benefits for the majority, the freedom of the individual must necessarily be regulated by that purpose. Yet he is not therefore to be treated as its mere creature. Far otherwise; for the most serviceable traits of his character are to be scrupulously conserved. The State which is actuated by these principles is warranted in carrying out the policies that advance them, in doing which the faith and morals of the citizen must always be matters of solicitude. Its attitude toward them is both negative and positive. The State can prohibit or compel as the exigencies of a given situation may determine. The exercise of force is its lawful prerogative, not only for the removal of obstructions to the welfare of the people, but also for the preservation of their rights. In this connection there is a place for punishment which is neither retaliatory nor retributive, but remedial.[5]

Bentham's contention that right is an artificial creation of the State, overlooks the truth that the State seldom, if ever, successfully introduces for the guidance of the community what does not already exist in the minds of its members. His further contention that law is intrinsically evil is oblivious to the fact that the law is largely negative. It is not made for the righteous man but for the lawless and unruly.[6] Its operation is conditioned by the abnormalities of society, and where society is normal, its jurisdiction is correspondingly limited. Equally fallacious was the plea of his distinguished disciple, John Stuart Mill, that we should assign to individuality that part of life in which the individual is chiefly concerned; to society, the part which interests society. Such an assignment

[5] The question of capital punishment is one to be discussed separately, with reference to the particular offender and to the society whose stability is impaired by his deed. Cf. Norman L. Robinson: "Christian Justice," ch. VII. "Justice and Punishment," p. 158, ff.

[6] I Timothy I. 9.

would be arbitrary and prove impracticable. Dividing human life into compartments of this kind is an oft-tried and useless experiment. It relieves it of nothing which is needlessly burdensome, and it opens the door for imaginary rights inspired by self-will, caprice or folly. The system of rights maintained by the State is to be appraised from the point of view of the whole community. Such rights, which also imply duties to be enforced by law if they are neglected or violated, derive their merit from the aid they render to a larger and better social life. Since they are subordinate to this purpose, their exercise is only admissible as it fulfills the purpose. No individual can assert a right actuated by his desire to do as he pleases. Before his will can be done it must have the consent of his fellows. The recognition by society of personal rights, even though these belong exclusively to the individual asserting them, depends upon the expression the rights make in service to society. The *laissez faire* principle is impossible except as a theoretical speculation. It may be true that perfect liberty is an equivalent to a total absence of government, but the truth is wholly relative to an idealized self-knowledge and self-control which make perfect obedience to a perfect law equal to perfect liberty. The State which combines these heavenly attainments has not yet appeared on earth.[7]

The juristic meaning of liberty is an absence of restraint. But in its application to the exercise of the rights of citizenship there is a negative aspect, which has to do with the presence of restraint so far as the rights of others are concerned, and a positive aspect which refers to the freedom of the individual more fully to become himself. Such, then, is the paradox of the State. And the problem it suggests is how to reconcile ethical with political obligations. Plato, fully aware as he was of the difficulty, set forth the function

[7] Cf. "The Idea of Public Right," prize essays in the competition of "The Nation," London, with an introduction by the Right Hon. H. H. Asquith.

of the State as an educational institution, to instruct citizens in one thing alone — the nature of the good. But could the lesson be given and learned, its values are lost so long as there is no united dedication of the citizenship to the practice of good. Nevertheless, the theory of Plato is as a lamp shining upon our darkness out of bygone days. He could not abolish the rivalries which obscured its wider illumination, but he grasped the essential truth of the upper side of the State's existence. Since he elucidated fundamental politics, many further possibilities of human good and ill have been discovered, in which, as I have said before, man's potentialities for right doing make a sad contrast with the low average of his actual moral attainments. He must be regarded as an incomplete being ever requiring, and to some degree making, a better environment. The social Elysiums of which some reformers dream indicate his infinitude of range, but they are not yet within his reach.[8]

Discipline is a necessity at the present stage of human existence, and in view of its exigencies the State is justified in the use of compulsion. Circumstances are conceivable when the common good could only be maintained by the coercion of malignants who themselves may be morally upraised in being made to obey. Nor are the educational results of a fearless enforcement of law to be despised. Though parliaments, congresses, courts, or even armies and navies are not primarily agents of instruction, but organs of the State, they have repeatedly taught that submission to civic rule is essential to its political integrity. Its right to exercise force upon recalcitrants is a prerogative in which no other human society shares. The knowledge that it has the right, and the reserve force to meet emergencies that may arise, is an indispensable bulwark of public safety. The ultimate arbiter and regulator of political and social

[8] Cf. Joyce O. Hertzler: "The History of Utopian Thought." A discerning survey of idealistic conceptions from the Hebrew prophets to Wells, with criticisms of their limited perspectives.

routine, to which the mechanism of the nation is attached, is the State, as the bearer of the swords of common justice and of common protection.[9]

The objection is raised that this conception of the State is altogether too militant, and favors the methods of armed violence which we have previously denounced. The enforcement of outward conduct by means of penalties, either threatened or inflicted, it is said, seriously interferes with the freedom of the citizen and with the spontaneous action of social interests. It is further objected that such interference checks the growth of the citizen's capacity to exercise his individual rights. As heretofore, the State must be viewed upon its positive as well as its negative side. Its single aim in penalizing offenders against social well-being is to insure the moral advancement of its citizens. It bids them do or not do, and assumes surveillance of their external life, in order that well-doing may be promoted and ill-doing prevented. Nor are their motives entirely left out of count. The moral sanction of the private and the public mind is always an accessory within the purview of the State, guiding its policies and adding to its authority. Sir Henry Jones truly observes that its educational work means nothing else than the enlargement and right disposition of man's intellectual and ethical faculties. He must be governed for his own sake, and not for an ulterior purpose. In this sense, a free State is the school in which nations learn the lessons of lawful sovereignty; and the curriculum should be arranged so as to instruct all alike. Better still, the State may perhaps be compared to a family which exists for the sake of its members. The school and the family have their strength in their *morale*, to which their united will and intelligence minister. Likewise the State should impart to the persons and groups composing it, the universalized knowledge which binds them into oneness, measurably corrects an errant psychology, controls way-

[9] Cf. Norman L. Robinson: "Christian Justice," Chapter VIII. "Justice and the State," p. 187, ff.

ward impulses, and instills nobler conduct. To lessen temptation, to widen opportunities for right living, to make loyalty to its own laws and institutions a welcome engagement: these are the duties of the State.[10]

The successful husbandman plants his crops when and where they will grow, selecting for them so far as is possible salubrious air and nourishing soil. He carefully considers their peculiarities, and adapts his methods of cultivation to them. He does not unduly meddle with Nature, but conspires with her to elicit the fruits of the earth as the reward of his toil. The successful State pursues a similar course for a similar end. Its rights are its duties, and its will is never more impressive than when it abstains from despotic measures and maintains, as best it can, beneficent purposes. Legal right often invokes opposition, and it has a troubled and vexatious record. But imperative right is in harmony with those moral convictions which are the cement of human associations, and testify to the ethical nature of the State. Reason sustains it, as it sustains all other rights which satisfy permanent human needs. Therefore such rights should have nothing to dread from any ordinary eventualities, since the consensus of human judgment is upon their side. When the founders of the North American Republic declared that all men are entitled to the enjoyment of life, liberty, and the pursuit of happiness, they spoke not alone for themselves, but for the human race. The limits of private conduct are determined by the ends they enumerate. Crime has no claim upon the State except to be exterminated; wrong opinion has no rights except to be corrected; a depraved conscience can assert nothing so much as its pitiful need of direction. At the same time the processes of extermination, correction and direction are always more effective when they are patient, sympathetic and educational.

The main cause of religious persecution, according to

[10] Cf. John A. Ryan and M. F. X. Millar: "The State and the Church," p. 195, ff.

John Stuart Mill, was "a resolve not to tolerate others in doing what is permitted by their religion because it is not permitted by the persecutor's religion." This resolve is not confined to religious persecutors; it is frequently held by social and political partisans.[11] The prosecution of radical or seditious views and actions in behalf of the nation, has sometimes been degraded by a furiousness that defeated its own ends. The great boons which the French Revolution conferred upon Europe were seriously impaired by the members of "The Committee of Public Safety." The political character of this Committee appeared the more tyrannical because of the freedom which it professed. These men are said to have been the children of circumstance, which may be described as the environment of the hour. But their real weakness was revealed in the ferocity which aggravated circumstance instead of wrestling with it. Those lords and ladies who exchanged Versailles and Trianon for the disastrous fortunes of the Temple and the guillotine, became heroes and heroines. Those who butchered them indiscriminately were hated as enemies of God and mankind. Incapable of pity as of justice, Marat, Barrere, Robespierre and their fellow Terrorists have received small consideration for their public courage, or for their resistance to feudalism. They died or survived with much murder on their souls. The Russian Revolution rests under the same incubus, which some of its defenders assert is an inevitable accompaniment of transitions from despotism to liberty. It would be nearer the mark to assert that it is the offspring of the most damnable of all despotisms; of the thing called the mob; the thing of moods, now mad with destruction, now brutally brave, now timid as a hare; a multitudinous appeal to fear; savage, violent, ominous; a hungry beast, which has often showed its fangs in the modern State, and also in our own country.[12]

[11] Cf. George M. Stratton: "Anger: Its Religious and Moral Significance," Chap. X. "Persecution and War in Religion," p. 161, ff.

[12] Cf. S. Weir Mitchell: "The Adventures of François," p. 170, ff.

The rack, the pillory, and the stake have propagated more opinions, heretical or orthodox, than they could ever exterminate. Miscarriages of justice reverse moral values, enthroning wrong at the cost of right, and repudiating the tolerance which tempers justice with mercy. Yet this tolerance is a delicate art, and can only be practiced by strong and efficient States. They may also push it too far. For what appears to be tolerance in the Executive is too often indifference. If there were a universal toleration of everything and everybody, chaos would follow as surely as it has followed intolerance.

In these and all other relations between the individual and the State, there is a constant interaction of wise and elevated sentiments which constitute the permanent well-being of both. Christian ministers, who have to subserve those sentiments, find their sources in divine truth. Nor need they fear for it, or for any of its derivative realities so long as freedom is the common good. In this connection the noble words of Milton's "Areopagitica" are pertinent: "Though all the winds of doctrine were let loose to play upon the earth, so Truth be in the field, we do injuriously by licensing and prohibiting to misdoubt her strength. Let her and Falsehood grapple; who ever knew Truth put to the worse, in a free and open encounter? Her confuting is the best and surest suppressing. . . . For who knows not that Truth is strong, next to the Almighty? She needs no policies, nor strategems, nor licensings to make her victorious; these are the shifts and the defences that error uses against her power. Give her but room, and do not bind her when she sleeps."

III

The dogmatic and fault-finding spirit which disguises itself as altruism, is not always a trustworthy guide. The citizen who pits his conscience against the corporate conscience may be right in so doing, but he has need to be sure of his ground.

Not every fulminator in the pulpit is another Chrysostom, nor every dweller in the Cave of Adullam another Aristides. Self-assertive, loudly advertised aversions to the average mind, or the empty peculiarities which covet publicity, must not be mistaken for that genuine patriotism which reveres precedents, and even laws, in its opposition to rulers who have violated both. If individuals who resent the control of the State would reflect that it supplies its citizenship with numberless opportunities for life and being, and the many needs which these entail, their impatience with its sovereignty might be abated. Evidently it is warranted in protecting communal existence from whatever hurts it; and when false statements are silenced for the benefit of the community, free speech is not hurt; it is only rescued from the hazards of personal eccentricity. No honorable citizen can be indifferent to his country's well-being, nor remain neutral in the time of its danger. He may plead exemption from its ordinary duties, or even from some of its lesser necessities, but riots, insurrections, wars, and the vicious policies which cause these outbreaks, demand that he act in concert with his fellow-citizens for the restoration of public order and safety. Social customs injurious to the State, even though authorized by its legislation, are not to be countenanced by him. He should strive for the repeal of such legislation, and protest against the customs which it sanctions.

In this connection, there are forty-eight different codes in the United States which attempt to regulate marriage and divorce. A person may be lawfully married in one State and become a bigamist when he enters another. Wives and husbands are still held in the marital compact in a given commonwealth, but are neither husbands nor wives, widowers nor widows, when they cross its frontier. Property rights and the legitimacy of children are wiped out by geographical accidents. The legality of divorce decrees, involving as they do domicile, jurisdiction, and other various causes which the different States assign for divorce, is confusion worse confounded. Marriages dissolved in one State are declared legal in another. In these and similar ways the reputation of honest men and women is often damaged, and that of social offenders is as frequently legally sustained. Judge W. H. Thomas, formerly an Associate Justice of the Court of Appeals of the State of California, is responsible for the statement that divorces are more numerous in America in proportion to its population, than in any other country which tabulates marriage statistics. The annual total of such decrees for the forty-eight States is in the neighborhood of 100,000, and is increasing three times as fast as the population. With one divorce for every seven marriages here, Japan is our only competitor, and her later record has fallen below ours. In 1870 we had 28 divorces for every 100,000 of the population; in 1922 the figures increased to 134 for every 100,000. "Much of this trouble," says Judge Thomas, "is chargeable to the chaotic condition of our marriage laws;" and he recommends "a uniform law, applicable to all American territory, and based upon wisdom and experience." The domestic tragedies perpetrated by this anomalous condition must be left to the imagination. Its prostitution of right living and decency breeds the shameful results that clutter the court records of the United States. The cry of its innocent sufferers sounds like the trumpet of God, calling every citizen to their relief. Such notorious iniquities, though fostered by unequal laws or by social usages, are not to be endured, still less condoned, but fought to a standstill.[13]

The same sense of obligation applies to the problem of possessions. Wealth, in whatever degree, is vitally related to the well-being of the community and the nation; and the attitude of the citizen toward it must be determined by what he feels he owes, and not by what he actually owns. The

[13] Cf. Lord Shaw: "The Law of the Kinsmen," address on "The Widening Range of Law," in which he asks whether the method of settlement and the solution of this and kindred problems is to lie "with the brutality of force, or with the ministry of substantial reason," pp. 97, 119.

protection specifically extended to property rights by the Constitution of this Republic evidences the wisdom of its founders. Their regard for property is justified by those ethical principles which should obtain in all constitutional law. The family is the unit of the State, and both exist by the accumulation of property. The right to gain a livelihood, and to acquire means for the education of children and the defense of age, has commended itself to all civilized States. English-speaking peoples, who are not prone to think or act nationally except upon the larger issues, long since realized the justice of that right, and have governed themselves accordingly. Upon nothing save the sanctity of human life, are they so completely agreed as upon the matter of property. Political or social propagandas which threaten its institutional character are predestined to failure in a real democracy. It should be added that those who direct organized politics are sometimes complaisant to fatuity when the claims of property are at stake. But notwithstanding their defense of some of its wrong uses, its conservation still stands. Relating, as it does, to men's dealings with all the physical instrumentalities of life, property is a necessity of human existence which has to be safeguarded. Provision for daily needs and future contingencies is incumbent upon the citizen. The physical and moral welfare of dependents stimulates his desire to work and to improve his property. The improvement is not made for self alone, but chiefly for the sake of others. Those who have not experienced the anxiety which uncertainty about the future inflicts upon the majority of toiling men and women, cannot realize the distress and indignation that such a condition provokes. It is one of the chronic sources of discontent in the labor circles whose numerical increase has kept pace with the growth of industrialism, and whose reactions should be carefully observed by all citizens. The removal of this irritant is advisable, for when the honest worker is insured against the evils of an unsheltered age, he will renew his task with hope and confidence. Some measures for this insurance have hitherto vacillated between stubborn opposition and panic-stricken surrender. Well considered legislation for the removal of the difficulty, and of those arising from loss of employment, or from prolonged sickness, would conduce to the safety of the State and of the rights of property. Such legislation is still in abeyance, or where enacted has often had a tendency to pauperization.[14]

In a true democracy there is no need to seek the material prosperity of the many by the ruin of the comparatively few who are rich. Artificial barriers to a more general prosperity are always being levelled in free and lawful States, where scrutiny of the sources of wealth is more likely to issue in constructive emulation than in destructive hostility. English-speaking peoples, as I said in the first lecture, are quite aware of the defects inherent in the capitalistic system, and the best citizens are intent on their abolition. But the fact that it is the only practicable system which has been devised for governing economic relations, weighs with thoughtful men and women, and forbids rash experiments. In less fortunate nations the non-producing and leisured classes have thriven in surroundings of ignorance, social subjection and political docility. But in the United States, the British Commonwealths, and other nations of a similar character, the hope of salvaging civilization, and with it the general economic structure, is founded upon a freedom which should not be denied to either rich or poor.

That freedom maintains the right of every worker, whether by hand or brain, to choose his work and his wage, and also the right of the employer to superintend the use of his invested capital. But in passing from theory to practice, the public welfare has required some advanced economic measures which, until recently, the State was loth to adopt because

[14] Cf. "Property, Its Duties and Rights: Historically, Philosophically and Religiously Regarded." Essays by various writers, edited by Vernon Bartlet.

its dread of paternalism carried it too far in the opposite direction. The industrial, social and moral attributes inseparable from an adequate economic system, have been delayed by the obstinate greed of capital and of organized labor, and by the indifference or cowardice of the public at large. To supplant denunciation with instruction, and the spirit of envy with that of good will; to show that mutual coöperation and not unlicensed competition is the life blood of free exchanges, are the duties of the State as well as of its individual members. It must place the privileges and the obligations of its corporate body before the public mind, and insist that every individual, every rank and condition of citizenship, shall share the solemn responsibilities which rest upon the entire nation.

IV

The general will of the State, which should deepen this sense of responsibility, is simply the consistent manifestation of countless individual wills. As a volitional unit it is obtained by extracting from each person's convictions those which concern the general interest. By combining, equalizing and balancing them, a single result is gained which is loosely defined as the will of the people. In so far as its verdicts are free and unified, as a rule they are reasonable. But when they are suborned, or compelled, or made mutually exclusive by group divisions, they are wont to be ineffective or injurious. Here opposite groups of facts have to be reconciled, since the letter of the law and liberty of conscience are occasionally found at variance with each other. Hegel contended that there was another group of facts in which the extremes of the opposite groups were synthesized. This group he defined as constituting "the ethical system," or "the moral life," or "social ethics." The "ethical system" affirms freedom in respect of the family, of the well-to-do and of the political organism of the State. In the words of Wallace, the modern State, according to Hegel, is "not something assuredly which lives in London, and has its holy of holies in the office of the Treasury; not something which lives for the time being in the Cabinet, and in the upper and influential circle of the bureaucracy." On the contrary, it is the concrete and indivisible unity of all the elements of human society that compose it. Whatever may be the contradictions and antagonisms within the State, it remains a permanent entity.[15]

Monarchy, aristocracy and democracy, as Hegel viewed them, were distinctions applicable only to undeveloped communities. The State's existence did not depend on them. It was complete in itself, and as such, the sole supreme and self-contained social form in which men and women found their ideal activities. The family was its natural basis, and the fountain of its intelligent, moral and artistic life. The interdependence of social effort, commerce, economic demand and supply, was compared to an ever-widening stream. So long as the more purely political organization, call it by what name one pleases, blended all these natural affinities and divergent interests into a single comprehensive nationality, its members could play their own parts well, and contribute their quota to the total of humanity. Hegel's theory of the State as the supreme end of human action, and therefore an end in itself, was really a segment of his pantheistic view of the universe. It has not found wide acceptance except by autocratic governments, and few political philosophers have adopted it. His conception of the State as a concrete part of the "Absolute" in which all opposites are reconciled does not correspond with the truths forced upon men by actual experience. This "Absolute," has neither organism nor purpose. Its asserted perfection is undefined and indefinable. It is neither personal nor impersonal, and therefore possesses no qualities for good or for evil. As a metaphysical hypoth-

[15] Cf. W. Wallace: "Lectures and Essays on Natural Theology and Ethics," p. 120, ff.

esis, skilfully conceived and expounded, but without moral character or consistency, it furnishes a striking proof of the mischief wrought by able but errant speculation. Any theory which attempts to destroy personality in God or in men, as Hegel's theory does, obstructs the spiritual communications that give their higher meaning alike to the individual and to the institutions of the State. Apart from its detrimental effects upon religion, one should mark its pernicious influence in modern politics, and its close connection with the World War.

Further, Hegel's proposition that the real will is the general will expressed in the social fabric of the State, and that the citizen has no will worthwhile separate from that fabric, ignores the freedom of the individual and confiscates him, body and soul, to the State. The essential difference between the State and society at large is lost in the process of confiscation. Much organized human life is outside the jurisdiction of the State; its social alignments traverse State divisions; and when properly made and kept are helpful to the State's integrity.[16] Extreme forms of individualism tend to deny the reality of these social alignments. Or again, the reaction against those forms tends to the view that society is an entity apart from individuals, and that they are merged in it without regard to their personal identity. The truth is that in society and in the State, the individual is both conditioned and unconditioned, ruled and ruler. The lawful intercourse of society, of the State, and of the citizen so interpenetrate, that genuine freedom is not curtailed but amplified.

Thomas Hill Green, one of the best thinkers in the British School of philosophic idealism, did valiant service for the ethical interests of our political heritage, by showing that the claims of the individual upon society and of society upon the individual are reciprocal. Certain powers are secured to

[16] Cf. L. T. Hobhouse: "The Metaphysical Theory of the State," p. 76, ff; also, Albert Schweitzer: "Civilization and Ethics," Chapter XIII.

every man by society, which must exercise authority to guarantee those powers. Both sets of claims rest upon the truth that those powers, in the man and in society, are absolutely necessary for the fulfilment of man's vocation as a moral being. Without them the self-devotion which leads toward better character in self and in others could not exist. The State does not absorb or suppress individuals. It is a body of persons, recognized by each other as having rights and possessing certain institutions for the purpose of the maintenance of those rights. Thus, while the State is more important than any citizen, it cannot be indifferent to the rights of any single citizen.[17]

In theory, as we have said, the common good is the aim of the State. But in reality, other motives and aims intrude, projected by illicit interests and desires. Contralized government resulting in mass tyranny, the ineptitude or unintelligence of peoples, or leadership itself misled by dogmatic prepossessions, have frequently buried the common good, and automatically guarded it from the inquiries of ordinary men. Nevertheless, a reasonable view of the situation upholds the belief that the maintenance of the State is by the power of good-will, not force; certainly never falsity nor treacherous diplomacy. Not a common greed but a common benevolence is the rock upon which political institutions must be built. Nor can this principle be overthrown by the facts derived from self-interest or from reckless national aggrandizement. When laws or their administrators violate liberty of conscience, history shows that, provided liberty of conscience is energized by the right, it triumphs, and enforces a change of antagonistic statutes and rulers.[18]

Sociology is a useful accessory in the determination of the citizen's relations to the State. It has systematized the interests of community life, and demonstrated that econom-

[17] Cf. Thomas Hill Green: "Principles of Political Obligation," pp. 347, 443. This volume and his "Prolegomena to Ethics" are of the utmost value to every student of ethical valuations.

[18] Cf. B. Bosanquet: "The Philosophical Theory of the State," p. 295.

ics and politics must be treated as collateral questions. Its surveys of ancient and modern peoples and States, though not of equal significance, have their special values. Modes of government, the different social methods and their respective advantages or disadvantages, are placed in a new and clearer light.[19] By its means we perceive that many political thinkers were hampered by the prevalent ideas of their age, and we also see how few were able to change those ideas. The science also includes the physiological branch, which has to do with the identities and differences of individuals, groups and races.[20] Social philosophy, to which Comte made an original contribution, simplifies these identities and differences, and teaches us to avoid erroneous distinctions between the State and the people. The idea that the sovereignty of the one necessarily implies the subservience of the other is abandoned. Those, who, imitating Rousseau, would practically annihilate the existence of the State, and those, who, imitating Hegel, would make the State the grand finality, are viewed as alike mistaken.

Viscount Morley is right when he says that Rousseau was the most directly revolutionary of all speculative precursors in this field; the first to apply his mind to those social conditions which must be modified. Yet the opening sentence of the "Contrat Social," which has been repeated around the world, "Man is born free and everywhere he is in chains," is utterly misleading in its bald literalism. Man is born for freedom, and this is attainable not by animal isolation in a fictitious state of nature, but by his subjection to social requirements, and to the law of the land. These are supposed to operate in harmony with the general will which aims at a community of interest. This general will, and not spasmodic majority or minority votes, is the substantial

[19] Cf. W. W. Willoughby: "The Nature of the State," p. 1, ff.

[20] Cf. W. McDougall: "Social Psychology," pp. 84, 170, 296 ff; id. "The Group Mind," Part I. "General Principles of Collective Psychology," p. 31 ff; Franklin H. Giddings: "Studies in the Theory of Human Society," p. 154 ff.

factor. The franchise may either hasten or retard its advantages. It can also help to relate particular wills, which while unrelated, have no controlling power. But it cannot exclude that community of interest which is the binding force of politics.

Those who assert personal rights over social rights should remember that the former are themselves, as often as not, imperilled unless subordinated to the latter. Government by one's own law is anarchy, but government according to equal law is approximate liberty. Locke held that the State is created to protect the rights which belong to the individual by nature, but he did not clearly distinguish between rights and obligations. Where much is given, much is required — a rule that emphasizes the closest alliance of rights and obligations for the sake of national efficiency. The political philosophy of Kant and Fichte was erected upon the conception of freedom as inherent in man. They were indebted to Rousseau for the idea, although it had been previously propounded by Locke in his "Treatise of Civil Government." "Men," he said, "being by nature all free, equal and independent, no one can be put out of this estate and subjected to the political power of another without his own consent." This proposition was derived from the sixteenth century Protestantism which appealed from traditional authority to that of the reason and conscience of the individual.[21] Moreover, far behind the Reformers one recalls Wyclif's bold thesis that "everyone in a state of grace has real lordship over the whole universe."

Let us further remember that the Puritan Revolution of the seventeenth century, and the American Revolution of the eighteenth century, were based upon individual liberty exercised under equal social restraints. These historic gains from distinctively Teutonic and Anglo-Saxon sources make us independent of the Gallican influences of the "Contrat Social." They reveal the slow and costly evolution of the

[21] Cf. D. G. Ritchie: "Natural Rights," p. 13, ff.

political privileges we enjoy, and require us to give credit to all concerned in their development. Thinkers of every school, notwithstanding their disabilities and difficulties, sowed the seed which has produced the harvest of democracy. This harvest in turn is being straitly winnowed by the Time Spirit which rejects the chaff and garners the grain. Two ideals of the State are now to the front: the one is that of the Germanic-Teuton who holds to the empire of a typical State over the world, or else the downfall of the State; the other is that of the Anglo-Saxon who believes in the freedom of the world or else its slavery. Much which distinguishes the day in which we live is created by the collision between these two ideals. It is a day of great burdens, but of equally great opportunities, and I am persuaded that from it will be dated the prevalence of the Anglo-Saxon ideal. For this reason future generations will view the World War as we cannot. They will see in it, not only infinite loss but infinite gain which far exceeds the loss. Yet I predict that before the Anglo-Saxon ideal does prevail, many vital changes must take place. It behooves us to observe the beginnings of these changes with the accuracy due to the beginning moment as the supreme moment. Contemporary governments, the work of their different departments; and contemporary peoples, their social and industrial pursuits, are also to be observed by the Christian pastor and the Hebrew rabbi, with a concern that visualizes their importance. Above all else, as citizens, they should discern in America what unfits her for the highest duties of a world State, and wherein she is competent for the discharge of those duties. To prove out self-government, freedom, democracy, in modern times, is not less but more difficult than ever it was. But the proof can be made by men and women who unremittingly devote themselves to the religious and educational enlightenment of the people, and who believe that God is the author of social and universal as well as of personal redemption.

V

If you ask for the sources of information, guidance and strength which are available for this inspiring task, I refer you to the ethical teachings of the Old Testament, and to the Life and Gospel of Jesus Christ. Compare them with their most strenuous opponent in civilized States; with the Socialism of Karl Marx, as found in his treatise of 1847, and quoted by Mr. John St. Loe Strachey, Editor of the "London Spectator," in a recent issue of that journal. Here you have face to face the two contestants for the franchise of the citizen in the modern State. None will treat the Marxian Manifesto cavalierly, if they reflect that in all probability it has made more converts in Europe and America during the last half-century than all the Protestant Churches of those two continents. Millions give it their unqualified allegiance; they look upon it, not as a political creed or a social theory alone, but as the sole religion of humanity. Here, then, is "Modernism" with a vengeance: not the cultured type of clerics and academics, but the type which is inseparably associated with the toiling masses, who have yet to learn from the Church the essential spirit and message of God's Evangel. Mr. Strachey describes the Manifesto as a sequestered document, from which the present tyranny in Russia gets its motive power; as one of the most alluring incentives to malignant thought and action which society at large has ever felt. Its propositions are, that overproduction is a peril; that class hatred and class war are obligatory; that the proletariat should rule by innate right, first, in the State, and eventually in the world. Their valid deductions are that abundance is created by artificial famine; that hate is a virtue; that strife is preferable to fraternity; and that the manual laborer is to form the next despotism because he stands in the logical succession of despots. Absolutism, oligarchism and constitutionalism have had their turn; now comes his, which he proposes to exploit to its farthest possibilities.

Democratic States instinctively oppose these propositions and their deductions because such States are the vantage grounds of that higher freedom which makes for social righteousness and not for a renewed tyranny. English-speaking States actively oppose them, because such States are measurably versed in the freedom of freedoms which is born of the Spirit of God. But all States that condemn Marxism must not reckon too much upon its financial and economic disasters. These it accounts for by asserting that the times are not ripe for its proposed deliverance of the underworld to universal empire. There is a likelihood that it will eventually dwindle and die in its own stench. But there is also a likelihood that the folly and covetousness we have observed in the modern State will make for Marxism some breach in society, through which its hosts of the discontented shall pour. If they are not to do this, States must get rid of their evasive diplomacies, their political fickleness, their emotional judgments, and their industrial treason. The riddance can only be made by a self-imposed religious regimen which gives to the citizen, whatever his creed may be, an inward and spiritual control; and admits him to actual communion with the highest law and the highest love. Science, politics, art, education, can prepare his way, but unless he finds divine fellowship at the end of that way, they will not save the State.

Again, religion furnishes him with the social and moral objectives that can unite the right-minded majority for their positive attainment. If society needs anything today it needs these objectives. The late war showed what it could become under the intoxication of battle. What might it not become if filled with the spirit of altruism and sacrifice for those ideals which few dare to dispute, but almost fewer still believe to be practicable? If some of Britain's best leaders have found the path to power by way of India, what power for right and justice awaits leaders of American politics, who shall assume our share of the burdens of humanity?

So far as the alienated workers of the world are concerned in this issue, it is safe to assert that they have never yet been able really to live without a spiritual center. If they, like multitudes who do not bear their heavy burdens, have at last become eccentric without first knowing where the true center is, here is a calamity which churchmen must overcome. Not the less, but the more, do wanderers from the central Source of social and moral life need support, encouragement, consolation and defense against oppression, whether from within or without their ranks. Church and State must realize that from this standpoint, politics, and the economic problems that cannot be separated from them, are psychological as well as prudential. Rabid nationalism, religious bigotry and class hatred are states of mind that do not readily yield to legislative measures nor pious protestations. They have to be encountered by a pronounced and reasonable fraternity, by the practice of just and generous living, by a far more inclusive sense of what St. Paul meant when he said: "Honor all men." [22]

But these qualities of heart and mind demand a supermorality which can only be supplied by religion. Here the problem is seen for what it really is: not merely political, economic, psychological, but always spiritual at its core. To solve it, the State should expand and redefine its ethic, stripping it of class favoritism, race prejudice and militant tendencies; formulating its foreign policies in those international organizations which have been recommended by the safest political guides of our time. Every object that may be considered contributory to the progress of the race should obviously be encouraged by the State. What retards its progress should be opposed by the State, despite merely domestic considerations. Then instead of rolling over the bodies and souls of men like a Juggernaut's car, political influence will breathe through their lives like a quickening wind. Nevertheless, when these things are done, and they

[22] Cf. "The Return of Christendom," by a Group of Churchmen.

are still a long distance from accomplishment, nothing but religion interpreted as love for God and all mankind, can save them from failure.

Here precisely lies the difference between two other views of the State and of the citizen's obligations. In the democratic or humanitarian view, it is the servant of humanity, to be judged by what it does for the lives of its members and by the part that it plays in the society of mankind. In the metaphysical view, it is self-sufficient, isolated, sovereign, the custodian of its own affairs, beyond which its interests fade away unless those affairs are in question. In the democratic view, the sovereign State is already doomed, and the nationalism it embodies will presently join the more primitive associations of the past. Nations, as we know them, are ultimately destined to subordination in a community of mankind. In the metaphysical view, the State must always remain as the supreme achievement of human organization, the best interpreter of the laws of God and reason, and the institution least likely to do wrong.[23]

One can find no middle ground between these two conceptions. Since life will do nearly everything else but stand still, it must express itself, as heretofore, in a further development of society, which will supplant nationalism as nationalism supplanted tribalism. The full logical idea of this expression is found in the New Testament. It is entirely free from narrow affirmations; entirely catholic in its outlook upon the future of the race. Though its documents were compiled beneath the political auspices of ancient Rome, it rejects the imperial unity of Roman politics, and refers all unity to the Federal Headship of its Risen Lord. It is the prerogative of Christianity to assert in unprecedented ways, the intrinsic worth of every individual soul and of all society; and to show how their worth can be realized in universal

[23] Cf. L. T. Hobhouse: " The Metaphysical Theory of the State," p. 137; John A. Ryan and M. F. X. Millar: " The State and the Church," p. 201; Frances J. McConnell: " Democratic Christianity."

fellowship. In this fellowship there is no trace of our modern distinctions: "neither Jew nor Greek, neither bond nor free, no male and female; for all are one in Christ Jesus."[24] Such is St. Paul's comment upon his Master's words: "Many shall come from the east and the west, and shall sit down with Abraham, and Isaac, and Jacob, in the Kingdom of Heaven."[25] This is the divine mandate which overrides all human mandates as we understand them. In this indivisible unity is the brightest hope and the last phase of the whole family named after the one Father.

Let us believe in the State, and in its inevitable movement toward the Father's purpose. But let us also believe that the religion we dispense is the future faith, not only of the leading States of the earth, but of the enslaved, the lost and the despairing. Neitzsche's sneer that it was only suitable for helots pays it a handsome tribute. For it began with outcasts and pariahs, headed by humble fishermen. Its doctrines of love and brotherhood constructed powerful nations out of the most unpromising human material, and taught them how to use their power; enabling them to establish beneficent governments and a growing civilization upon the débris of once mighty kingdoms.

In summary, the Christian Scriptures recognize in the State a divine institution, and speak of its administrators as officers of a Higher Authority. They inculcate civil obedience, exhort the converts of the early Church to be in subjection to political authority, and to pray for those appointed to exercise it. But their obedience and subjection are given as unto God; for the sake of their Lord, and not for the sake of man. Here are not two governments, each independent of or opposed to the other, but one unreserved allegiance, including political loyalty, and always superior to it. The ideal State is foreshadowed by the Apostle to the Gentiles, whose concepts had been moulded by Rome as well

[24] Galatians III. 28.
[25] Matthew VIII. 11.

as by Jerusalem, and whose being had been transformed by his contact with Christ. St. Paul saw it as it should be, if it fulfilled its true end, when rulers are no longer a terror to the good, but to evil doers. He advises those who would be free from fear of the State, to be and to do good; and they shall have praise from the prince, who is God's steward for righteousness. The gap between the State he portrayed, and that which we know, must be closed by the Christian Ecclesia, whose creation and growth are reviewed in the following lecture.

SIXTH LECTURE

THE CHRISTIAN ECCLESIA IN THE TWO EMPIRES

"Unto me, who am less than the least of all saints, was this grace given, to preach unto the Gentiles the unsearchable riches of Christ; and to make all men see what is the dispensation of the mystery which for ages hath been hid in God who created all things; to the intent that now unto the principalities and the powers in the heavenly places might be made known through the Church the manifold wisdom of God, according to the eternal purpose which He purposed in Christ Jesus our Lord; in Whom we have boldness and access in confidence through our faith in Him. Wherefore I ask that ye may not faint at my tribulations for you, which are your glory."

Ephesians III. 8–13

SIXTH LECTURE

THE CHRISTIAN ECCLESIA IN THE TWO EMPIRES

The ideal and actual history of the Christian Ecclesia — Our Lord the Founder of the Church for a mission to all nations — Authority exercised by the apostles in fellowship with him — Development interrupted by deviations from Christ's ideals which, however, repeatedly asserted themselves — Persecutions due to misunderstandings of the real purpose of the Church — The significance of Constantine's conversion for the further spread of Christianity — The transition from Apostolic into Catholic Christianity marked by sacerdotal claims and questionable policies — St. Augustine's crucial influence over Christian thought and behavior — Hildebrand's notable Pontificate — The rise of City-Republics and the emergence of popular rights and liberties.

THE ideal history of the Christian Ecclesia does not exist. Such a history would have no predilections. Its viewpoints and appraisals would not indicate the particular denomination, if any, to which the author belonged. Its critical merits would survive the keenest scrutiny, and the book itself would remain as the permanent authority of all intelligent churchmen. But since so unique an example of profound scholarship and dispassionate statement is unavailable at this time, we must be content to consult the more modest yet trustworthy Church histories that serve the student well, and contain the latest results of original research. The best of these do not set out to prove a case, but to state it as it is, divested of prejudice and of doubtful or untenable theories. Many of them cover only a single personality, event or period of the Ecclesia. They give accurate and exhaustive accounts of Councils, controversies, schisms; of the rise of the Episcopacy, its monarchical essence, the revolt against it, and similar issues relative to doctrine or polity. Other histories weave these matters into a connected story, fascinating, powerful, convincing, and one which does not cause the student to be of the mind of Falstaff's tailor, who wanted better security than Bardolph could supply.

I confess that I am largely dependent upon the material thus placed at our disposal by competent historians from Eusebius to Hort, Harnack, and the goodly number of modern Church annalists. So I do not have to collate authorities, collect evidence, nor reproduce a given era with photographic detail and fidelity. I have no desire to gain kudos among the scholars absorbed in these useful pursuits, to whom I am indebted for nearly all I know about the subject. Descriptions and references that I make must imitate the modern painters who project upon the canvas the broad contours which have caught the eye, and which also express the feeling and rhythm of the objects they depict. The first impression derived from the reading of Church history is that, unlike some themes, one cannot have too many books upon it. The Christian Ecclesia, her creation and growth, faith and practice, present to us the progressive stages of what is conceded to be the foremost spiritual achievement in the world. It is with the concrete aspects of this achievement that we have to do; with its wonderful birth, experience and work, its seeming defeats and real victories.

The fact that "The holy Church throughout all the world" was a definite divine creation, when Nicetas, bishop of Remesiana wrote these words in the fourth century, is far more important for present and future civilization than all the theories or institutions of politics. She existed then, as now, visible to all men, an organization that had antedated the Bible, as we have it, by nearly two centuries: the Witness from the first century until the present day of invisible realities. The Church of that far off time was co-extensive with Roman rule from Hadrian's Wall to the Euphrates River. Her evangelists went beyond the frontiers of the Empire into the unknown East and West. She maintained in all the regions indicated substantially one teaching and one worship.

Her essentials have changed less than those of any other organization except the home. The federal rule of the Episcopacy knit together scattered tribes and peoples. Among the Pontiffs and bishops who exercised it, those of Rome, Alexandria and Antioch stood out in an undisputed priority. True, separate and minor societies were found circling round the major Society like planets round the sun, but they only made her unity the more conspicuous.

The Ecclesia proper was first called the "Great Church" by the pagan Celsus, who thus distinguished her from seceding sects. Her claim to have been such is indorsed by Harnack, and Bishop Headlam asserts in his Bampton Lectures that she was at that time recognized as the Church Universal by non-believers as well as by believers.[1] Those who are convinced that she was divinely originated will explain this marvellous advance by that conviction. Her preservation and enlargement since the fourth century and in the three centuries before it, are not readily explained in any other way. Origins in general, and that of the Ecclesia in particular, are thorny issues, about which numerous disputes foregather. The ancient world in which she appeared, as something apparently born out of due time, has vanished. It can never be fully recovered to us. Many of its factors remain shrouded in the mists of the past. The search for them is hindered by numerous erroneous speculations and assumptions. The competent scholars who conduct it concentrate upon the memorable literature of antiquity; upon its philosophers, poets, prophets and apostles; upon the principal events of the period that covered the four hundred years before the birth of our Lord, and the two hundred years after His death. The teachings and happenings of those great pivotal ages are still of supreme interest to mankind.

The chief thing we know about them is that Christianity emerged from their heart as the united testimony of various

[1] Cf. Arthur C. Headlam: "The Doctrine of the Church and Christian Reunion," p. 75 f. 210 ff.

races, over whom it had won a moral triumph of the first magnitude. Doctrinal theology deals with their testimony to the Faith from one standpoint; ecclesiastical theology from another. Both are often too abstract and technical to serve the purposes of historic narration; certainly both are prolific of differences. If one may be pardoned for saying so, what really matters is the emergence I have named. The greatest proof of Christianity is Christianity itself. Doctrines and methods of government are first-rate secondary things, but they are secondary. And even origins can be overdone. If we are prepared to believe that the life of the Crucified and Risen Lord animated His disciples and resulted in the creation of His Ecclesia, by the Will of God, upon the foundation of Christ's Person and Mission, then the process becomes explicable. However it is explained, the Church, like the sun, shines as a vital organization. She imparts great gifts to men, and they reverence her for the spiritual benefits which they receive from her. The majority do not trouble about the exact manner of her origin. To them its problems appear to belong to another world. They do not debate them; they live in and love the Church apart from them, and this, notwithstanding that those problems are forever recurring, as they were at Nicæa and at Chalcedon. It suffices for the body of believers that the Church has had an unbroken tenure of existence in the world from what is, to them, an immemorial past.

It is generally understood that she stoutly resisted the Paganism which at times seduced her outward being. Her children praise her because she has often enthroned humility and lowered the pride of earthly rank. They treasure her for her insistence upon sacrifice, and her denunciation of selfishness. They honor her for her opposition to the encroachments of unlicensed power, and to the provincial or racial arrogance which incited conquest and oppression. These are some of her credentials, not only for Christians, but for all lovers of justice and freedom. Had she done no more than they indicate, she would have proved herself worthy of human confidence. But the Church also denied the theory of separate descent which has served as the defense of slavery. She addressed her Evangel to men as men, regardless of race, color or condition. The first choice of her youthful period was for the poor, the helpless, the abandoned and the depraved. Her backslidings and infidelities, the repeated outrages of her inferior breeds upon the spirit and letter of the message committed to her care, should be recalled by us even if they are ever to be forgotten by the world. But they did not destroy the human hopes fixed upon her as an eternal institution, nor alienate the love and confidence of her devoted members. When evil days came, and corruption or tyranny deeply infected her visible rulers, she continued to adore her invisible King, and was usually in health and vigor of soul on the borders of her missionary activity.

Those who turned from the transgressions of earth-bound ecclesiastics to the ideals they distorted or denied, found in those ideals a perennial source of consolation and of power. False doctrines and opinions which claimed her sanction; evil devices and deeds paraded under her name; jailings and burnings of Christians by those who professed the same Faith, could do everything possible against the Church, except destroy her. She remained alive, resumed her original teachings, enriched them from contemporary systems of thought, preached them everywhere. Her records are resplendent with pure, serviceable spirits whose names should be as familiar to us as those of the distinguished statesmen of one's country. Her reformative epochs, when she threw off the old, put on the new, and crystallized her energies afresh for the salvation of men and nations, have a fruitful significance for the present age. Her religious revivals, even revolutions, are as verifiable and recreative as any other methods she has employed. Thus she became what she still is: an indestructible reality which no explanations can belittle without introducing more difficulties than they remove.

II

Contrary to natural expectation, our Lord expounded no stated system of doctrine or of organization. But it is reasonable to affirm that the essence of His Message, and of the forms and institutions in which it took shape, were held as a unity by Him, and that what He revealed was germinal of its after developments. He used the language of life, not of philosophy; of parables, not of formal discourse. The fiction which conveyed the highest truths in lowliest terms, was His chosen method of communication. He concentrated upon a few fundamental verities that became the property of every conscience and of every age. His words contained explicit realities understood by all who heard them, and also implicit depths of truth to be understood later by the initiated. Their spirit and life, immensity and freedom, could not be coffined in one interpretation. God's seed was in them to germinate, and to bear fruit after its kind. They were certain to be variously construed; to undergo those adjustments demanded alike by their infinite content and by the ever widening necessities of the Faith.[2]

His followers felt, as we feel, that He *was* the Gospel; its personalized center and the source of its regenerative power. Hence they endeavored to discover the inmost mystery of His Being. What in itself was actual, belonging to His very mind, was paramount with them. They differed honestly among themselves, as we differ, in proclaiming Him to others. These differences, which did not disturb their substantial agreements, indicated that He transcended all explanations. No categories, whether Synoptic, Pauline or Johannine, could contain Him, His works, or His words. I see no need, therefore, to view them as contradictory because they are separate accounts. Are they not rather to be coördinated beneath the inherently selective principle already named,

[2] Cf. Arthur C. Headlam: "The Life and Teachings of Jesus the Christ," chapters V and VI.

as the most available hypothesis for the known facts of Christian history? Not a few who reject the evolutionary hypothesis in this connection, admit it in the physical realm, in society, in the State, in politics, in nearly everything save the Christian Faith. One is tempted to ask why that Faith or the Ecclesia should be exempted from what is, beyond question, a cardinal method both in Nature and Humanity. As a theory it was used by Newman in his "Essay on the Development of Christian Doctrine"; through which he hoped to silence the objections against Roman theology, by showing that it was an expansion of the original principles committed to the Apostles. Much that he advances in the Essay is admissible by Protestants, and his idea of the Church as a living growth, to be developed by its own potentialities, reacting upon society, and beneath the direction of the Spirit of God, proves how well Newman could have handled some theological problems of our age, by the aid of the biological learning which he unconsciously heralded. Upon its constructive side, his argument makes him to some extent the progenitor of Modernism.

The theory of development, as applied to the Ecclesia, ranks high in correspondence with the facts. It forbids the isolation of our Lord from the Church which bears His name, and which carries on His work in the world. Further, its application relates the Christian to the Jewish Ecclesia. This name itself had associations that linked it with the Hebrew Scriptures, and it was used by the Greek translators of the Pentateuch in their rendering of the Hebrew word "qāhāl", which means a gathering of men, or again, of nations. They were called out, not to be separate, but for purposes of assembly. This was its precise meaning in the Old Testament, and when the use of ἐκκλησία was adopted by the New Testament writers, it already had a local, national and religious history connecting it with that of the Mosaic Commonwealth. Its actual use by Jesus is confined to St. Matthew. Doubts have been cast upon the credibility of his references, but Dr. Hort asserts that there is no *a priori* reason for suspecting them. In St. Matthew XVIII. 17, our Lord speaks of the existing Jewish Ecclesia, before which an offending brother is to be summoned as a last resort. In St. Matthew XVI. 18, He elicits St. Peter's great Confession, and declares that upon the Apostle as upon a rock of constancy, He will build His Ecclesia. This declaration established it in lineal succession with that of Israel, but to be completed and perfected in the Covenant which He was yet to ratify.[3]

The Church of Christian history does not have to be identified with that to which our Lord referred in this familiar passage. In a specific sense it was His own Ecclesia: the outgrowth under His personal direction of the revelation of God in history, of which Christ was the culmination. One may maintain the belief that this universal Ecclesia, which He called "My Church," and linked by inference with the Jewish Israel, has been from the first the inner soul and selfhood of all existing organizations which bear His name, and as such, the source of that indestructible unity now revived among Christians after their prolonged stay in the wilderness of sectarian divisions. The distinction is not negligible, since the truth often lies in such careful interpretations, and it is always wise to recall them if we would reduce the large sum of errors which obscure the issue before us. The gist of our Lord's saying is its naming of the Christian Ecclesia, connecting it with that of Israel, and proclaiming its immunity from future decay and death. Endurance, continuity, newness of life and power were the enduements with which He enriched it. It was built upon St. Peter and upon his fellow Apostles, who were equipped for their mission under our Lord's authority, and because of their confession of His Messiahship.

In the last hours of His Passion that mission was transferred to them; with the accompanying symbols of the Holy

[3] Cf. F. J. A. Hort: "The Christian Ecclesia," p. 9 ff.

Supper as the Sacrament of their fellowship, and of the washing of feet as the pledge of their service. The commandment that they love one another, enhanced with new meanings which Christ alone could impart; the parable of the Vine and the Branches, the promise of the Paraclete, the dedicatory Prayer, were one solemn ordination of the discipleship as the infant Ecclesia. Here she was patterned in sacred conference and after the mind of her Lord; at Pentecost she was manifested to the world as a single visible Society, sustained by His Risen Life and its purposes, and held together by a common allegiance to Him. Professor Benjamin W. Bacon elucidates the matter at length, and says that there was "already a brotherhood in Jesus' time"; "its law of mutual service was formulated"; its "bond of perfectness which Paul makes the basis of a new sociology did not have to be invented for the Churches of Asia." But Professor Bacon emphasizes the fact that "the word 'Church' never occurs in the Gospels, save in two passages of Matthew, one textually doubtful, both recognized by all modern students as belonging to that element of Matthew which is latest, and has least claims to authenticity." To Pauline propaganda must be ascribed, he contends, the later content of the term Ecclesia. "If Jesus used this Greek word it could only be in its Old Testament sense." In the one instance, we have "a mere rule of ecclesiastical procedure"; in the other, "at best a prediction of the future, whose significance could only transpire after Jesus' death." The "brotherhood" which began even in Galilee, and grew to something more at Jerusalem "had no sense of its real mission until it became conscious of a work entrusted to it, together with the power to fulfil that mission." If the disciples conceived of our Lord, "in any sense or degree as the Redeemer, it was only by virtue of being placed at the head of the Old Testament 'Church', the people of Israel." "Nothing," insists this author, "can be more certain than that 'the Church', as we understand the word, is an outgrowth of

Jesus's rejection and crucifixion, as these were reacted against by the faith and loyalty of His followers. Our conclusion then must be that the beginning of the conscious life of the Church was its endowment with power through conviction that God had raised Jesus from the dead." [4]

The end justifies the scholarly caution with which Dr. Bacon treats this great issue. There is little in his exposition which does not commend itself to those who apply the theory of development to the Ecclesia. He views it from its strictly historic side, as well as from the spiritual viewpoints which so phenomenal a creation demands. What he says is entitled to our respectful consideration, both for its own sake, and for the sake of his reverent and constructive learning. Changes were easily effected in an organization which, as yet, had taken on no rigid outlines. Processes that required centuries for their maturity were introduced without friction. From the moment at Antioch, when believers who previously had referred to one another as "of the way" were first called Christians, to the end of the Apostolic age, the Divine Society, as a vital entity, was susceptible to fresh impulses because unfettered by hard and fast regulations. St. Paul's successful resistance of the Judaisers who sought to inter the new Faith in their old traditions, freed him for his evangelization of the Roman world. His conceptions of the Ecclesia were for him a requirement of that revolutionizing crusade. In his letter to the church at Colossæ, and still more in his letter to the Ephesians, the Apostle uses mystical terms to set forth the Ecclesia as the Body of Christ, in which all believers are forever one, and of which He is the Head. The Church is indissolubly joined to Him, she is His chaste and beautiful Bride; her presence among men reveals the redemptive wisdom of God, which began in the past of the Creation, and was to be consummated in the future by the palingenesis of the earth through her.

[4] Professor Benjamin Wisner Bacon: "The Founding of the Church," p. 13 ff.

The pivotal saying already mentioned and ascribed to our Lord: "Thou art Peter, and on this rock I will build my Church," echoes throughout New Testament literature. Influenced by it, the Apostles assumed and exercised an authority, not clearly defined, over the corporate life of the Ecclesia. This authority was the legitimate outcome of their fellowship with Christ. I need not discuss here the controversial issue of their relation to the historic episcopacy, except to repeat the statements of one of the foremost of modern Anglican scholars, that "it is not to the Apostles we must look for the prototype of the bishop," and that "the episcopate was formed, not out of the apostolic order by localization, but out of the presbyteral by elevation; and the title, which originally was common to all, came at length to be appropriated to the chief among them." [5] The first officers of the Church were the seven named in Acts VI. 5: Stephen, Philip, Prochorus, Nicanor, Timon, Parmenas, and Nicolas, upon whom the Apostles laid their hands to symbolize their approval and benediction. The priestly function was incipient, if not active, since the Priesthood and the Sacrifice of the Lord Himself as sole Mediator predominated in the consciousness of the Apostolic Church. The title *Episcopos* indicated the office of the Elder or Presbyter, and these names were used interchangeably. The apparatus was simple, democratic, and from the Protestant standpoint, constitutional. Its officers did not supersede the freedom of the Ecclesia. On the contrary, they invoked it for the safeguarding of the important interests committed to their oversight. The monarchical principle, which was of the nature of patristic and subsequent episcopacies, received a limited recognition in the case of St. James at Jerusalem, and to a lesser degree in the temporary functions entrusted by St. Paul to St. Timothy and St. Titus at Ephesus and Crete respectively. The conclusion warranted from these and other relations is that Apostolic history was not a depository of infallible pre-

[5] J. B. Lightfoot: "Commentary on Philippians," p. 196 ff.

cedents to be strictly obeyed at all times and in all places. It imposed no Levitical code upon the vigorous and progressive life and liberty of the Church. Quite otherwise, it was a stirring record of victorous campaigns waged against apparently overwhelming odds. As those who accept the development theory would expect, it contained no series of final precedents or laws, made regardless of divine teachings and purposes which were capable of still further adaptation, and it was therefore inherently competent to meet changing needs and circumstances. The firm belief of the Apostles and their converts that the prerogatives of the Ecclesia were inspired and guided by the Spirit of God, adds to their impressiveness and accounts for their success.[6]

III

The Church of the sub-Apostolic period was grounded in the fundamental truth that man's salvation was accomplished by the Crucified and Risen Jesus. He, as Lord and Redeemer of the World, enabled her to speak with a universal voice. Before the end of the second century she was looked upon as the ark of safety for the human race, and eternal life as the gift of Christ was regarded as an impossibility outside her pale. St. Cyprian's dictum: "Extra ecclesiam hanc visibilem nulla salus," gave terse expression to a then prevalent belief which was influential before his day. The bishops were no longer viewed as local officers, but as the inheritors of the Apostles, and the dispensers of that redemptive grace which had been communicated by them through a direct ordination. The teachings of the New Testament were to be understood only as an increasing body of traditions explained them. With the growth of the Christian Societies, these traditions became more complex and required the application

[6] Cf. F. J. A. Hort: "The Christian Ecclesia," lecture V on "The Exercise of Authority," p. 76 ff. I am indebted to this instructive volume for many of the positions taken.

from time to time of orthodoxy's multiplying articles. Absolute correctness of creedal expression was regarded as a theological virtue, apart from which the character and meaning of primitive Christianity would have been lost to mankind. So the Holy Catholic Church developed out of the jurisdiction of the episcopal hierarchy, with whose existence it was identified, and apart from which there was no Church. Their prerogatives were enlarged by the deepening contrast between the ideal, unified and spotless Society of the Pauline letters, and the actual, struggling, local communions. These prerogatives were exercised for the enactment of laws, the administration of discipline, and the authorization of beliefs. The light which is inseparable from the life of religion waned; while faith, no longer regarded as a spiritual dynamic, depended upon stereotyped rules rather than upon affection, conscience and reason The intellect became a drudge to what was called "the believing mind," which in many instances was an ardent use of imagination, to sustain theories about Apostolic succession and its sacerdotal attributes. Any attempt to disparage these was set down as indicating a want of piety, or an intractable and rebellious disposition. In brief, the organization which has since been arraigned as a fantastic invention of ecclesiastical sophistry, and a flat contradiction of the purpose of our Lord, was the first charge of bishops and the idol of their flocks.

That it had carnal elements and produced disappointing results is beyond cavil. Yet it protected and transmitted the Chrisitanity which it repressed. During those eras when God's gifts had to be accommodated to the limitations of their earthly stewards, the contemporary literature was scanty enough. The "Teaching of the Twelve Apostles," discovered by Bryennios in the Library at Constantinople in 1875; the "Shepherd of Hermas"; the two letters of Clement and those of Ignatius, the Martyrdoms of Ignatius and Polycarp, and the Epistle to Diognetus complete the list. They reveal little of an inspirational sort, and simply serve to connect the Apostolic age with the later hierarchy to which Ignatius gave vehement adherence as the living nexus of the Ecclesia, derived from the Apostles themselves.[7]

The surprising progress of a despised and foreign sect in every province of the Roman Empire is partly explained by its exclusive character. The first Christian Societies lived precariously, and the civil power which dealt with them was in many respects an ironical comment upon St. Paul's portrayal of the ideal Ruler and State. Doubtless some believers felt strong impulses to assert their higher freedom in Christ in premature ways. Their loyalty to Him, like that of the whole Church, was undivided and indivisible. It suffered no rivalry, not even that of imperial Rome, to infringe upon the lordship of the Risen Reedemer and King. St. Paul's sentiments toward the State were those of an educated Roman citizen, well aware of his civic rights, and not averse to asserting them in the hazards of his missionary journeyings. But these were not shared by the leaders of the Ecclesia of after days. They viewed the imperial government with obstinate and long-lived distrust, and Tertullian openly declared that the Christian preferred any other interests to those of the State. Origen's defense of this indifference has been pointed out by Professor Gwatkin as a quibble. Others insisted that the Church could not be an enemy of the State, since her precepts furthered good morals, and so promoted national well-being. But officials of the State were slow to understand how any one who thus argued could refuse to support its institutions.

It was an ambiguous moment, when Christians had not clearly differentiated between the evil elements of statecraft and those which made for just political conditions. Nor was the differentiation always apparent, especially where the practice of Emperor-worship had left its polluting traces on all departments of civil rule, affecting both public and private

[7] Cf. Oscar L. Joseph: "Freedom and Advance," Chapter VI on "The Christian Ministry," p. 107 ff.

life. Those who held that Christ was universal Lord, could not profess a dual allegiance which would have degraded beliefs dearer to them than life itself. It was not a case of Christ and Cæsar, but of Christ or Cæsar. Upon this issue, often inseparable, the Christians did not consider convenience first, and conscience second. Upright dealing with their own convictions was one of the sources of their fortitude: a virtue, however, which they are charged with having mistaken for what was really obstinacy. Why did the martyrs refuse to satisfy the requirements of the Roman Law? These, it is urged, were not excessive; in fact, they compare favorably with those imposed by Christians upon their fellow believers in a later age. A mere ceremonial offering of incense to the Genius of the Emperor was often sufficient to stay persecution, and enable the accused to leave the tribunal in safety. Casuists who quoted the case of Naaman bowing blamelessly in the House of Rimmon, would have had little difficulty in framing a plausible plea for obedience to this demand of the State. But the Roman Christians refused to infringe upon the worship of the one God and the one Lord.[8] Their spirit of exaltation may have carried some martyrs beyond the bounds of discretion. Probably others felt a certain luxurious spiritual sensibility in daring the bitterness of death. But there was no softness in the sequel of their transports. If they anticipated joy in suffering, the suffering itself was real and frequent; and its brave endurance by them lifted Christianity to higher heights of conduct and influence than could have been attained by prudence and restraint. Thus the evolutionary process persisted, patient with human errors, conservative of divine elements.

The further fact that the Church was organized from the first as universal, gave color to the plea that she was antagonistic to an imperial World-State. Christianity was regarded by its followers as an independent, catholic and self-suffi-

[8] Cf. W. Emery Barnes: "Hermas: A Simple Christian of the Second Century."

cient religion. It stood out in contrast to national religions like Judaism, or to any other cults of the age, and appealed to the soul's deepest needs, not to financial endowments or political patronage. The idea that its Risen Master was about to return in glorious might and save His people from their enemies, made superfluous the identification of Christianity with earth's temporalities. So the Church insisted on going her own way, while the Imperial State regarded the Church as an enemy in disguise. Conspiracies and plots were quite common, and consequently Christians fell under the general suspicion that their organization was secretly seditious, with rules, ceremonies and pass-words peculiar to itself. Although no systematic effort was made by the imperial authorities to put an end to the movement until the reign of Decius, (249–251) for many years before this date, the misunderstandings and hatreds of jealousy or ignorance brought serious trouble upon the Church, and led to her ostracism, or to occasional acts of governmental repression as a result of popular riots. So far back as 64 A. D., when Nero was Emperor, he took advantage of the widespread prejudice against Christians to accuse them of having set fire to Rome, and to institute a short but savage persecution. Their traducers imputed to them, and to their strange and despicable religion, a concealed flagitousness which made it hostile to the government and to mankind.

About the year 111 A. D. and under the Emperor Trajan, the relation of Christianity to the law was more definitely ascertained. The younger Pliny, who had been sent as governor to Bithynia-Pontus, found there a great number of Christians, some of whom he examined and put to torture. He wrote to Trajan, proposing that he should give his victims the opportunity of escaping execution by sacrificing to the gods, and cursing Christ. The Emperor by his rescript, which then had the force of law, approved of Pliny's course. Thus the administration, even in the charge of a humane and scholarly proconsul, and under the direction of an able Emperor, outlawed the profession of Christianity, but showed that it should be penalized with discretion as well as zeal.[9]

One of Rome's noblest historians, in referring to the Christians said: "The name was derived from Christ, who in the reign of Tiberius suffered under Pontius Pilate, the procurator of Judæa. By that event the sect of which he was the founder, received a blow, which for a time checked the growth of a dangerous superstition: but it revived soon after and broke out not only in Judæa, the original home of the pest, but even in Rome, where every thing horribly shameful collects and is practiced. Nero proceeded with his usual caution. He found a set of profligate and abandoned wretches who were induced to confess themselves guilty, and on the evidence of such men a number of Christians were convicted, not indeed upon clear evidence of their having set the city on fire, but rather on account of their sullen hatred of the whole human race." [10]

A great change was soon to take place when the principle of toleration for all religions was adopted. "The most remarkable document on the relation of the Pagan State to Christianity — more remarkable than the rescript of Trajan to Pliny — is the edict which, in 311 A. D., closed the last great persecution. It was primarily the edict of Galerius, the fierce Dacian soldier, at whose instigation, Diocletian, his father-in-law, commenced the attempt at suppression. But it bears the names also of the other Cæsars, Constantine and Licinius. And while it justifies the motives which had originally led to that most savage and persistent attack, it confesses the futility of the attempt, and extends toleration both to individual Christians and to their Churches. Yet what is really conceded is a mere arbitrary toleration (*venia, indulgentia*), grounded on special reasons rather than on general principles." [11] It nevertheless marked the repulse of the

[9] Cf. A. Taylor Innes: "Church and State," p. 10 ff. Principal Herbert B. Workman: "Persecution in the Early Church," pp. 210–214.

[10] Tacitus: "Annals," XV. 44. Murphy's edition (1822).

[11] A. Taylor Innes: "Church and State," p. 21 f.

civil power, after which Christianity remained the acknowledged master of the masters of the world, in which all religious beliefs were now tolerated. The Roman distrust of religious or any other secret orders was embodied in its constitutional law, and it remains to the present time as a somewhat dreary bequest from that law.

Though there were a few converts in Cæsar's household, no large numbers of the aristocracy were reached by early Christianity. But in learned and philosophical circles many were won, both by the religion's ethical superiority, and by its provocation of philosophical thought. That it could seem to be at once a simple way of living for the plain person, and a profound interpretation of the universe for the speculative thinker, meant much for its success. In spite of all opposition the Church steadily grew, until in March, 313, the Emperors Constantine and Licinius published the Edict of Milan, proclaiming the principle of complete religious liberty, and constituting Christianity a legal religion. Under Theodosius the Great (379–395) its orthodox forms, as established by the decisions adopted at Nicæa in 325, were recognized as the State religion, and heathen worship was banned.

The Edict of Milan, preceded as it was by Constantine's so-called conversion on the 27th of October, 312, marked a decisive stage in the outward growth of the Church. The Emperor was conscious of her increasing strength and sought to enlist her membership for his rule. But it was not until his final triumph over Licinius, that pagan symbols disappeared from the current coinage, and the Christian monogram or labarum, originally adopted from heathen temples, became a prominent device. From this time onward the Arian controversy demanded Constantine's attention. He appointed the time and place for the Council of Nicæa, summoned the episcopate, paid part of the expenses out of the public purse, nominated the committees in charge of the order of business, and used his imperial office to bring about the adoption of the creed, punishing those who refused to subscribe to it.[12] By presiding at the Council and afterwards pronouncing sentence of banishment against Athanasius, the Emperor closely identified himself with institutional Christianity, and showed his determination to act as Pontifex Maximus in the regulation of religious matters. Although his baptism by Eusebius did not take place until 337, when Constantine lay upon his death bed, the reconciliation he effected had become a reality, and Christianity was installed as the official religion of the Empire. The Emperor's motives may have been dictated by political convenience, but his public acts were an hitherto unparalleled submission to the Church by the most powerful existing temporalities. If he hoped that she would, in turn, become the willing instrument of imperial absolutism, his hopes were doomed to disappointment. In the outcome she became its formidable and subtle foe.

Thus, in a Council which elicited universal esteem because it was the first attempt to assemble the entire Episcopate, and after which subsequent Ecumenical Councils were modelled, the Rome that had formerly forbidden religions to proselytize outside their pale, least of all among Roman citizens, now publicly authorized the rule of Christianity. For centuries afterwards the chief religious and civilizing forces in the West were dated from this memorable surrender. It meant that the habitable world relinquished an alien and antagonistic position, and pledged itself to conduct its secular affairs in the embrace of the sacred life for which the Church was the channel.[13] Out of this new relationship came a universal ecclesiasticism independent of the civil power. How it could exist without absorbing or destroying the State soon became a vexed question; and Constantine, the son and successor of the first Christian Emperor, showed a spirit of resentment mingled with rashness against the toleration and

[12] Cf. "Encyclopædia Britannica," (Eleventh Edition) Vol. VI, pp. 332, 990; and Vol. VII, p. 310.
[13] Cf. William Temple: "Mens Creatrix," p. 325 f.

freedom of the Edict of Milan. Later, in the reign of Julian the Apostate, the reaction from the Edict took decided shape, and Pagan rule resumed control, only to be finally subdued by the growing dominacy of the State Church.

IV

The events narrated and the changes they wrought gradually developed Apostolic and sub-Apostolic into Catholic Christianity. In some respects the development was beneficial, in others a hated despotism became the symbol of the Kingdom of God. Absolutism and imperialism, as well as oneness of doctrine and discipline, were the salient features of the Church of the Fathers. Paganism, vanquished in the political realm, retaliated by impregnating clericalism. The decadence of the State naturally infected its official religion, and the Emperors assumed a control over the Church which was detrimental to her spiritual life. The bishops, who were primarily responsible for her witness to the Divine Order in the world, made deplorable concessions to the State. Her discipline was subordinated to notorious evils against which they seldom invoked the authority of their episcopate. Theological ideas characteristic of the time, made Baptism the means and not the sign of salvation, and a similar logic evolved the perpetual sacrifice of the Mass out of the Eucharist. The tradition of Apostolic Succession was magnified until it implied the setting up of the Papacy as the Vicariate of Christ. The impressive feature of this growth was its continuity. Sacerdotal rule was not established by deliberate usurpation, but by an apparently intrinsic process evolved from the original propositions of the Faith. In the most depressing intervals of society and of the Church, the beauty and holiness of that Faith were expressed in the devotion of saints who were also theologians, evangelists and martyrs. Some whose names are connected with measures which were disastrous from the modern viewpoint, took joyfully the spoiling of their goods and the burning of their bodies. But these exemplary instances of consecration to higher things than offices and emoluments, did not rescue the Church from that self-distrust of her divine origin which induced her to behave like an extraordinary State. The State retaliated by exhibiting a contemptuous indifference for the real nature and mission of the Church.

We have to keep steadily before us the genuinely conscious oneness which enabled her to withstand an enormous pressure of internal and external opposition. This unity was the sanctuary of God's Spirit: the secret of a life which ecclesiastical misdemeanors and crimes could not kill. A common dependence upon the Church preserved many values for us and created many precedents to which we still resort. She often made politics the instrument of morality, impressing upon after ages the fact that civilization was not only the heir of Hellenism, but still more of Hebraism; and, most of all, of the New Testament Evangel. The conviction that our Lord had founded, and had intended to found, a visible Church as the organization in which His truth should have rightful power, was firmly fixed in the contemporary mind. It also predominated in the mediæval mind. Nor has modern research discovered anything in the New Testament that sets aside this historic conclusion. Christianity, as conceived by its past leaders, could not have survived had there not been a Church built according to their plan as its fortress. One need not recite the names and deeds of Pontiffs, Bishops and Fathers, who were then reverenced and obeyed. It is enough to say that while we do not render them blind homage, we should consistently esteem and love them as Elder Brethren of the Household of Faith and Princes of the Christian Israel. Their rule was a kind of reckless idealism, with spiritual aims too often vitiated by false methods. If the Church was all that they insisted she was, the people realized that she ought to govern the whole of life. But in attempting to do this she descended to policies and agencies which lowered her claims and contradicted her professions.

In the West, the City of Rome captured the patriotism of the Imperial State and the imagination of the Church. The removal of the seat of government to Constantinople, with a deputy at Ravenna, increased the importance of the Roman Papacy, which reached a height the Patriarchate of the Eastern Church could never have attained. Antioch, Jerusalem, Alexandria, and even Constantinople were provincial when compared with the metropolis on the Tiber. Although many outstanding dignitaries of the Church were frequently found elsewhere, a hieratic atmosphere enveloped the Roman See, whose Pontiffs were notable for their sound practical judgment and administrative ability. The work of Leo had been the decisive factor in the conflicts waged at Chalcedon and Nicæa. Yet men of the stamp of Tertullian and Cyprian belonged to the African Church; Clement, Origen and Athanasius were of Alexandria; Polycarp, Irenæus, Theophilus and Ignatius were of the Eastern Church.

But St. Chrysostom and St. Augustine were the preëminent representatives of the Catholic Christianity of the time. In the East, the great John of Antioch was renowned for his complete mastery of all the arts of sacred discourse, and for the calm courage with which he endured his banishment from the scenes of his moving eloquence. In the West, St. Augustine showed a constancy, resurgent over the appalling catastrophe of the fall of Rome in the early fifth century, when he wrote "De Civitate Dei." The occasion of his famous apology encircled it with a solemn grandeur. After ten hundred years of unequalled political organization and government, the Eternal City had been captured and sacked. Her collapse shook the habitable world; the wild rumor spread that her fate was but the prelude to the dissolution of the globe itself. "My voice falters," cried St. Jerome, "sobs stifle the words I dictate, for she is in the hands of her enemies who enthralled the earth!" In the subsequent crisis, St. Augustine overcame his dismay, which had been overwhelming, by idealizing the City of God. He had witnessed a stupendous calamity which for the time being crushed the fabric of civilized society. Further reflection convinced him that no temporal State, though it persisted through the centuries, could postpone by an hour its appointed doom. If Rome could be overthrown; if an Empire to which men had attributed an inviolable sanctity, and an authority which stretched from the borders of India to the western coasts of Britain, was vulnerable, then everything visible was but a fleeting show.

Moreover, the Church was denounced as the chief conspirator against the Empire. Multitudes who were still pagans at heart attributed its sorrows to her. Their accusations were as false as some others afterwards made against Alaric and his invading hosts. The disintegration of the Empire began long before he appeared at the gates of its capital. Its work was done and could not be undone. Its permanent elements were absorbed in later forms of society. Its assimilating force, preparatory though it was for freedom, was not that freedom. When the agonies of its dissolution had subsided, visioned men perceived that they were the pangs of rebirth, not of death. Nevertheless, while the chaos reigned, St. Augustine girded himself for the defense of the Church against her foes. His work, the most learned product of his matured genius, was a recognition of theocracy as the foundation of human rule, and of religion as the determinant of human welfare. It pulverized the charges levelled at the Church. But its lasting values are found in its original treatment of history as the registration of the Divine purposes. Had he been more of an individualist, like Origen, St. Augustine could not have become so aggressive and constructive a thinker. Though the main burden of his treatise was to vindicate the God of the Christians against the attacks of heathen orators, and to absolve the Church of any guilt for the wreck of the imperial State, he presently passed from these themes to deal with the visible militant Church, and with the *communio sanctorum*, of which that Church was an imperfect embodiment.

His truly great mind was not always clear and compact in its thinking. Such minds seldom are. They have few qualifications for well-rounded magazine articles. But his thought has been plundered by far lesser men who were not always consistent with their source, some of whom he would have vigorously repudiated. Nor did he carry out to their logical conclusions the reasonings he advanced. He wrote as a mystic as well as a statesman; as a prophet whose words went beyond immediate conditions, and who foresaw some ideals still to be fulfilled. His weightiest argument was that the organization of the world, as a human society separated from God, was a capital offense sure of punishment. He had no intention of explaining the respective policies of Church and State. But he clearly understood the nature of the conflict between them. It was more than the clash of two antagonistic institutions; it was the passion for self as opposed to the passion for God. As one of the few really great spirits who have loved God with consuming fervor, St. Augustine spent his magnificent strength on this opposition. He denounced the Donatists for their efforts to evade all civic responsibilities, and asserted that the latent anarchy of their attitude warranted the exercise of State authority against them.

In the section of "De Civitate Dei" entitled "The Mirror of Princes," he drew a portrait of the righteous ruler under whose guidance the ideal State and the ideal Church co-existed and were complementary. Dissensions occurred between them, not because they were congenitally antagonistic but because they were imperfect. Were both what they were intended to be, a natural harmony would govern their intercourse. On the other hand, there could be but one Kingdom: that in which Christ was the acknowledged King. The true Commonwealth was composed of just and enlightened spirits, consecrated to their Risen Lord, and obedient to His teachings. His conceptions of divine sovereignty, of the Ecclesia as the Second Parousia, which also made her, in this sense, the actual Kingdom that some anticipate, do not call for discussion here. It was a distinct descent, however, for so practical an idealist even to advise that physical compulsion should be employed against the Donatists. Given by lesser men, the advice might not have been so mischievous; given by St. Augustine, it was employed to sanction the persecutions which afterwards disgraced ecclesiastical dominion. For those who believe that the State is concerned with things temporal, the Church with things eternal; that the State coerces, and appeals to fear, the Church to the love that casts out fear, much that St. Augustine advocates will not be attractive. He was not always careful to distinguish between the ideal and the actual Church, and in other ways he showed that consistency was no foible of his massive mind. But he stood at his post in a cataclysmic age, when other noted Christian leaders forsook their duty for a useless seclusion. It would be superfluous to further praise a Saint and Father, a philosopher and theologian, a laborious bishop and statesman, whose ideas, despite the changes of sixteen centuries, have moulded the politics and the religion of the Western peoples; and whose treatise, "De Civitate Dei" was the precursor of nearly all similar speculations upon the universal Commonwealth of man.[14]

V

The Roman Pontiffs were not of equal intellectual rank. But the great majority of them, however, realized their grave responsibilities and faithfully exercised their functions. Gregory the Great (590–604) was one of the first Popes to consolidate the European nations in behalf of a central au-

[14] Cf. J. N. Figgis: "The Political Aspects of St. Augustine's 'City of God'"; W. Montgomery: "St. Augustine, Aspects of his Life and Thought"; Adolf Harnack: "History of Dogma," Vol. V. p. 3 ff; "The Cambridge Mediæval History," Vol. I. Chapter XX.

thority. As the wealthiest citizen of Italy, the eleemosynary work undertaken at his initiative and expense, virtually made him the superior of the Emperor in the East. The worth of Gregory lay in his candid expression of his own time. Its strength and weakness were dramatically displayed in this Pope who saved Rome from the Lombards. Not a little acrimony was evinced in the correspondence between him, the Emperor Maurice and the Patriarch of Constantinople. But Gregory held and justified his strategic position at a transitional moment. He deserves our grateful remembrance, because, though burdened with the cares of the Pontificate, he seized the opportunity to despatch the missionary Augustine to England for her conversion. Moreover, the two main pillars of the Mediæval Church — Monasticism and the Papacy — were set up by Gregory; and they sustained its superstructure for four fiercely contentious centuries to come.[15]

The Holy See now became an empire in itself. Its officers rivaled the territorial princes, and assumed prerogatives which forced Church and State into collision. A general peril temporarily arrested their disputes between the years 717 and 732, when Mohammedanism's military prowess conquered Spain and threatened the conquest of Christendom. The danger was averted by Charles Martel, who defeated the Moslem invaders at Tours (732) and earned the title of the Saviour of Gaul. Leo III also delivered Constantinople from the attacks of the Moslem prophet's fanatical soldiery. Both these celebrities were champions of the Cross, yet ecclesiastical prejudice prevented their receiving the rewards due to their brave exertions. The one was accused of interfering with Church property; the other of heresy. Although Nicholas I (858–867) had only a short Pontificate, he advanced the papal claims by his defiance of

[15] Cf. F. Homes Dudden: "Gregory the Great, His Place in History and Thought," two volumes; "The Cambridge Mediæval History," Vol. I. Chapter VIII.

the Eastern Emperor Michael the Drunkard, in defense of Ignatius, the deposed patriarch of Constantinople. His inflexibility concerning the sanctity of marriage against Lothair, King of Lorraine, and his chastisement of certain rebellious prelates made his administration famous. Such a Pontiff did not need the argument of the "False Decretals" in his behalf. His lasting influence emanated from his character and policy, not from a spurious document which voiced contemporary sentiments upon Church authority, but was not, as so advertised, of ancient origin.

The growth of Canon Law in Western Europe created a conception of the Church that afterwards culminated in the Pontificates of Hildebrand and Innocent III. That Law was emphasized by the circulation of the "False Decretals" referred to a moment ago, and which included the forged Donation of Constantine.[16] As we have noted, after the Peace of Milan the whole problem of Church and State had passed into a new phase. The Empire recognized Christianity, but in so doing it did not intend to relinquish its own supremacy. In various ways Constantine's successors showed that to them the Ecclesia was a branch of the Civil Service, side by side in particular instances with the heathenism it had displaced. This conception has never been entirely eliminated in the Eastern Church. The Emperors of that division of the imperial Roman rule always ranked above the Patriarchs, for which reason, the Russians, at the time of their conversion, adopted Eastern rather than Roman ecclesiasticism, because the former left much more authority than the latter to the autocracy of the State. Hence the late Russian Tsardom carried the theories of Constantine into the

[16] The Decretals originated in the efforts of the bishops of Northern France to escape from the overlordship of their archbishops by developing the idea of appeal to Rome. The Donation of Constantine was embodied in the Decretals as a part of the process and emphasized his gift of the "Patrimonium Petri" to the Church. Cf. "Encyclopædia Britannica," (Eleventh Edition) Vol. III. p. 916; Vol. VIII. p. 409; M'Clintock and Strong: Vol. II. p. 734, 861; "Schaff-Herzog Encyclopædia," Vol. III. p. 486; "The Catholic Encyclopædia," Vol. V. pp. 119–121, 773–780, Vol. XIV. p. 257.

twentieth century, combining the spiritual and temporal sovereignties in itself.

Until the ninth century the Roman Church kept inviolate her resolution that secular rulers should not control the Pontiffs, who were still nominal subjects of the Emperors. The three factors conducive to this end, Feudalism, Chivalry and Monasticism, have been previously mentioned. Two main ideas were crystallized by their united aid. The first was a world-federation of Christians to be achieved through the Empire; the second, the sovereign authority of the Church as residual in the Papal States. Perhaps "the safest judgment which we can form on the whole character of the ninth century is this, that men were convinced that each power had its own appropriate sphere, but that they were also keenly alive to the fact that in practical life the two spheres intersected, and that no general principle could enable them to determine with regard to many questions, what exactly was the sphere of the State and what the sphere of the Church." [17] It was not until the middle of the eleventh century that the political upheavals in Germany, and the incipiency of the conflict between the Papacy and the Empire, forced men to reëxamine the principles that underlay the social order.

So much in anticipation. To revert to the sequence of events: the work of resettlement begun in Northern France was completed on Christmas Day, 800, when Charles the Great inaugurated Mediævalism by the foundation of the Holy Roman Empire. It rested on the declaration that while the old Empire was continued, it was no longer Eastern but Roman, and owed no further allegiance to the Emperors at Constantinople. For the second time Rome became the mistress of the Western world; and its Cæsars, who were elected at Rome and crowned by the Pope, were allied with the Vicars of Christ. In an age when ideals were everything and practice was meager, such an alliance was almost sure

[17] R. W. Carlyle and A. J. Carlyle. "A History of Mediæval Political Theory in the West," Vol. I. p. 257 f.

to be effective. In theory, Church and State were equal, but in the outcome, vigorous and able Emperors like Otto the Great and Henry III bore down upon the Popes, even electing and deposing them when they deemed it necessary. From 800 to 1050 the Pontificate had also to contend against the factions within the Church, and against the militant Roman nobles. But after the reign of Frederic III imperialism declined, became subordinate to the Holy See, and so remained until the rise of Nationalism. A great deal of contemporary literature turned upon the transference of the seat of empire from East to West. By what legal right had the transfer been made? The answers varied: some dwelt upon the fact that an Empress then reigned at Constantinople; others discussed the lawfulness of the act in the light of the Pope's coronation of Charles as the first Emperor of the West.

During the opening days of the eleventh century, the theory of imperial rule was recast by the revival of papal authority. The leader of the revival was Hildebrand, one of whose immediate predecessors, Gregory VI, had been deposed by the Emperor. A man of genius and courage beyond words, Hildebrand's title, Gregory VII, was chosen for him by the Cardinals of the Conclave, as a protest against the imperial despotism. He became Pope on April 22, 1073, at a time when the Church was wide in domain and united in doctrine, but disorganized and weakened in her centralized rule. For a hundred years before Hildebrand's restoration the Holy See had been the sport of Roman factions and their chiefs. Yet despite political disturbances of the capital and of Europe, the Church remained a single body, supernational, with her own government, laws, and language of worship. For some years before his elevation to the papal throne, Hildebrand had been its trusted counsellor, who ceaselessly proclaimed its spiritual dignity and renown, and after his elevation he revolutionized the conception of his great office. As the Cardinal Deacon who inspired the policies of Leo IX,

Stephen X, Nicholas II and Alexander II, he had been largely instrumental in placing the election of Popes in charge of cardinal-bishops, whose choice was to be confirmed by the clergy and the Emperor, although the participation of the latter was left somewhat nebulous. The purpose of the change was not only to prevent the invariable disorders hitherto attending papal elections, but especially to free the Church from the secular interference of the Empire. Hildebrand "was determined to put down simony, the buying and selling of ecclesiastical offices, and to restore the spiritual independence of the Church as represented by the freedom of election to great pastoral and administrative offices." [18] It was this determination that precipitated the approaching struggle. The best scholarship shows that its governing conceptions were neither solely original with Hildebrand nor to be attributed to the influence of Cluniac Monasticism. Although he has been claimed by French authors as a monk of Clugny, he had no connection with that celebrated retreat, nor was he ever a monk.[19] To Waso of Liège, whose interpretations of Canon Law were widely received in the Rhine provinces, and to Cardinal Humbert, whose "De Simonia" voiced the views of the reforming group in the Curia, must be ascribed in part the intellectual genesis of Hildebrand's gigantic scheme. He doubtless studied Humbert's treatise, in which the author depicted Henry II in hell, notwithstanding that monarch's service to the Church, because of his unwarranted intervention in her affairs. But Hildebrand's ideas were to a large extent his own, and he was the real founder of the unique hierarchy of Mediævalism.

[18] J. Vernon Bartlett and A. J. Carlyle: "Christianity in History," p. 415.

[19] The only contemporary source for this claim is a voluminous work by Bonizo of Sutre, amplified in the next century by Otto of Freising, who even asserted that Hildebrand had been prior of Clugny. The confusion arose from another cleric of the same name. For a decisive study of the issue see Marteus: "Gregory VII" Vol. II. p. 281 ff.

VI

He struck at the source of interventions by impeaching the dual headship of the Empire. Hitherto this had been regarded as the covenant of covenants, the "imperium" and the "sacerdotium" formally accepted by all, and previously acknowledged by Hildebrand himself as comparable to the two eyes of the human body. He now discarded the theory and changed the metaphor. The sun stood for the Church; the moon for the State. What light temporal jurisdiction enjoyed was borrowed from the spiritual supremacy. This he proposed to organize afresh in a vast United States of the world, over which the Pontiff of Rome should preside as the very Vicar of God. To the several states of the new Federation could be delegated the maximum of domestic autonomy, consistent with the full control and duty of an infallible and ghostly sovereignty. The Pontiff, and he alone, must answer "on the dreadful day of Judgment before the just Judge," for the conduct of his royal underlings, as well as for the discharge of his own measureless obligations. The business of kings and princes, whose very being, as Hildebrand contended, was in itself a result and proof of the fall of man, was to maintain order, dispense justice, extend trade and promote the general welfare in correspondence with local needs and usages. They were but the pro-consuls of a universal spiritual empire, from every province of which appeal could be taken to the Holy See. To quote Hildebrand's own words, the Pontiff "alone held the keys of heaven and hell, and he alone was able to bind on earth and loose in heaven, to give and to take away, according to the merits of each man, empires, kingdoms, duchies, countships and the possessions of all men."

Two corollaries of this amazing theory must not be overlooked. If the Pope was supreme over the State, by so much the more was he supreme in the Church. The centralization of all government in the Holy See naturally involved the centralization of ecclesiastical government. To Rome all its disputes must be referred; by Rome all offices of the Church must be filled; from Rome all her legislation must proceed. Without the papal sanction neither the canons nor the acts of provincial councils or of metropolitan bishops were warranted. These views, of which Hildebrand was perhaps not the sole author, but certainly a more thorough and fearless exponent than any of his predecessors, necessarily curtailed the power of the episcopacy, and of the rest of the higher clergy. The records of his reign tell of his continual controversies with abbots and prelates as well as with secular princes. A second consequence of his theory was the increased importance of the papal legates. In the practice of Hildebrand they became his vicars, holding within the limits of their instructions the plenitude of his powers; therefore, above ambassadors or proconsuls of imperial Rome, and superior to all local authority, temporal or spiritual.

The modern mind is dazed before the magnitude and boldness of such assertions. Nor is its wonder lessened when we find that Hildebrand invested individual Pontiffs with an infallibility which went beyond that of the Vatican decrees of 1870. As he held it, the Pope's word was simply and purely God's word. It has to be remembered that for the Christians of that day such conclusions were the accepted creed of the Church. The premises upon which they rested dismayed few, and were denied, if at all, by a very small minority. The majority of thinkers, and all the unthinking, believed in the absolute right of consecrated rulers as implicitly and as unreservedly as we believe in the law of gravitation. Hildebrand interpolated one further remove in the absolutism everywhere extolled. Since the divine right of kingship came to the throne through the consecration of the Popes as God's vicegerents, they must be above the thrones they consecrated. One of his favorite syllogisms puts the issue: "If Peter and Paul judge spiritual things, what must we believe to be their power over earthly things? If they judge the angels who rule over princes, what can they not do to their slaves?" When he applied to his Pontificate the words addressed to Jeremiah: "See, I have this day set thee over the nations and over the kingdoms, to pluck up and to break down and to destroy and to overthrow, to build and to plant," there was no criticism, high low or middle, to question his exegesis.[20] There is not a scintilla of evidence that this great Pontiff trembled at his own deductions, or foresaw that they made political rule negligible. The story current of his writing to the Emperor Henry, beseeching him to refuse to confirm his election to the papal chair, is one of those inventions that testify to a hidden truth which Hildebrand's private letters to Lanfranc and other intimates corroborate. They are full of the agitations of a very noble nature deeply aware of human infirmities while called upon to bear infinite burdens. The sincerity of his beliefs and convictions is beyond question. In his speeches, and in his excommunication of Henry IV, one can visualize him with uplifted hands and eyes addressing St. Peter in Paradise. It appears to us as though to him that Apostle was the living captain of God, for whose command he waited; with whom he identified himself so completely that their union was perfected. The mortal head of an immortal dynasty, he lived in an exalted consciousness that the spirits of light or of darkness attended every motion of his heart and mind.

Nevertheless, as Pope he knew neither shrinking nor timidity. The King of Denmark and the Duke of Poland were informed that their States owed tribute to the Holy See; and they promptly paid it, for over their devoted heads Hildebrand brandished what he described as "the sword of apostolic punishment." He demanded that Hungary should be a papal fief by virtue of the supposed transfer of that country to the Papacy by St. Stephen. Corsica, Sardinia and Spain were bluntly told by him that they were a part of Constan-

[20] Jeremiah I. 10.

tine's Donation. He wrote to the reigning princes of Castile, Aragon and Leon, within a few days of his election as Pope, that "their countries were of old time the property of St. Peter, and, that notwithstanding their long occupation by pagans, they still belonged to no mortal." The territories wrested from the Saracens must also be held in fief from St. Peter. When Philip I of France refused to desist from his traffic in holy things, his subjects were released from further obedience to him, and the whole realm was laid under interdict. As for the Gallican bishops and their dread of the royal displeasure, "it is useless," wrote Hildebrand, "for the strenuous soldiers of Christ to speak to them." They were no more than dust in the balance of a Pontiff who at one time had excommunicated every archbishop in France. When Solomon, King of Hungary, proved refractory, Hildebrand dethroned him for a rival who was glad to acknowledge himself as the Pope's vassal. When his Norman feudatories repudiated their allegiance, he did not hesitate to excommunicate his own allies. He wrote to Svend, King of Denmark, that there was "a very rich province on the sea coast, not far from us, held by a vile heretic," which one of Svend's sons might well acquire and hold in the name of St. Peter; thus setting Norman against Norman.

In every part of Europe his legates reduced the royal prestige, and executed the behests of that clear and intrepid brain which controlled from the throne of Rome the temporal and spiritual jurisdiction of Christendom. Nothing seemed to escape his notice. The cruel treatment of shipwrecked sailors, the sale of their wives by the Scottish tribesmen, the outrages of some petty chieftains in Ireland, were as vividly before his gaze as the weightiest matters of divine law. Only in England did this imperial overseer of rebellious princes and prelates meet a repulse, to which I have already referred. In May, 1080, after Hildebrand's famous victory at Canossa, his legate, Cardinal Humbert, was instructed to exact from William the Conqueror a recognition of his feudal dependence upon the Pope. The message, though verbally conveyed, was couched in terms which ran through Hildebrand's letters from the time of the excommunication of Emperor Henry IV. In the abstract, it insisted that William should do homage to the Pope's position as the suzerain of all earthly potentates, and their personal representative before the judgment seat of Christ. But in turning this abstract idea into a command Hildebrand mistook his man. "I hold my own Kingdom of God and my own sword," was the answer of the stark Conqueror, as he spurned the required oath of fealty.

We need not tarry to pass lengthy judgment upon Hildebrand's conception. No unprejudiced intellect can withhold its tribute of reverent admiration from this matchless ideal of a spiritual power upraised far beyond all worldly strife: arbitrating between warring monarchs and turbulent States in the inerrant light of divine truth and righteousness. A grim fact-facing attitude was Hildebrand's primary reaction to the tempestuous life around him. Here and there, in his private self-revelations, we catch the echoes of a thwarted religious romanticism. For his was a short-lived triumph destined to defeat. Yet its intense psychological interest subdues our moralizings. Sympathy, rather than censure, is appropriate for this superman who, nevertheless, found the world's problems too great for him. He chose to be human life's foremost partaker rather than its mere spectator; and he lived tremendously. Consider also the wastrels, the caitiffs, the crowned tyrants and titled rascals, who were then more plentiful than honest leaders and princes. Their plottings and murderings furnish the dark background for an unparalleled pontifical mission, the prerogatives of which are not to be determined by ordinary standards of success or failure. Its faith in the powers of the world to come was a radiant gleam playing on the prevalent darkness. The supposition that he who held it could build a cage from which none could escape the Highest Will was a mistaken one. But what lover of God has not felt at intervals Hildebrand's desire to protect humanity from its intolerable iniquities and sufferings. If this priestly king and kingly priest revolted against the sorrows and tragedies which seemed likely to stretch out till the crack of doom, his revolt was pure in its motive and magnificent in its daring.

Human beings hidebound by custom and tradition, entangled in a social environment which made the slightest progress almost impossible, slaves to the apparitions of their forefathers as well as to very visible and merciless monarchs, were the raw material with which Hildebrand had to work. The least imaginable scope was allowed his remarkable gifts for change and betterment. His titanic strength was of necessity dragged down by the weakest and the dullest who abounded everywhere. He could not rise alone while he essayed to carry so many others who were falling. The surface of the universal society he encountered presented natural inequalities, aggravated by harsh and stubborn customs of ignorance and superstition, of pride and power. From this low malarial general level he undertook a flight which visionaries and enthusiasts in later times have lauded as the ideal of humanity. It would have dispensed justice and compassion, so they believe, alike for the evil and for the good. Yet it is the verdict of history that Hildebrand's system, when well weighed in the balance, is found wanting. Its roseate glow faded with the light of common day. Hidden beneath its dreamy splendors and actual achievements were untold corruptions and abuses which it could not exterminate. Its Pope Angelico is as imaginary as Tennyson's King Arthur or Plato's ideal Republic. Its very intensity, which gives one pause, proved its impossibility; its partial realization was a mixed benefit; its triumph would have been the death knell of liberty.

But for these fatalities we cannot justly blame Hildebrand. From the Nebo of his bold speculations, he surveyed a future which appeared to him overflowing with milk and honey. Behind him were the dreary sands and the sterile wastes of misspent ages; the hopeless, bloodstained struggles of monarchs and mobs; and the slow sure stagnation of social death. Who does not share his throb of spiritual delight as, from his lonely elevation, he descried a new world in which righteousness would dwell? In that perfect society, the lion and the lamb should lie down together; fraud and wrong should give way to truth and peace. There the sword of the Lord and of His first Apostle should put to flight the hosts of darkness. All this the great Pontiff saw or thought he saw. What he did not see was that with such observation the coming of the Kingdom was not to be ascertained. Like the Puritans, many of whom so often have too hastily condemned him, he attempted the impossible. They attempted it on the more democratic lines of Geneva, he, by the autocracy of one supreme Pontificate. Both failed, but theirs were the splendid failures that have ennobled and enriched humanity. The prophet, priest and statesman, whom Voltaire characteristically called a fool, and Condorcet a knave, but whom Gibbon with justice recognized as a second Athanasius, was one of the rare dreamers who have left their impress on the history of succeeding ages. We may allow with Gregorovius that if his policies could have been carried out in the purity and breadth of their creator's intention, they would have constituted "almost the highest earthly form in which mankind could have seen the expansion of its unity and harmony." Whatever his shortcomings, and judgment on the great Gregory VII perhaps can never be unanimous, this much his bitterest enemies must concede: he demonstrated that ideas are more powerful than the sword, and that the mailed fist is impotent against spiritual convictions.

VII

These ideas and convictions held good for two hundred years after his death, during which period the Church more and more became a State within the political State, with its own inquisitors, police powers and international emissaries. The friars and other regulars who travelled the length and breadth of Christendom were devoted to the Holy See, whose Pope had deposed Henry IV at Canossa, and compelled him to wait three days in the snow before granting him absolution for his contumacy. Freed from secular service to the State, strictly clerical interests were naturally attached to the Papacy. The bishops and their parochial clergy who showed some traces of national feeling were denounced by thousands of friars in every land, who swore by the Pontiff at Rome. They and their superiors had yet to learn in the costly school of experience that the influence of the Church was to be exercised, not as a governing body with frequent resort to physical compulsion, but as a holy brotherhood, after the fashion of the Apostolic Church, and of the Mediæval St. Francis. The mistake which clericalism inherited from Hildebrand: "of substituting the Jewish ideal of righteousness by means of government, for the Christian ideal of government by means of righteousness," [21] resulted in the battlings between Popes and Emperors during successive generations. Both Church and Empire grasped for power; each was jealous of the other; each viewed their mutual functions with suspicion and undermined each other's moral authority, in pathetic forgetfulness that their service for mankind was complementary and not contradictory.

The twelfth century witnessed the rise of the City Republics of Italy, which the reigning House of Hohenstaufen endeavored to suppress. The instinctive enmity between the Latin and the Teuton blazed out in the resistance of these independent municipalities to the aggressions of Frederic Barbarossa. Their cause was espoused by the Papacy, but that of the Empire also found supporters in Italy. The two parties, known as the Guelf and the Ghibelline, supported the divine authority of their respective leaders, the Guelf asserting that God had set Pope over Emperor, and the Ghibelline

[21] A. Robertson: "Regnum Dei," p. 368.

maintaining the opposite. The papal faction had a formidable intellectual array, but it lacked the material means to enforce its plea. The Empire though strong in military resources, was weakened by internal quarrels, and some of its temporal princes were also ecclesiastics who relished the height of the papal supremacy. This had reached a pinnacle of solitary state upon which the Pontiffs were set to "pluck up and to plant." Monarchs were their vassals, their interdicts paralyzed nations, and the threat of excommunication brought the haughtiest rulers of Europe to their knees. Louis IX of France, who afterward became a canonized saint, and that great prelate, Robert Grosseteste of Lincoln, whose learning and piety were the admiration of his countrymen, remonstrated in vain against the exorbitant demands of the Holy See. The German Cæsars equalled it in arrogance, and almost exceeded the Pontiffs in their ambition to exalt their monarchical estate. It was an open race for world dominion led by two unyielding personalties, Hadrian IV and Frederic I.[22] Hadrian was the only Englishman who ever sat on the papal throne, where he revealed a more liberal spirit than any other occupant of that exalted station, but damaged it by granting Ireland to Henry II. His temperament and traditions fostered the democratic tendency in the Mediæval Church to recognize ability wherever found, and to bestow its offices according to merit. However wide were the departures from these ideals, they survived and reasserted themselves. Dean Church states in his volume, the "Beginning of the Middle Ages," that the Church was the repository of nearly all that was praiseworthy, the conservator of letters and learning, of the human virtues and of the best tendencies of the age. The Empire was characterized by a radically opposite spirit, and proceeded to extremes which enraged the Italian people, specifically those of the Northern provinces. Conscious of the ancient glory of their civiliza-

[22] Cf. F. J. Foakes Jackson: "An Introduction to the History of Christianity, A. D. 590–1314," p. 247 ff.

tion, and of its rapid development at this time, the Romans resented the lordly insolence of the Emperor Frederic I on the occasion of his coronation, June 18, 1155. They closed the gates of their city against him, and allowed him no sufferance beyond the Leonine City. He was crowned at St. Peter's, but he was not permitted to visit the Lateran Basilica.

While Guelf and Ghibelline quarreled and fought, other interests foreign to their intentions were aroused. Lord Acton pertinently observes that it is idle to look for the spark of freedom in flint and steel. It arose out of their violent contact. The object of both parties was an unqualified supremacy. The rulers were absolutists to a man. But they forsook their theory under necessity, and indirectly encouraged popular control by seeking the aid of those City Republics which were its nurseries. The commonalty, which was really everything yet seemingly nothing in the great debate, was awakened by its tumult. The people at large, who far outnumbered princes, prelates, monks, scholars, philosophers and retainers of courts and camps, supplied the flesh and blood and the taxes exacted by these endless conflicts. They did those daily tasks without the doing of which civilization would have faltered. Yet they had no voice in the administration of Church or Empire, nor in the pacification of affairs which meant life or death to them. Although legislation was ostensibly enacted in their behalf, and religious, academic or political theories had to be verified in their experience, there were no very apparent relations between them and their governors and guides. Nevertheless, democracy had its obscure genesis at this particular juncture, as an untoward result of the appeals which Church and Empire alike made to the people. The same pontifical policy by which Hildebrand established the independence of the Papacy, and thus engendered the conflict between it and the political power, unwittingly conceded the sovereignty of the people. The Papalists argued that since the Emperor derived his authority from the nation, it could always take back what it had given. The Imperialists replied that nobody, not even the Pope himself, could deprive the Emperor of that which the nation had bestowed on him. It was therefore a valid conclusion that the people were the arbiters of the controversy. When Hadrian IV and Alexander III incited the Italian City-States to rebel against Frederic I, because rebellion advanced their schemes, they ignored the possibility of a similar revolt against the temporal powers of the Holy See. In the plottings and counter-plottings of Popes and Emperors we may trace the growth of a third estate. While it emerged out of the surrounding chaos none was aware of its latent might; none seems to have suspected that a greater social force than the Papacy or the Empire had at last appeared.

In summary, it may be said that the Christian Ecclesia had to combine with the Latin and German Empires in order to exorcise the spirit of ageless paganism which possessed society. Christianity had been superimposed upon that paganism, and taught principles and beliefs incompatible with former views of life and conduct. The antique cults and practices formed the soil from which many personal and social habits grew. Their dross and gold were deeply related to ancestral instincts which could not be speedily exterminated. Hence the conviction of Church and State that their union was essential to that extermination created the despotism of the Eastern Church, and also, in the sequence, the liberalizing policies of the Western Church.[23] The theologians and ecclesiastics who could not imagine Christianity flourishing beyond the confines of the Empire favored its jurisdiction, and insisted that the Church was in the State. But as hosts of pagan invaders, who in religious matters were usually led by their rulers, surrendered to the Cross, the outlook changed, and Pontiffs and bishops came to believe that the State was in the Church. Lord Acton observes that the process in-

[23] Cf. Henry Osborn Taylor: "The Mediæval Mind," Vol. I. p. 8 ff.

duced the Church, which in earliest times addressed itself to the masses and relied upon the principle of liberty, to throw its mighty influence into the scale of authority. She supplied the wherewithal for the establishment of new and nominally Christian States which had been redeemed from barbarism. She taught the princes of converted pagan tribes the rudiments of government, and gave their peoples what little knowledge they acquired. It is not surprising that these princes and peoples felt a strong attachment to clerics whose minds were the sole sources of national light and betterment, or that the Church was made exempt from taxation, from civil jurisdiction and from political interference. But as the peoples advanced in self-consciousness and formed their national integrity in the hereditary succession of the Crown, Church and State drew apart, and presently drifted into open antagonism. To the conflict which ensued for four hundred years, civil freedom owes its beginnings. "If," says Lord Acton, "the Church had continued to buttress the thrones of kings whom it anointed, or if the struggle had terminated speedily in an undivided victory, all Europe would have sunk down under a Byzantine or Muscovite despotism." [24]

Out of the seeming wreckage of these centuries that have passed beneath our rapid review arose the doctrine abhorred by its principal contestants on both sides. The divine right of Popes and Emperors was at last countered by the divine right of the People to set up and pull down princes. Once it reached broader grounds and obtained the sanctions of religion, it spread apace until it was sturdy enough to defy Church and king. The disparagement of civil authority by ecclesiastics who detected its manifold infirmities returned to vex spiritual authority. Even in Hildebrand's time, he and his opponents were driven to acknowledge the embryonic democracy to which two centuries later both Guelf and Ghibelline alike appealed for approval. We shall see in the next lecture that the sentiments of the most celebrated

[24] "History of Freedom," p. 35.

Guelfic writer were destined to go far. St. Thomas averred that a king who is unfaithful to his duty forfeits his claim to obedience. "It is not rebellion to depose him, for he himself is a rebel whom the nation has a right to pull down. But it is better to abridge his power that he may be unable to abuse it. For this purpose the whole nation ought to have a share in governing itself." This language, which sounds appropriate for a modern revolutionist, was enforced by the further declaration of St. Thomas that "all political authority is derived from popular suffrage, and all laws must be made by the people or their representatives. There is no security for us so long as we depend on the will of another man." It is worth while to observe that he penned these illuminating opinions at the very moment when Simon de Montfort summoned the English Commons. The politics of this Scholastic and Neopolitan Friar were the advance guard of the present constitutionalism which, after its world-wide acceptance by civilized States, is now being subjected to criticism and accusation.

SEVENTH LECTURE

THE COLLAPSE OF MEDIÆVAL IMPERIALISM

"Is it so small a thing
To have enjoy'd the sun,
To have lived light in the spring,
To have loved, to have thought, to have done;
To have advanced true friend, and beat down baffling foes—

That we must feign a bliss
Of doubtful future date,
And, while we dream on this,
Lose all our present state,
And relegate to worlds yet distant our repose?"

MATTHEW ARNOLD: *Empedocles on Etna.*

"Before the fear of ridicule and the touch of reality, the illusions of youth pass away, and with them goes all intellectual courage. We have no longer the hardihood, we have scarcely the wish, to form our own creed, to think our own thoughts, to act upon our own beliefs; we try to be sensible, and we end in being ordinary; we fear to be eccentric, and we end in being commonplace."

WALTER BAGEHOT: *Collected Works*
Vol. III. p. 128.

SEVENTH LECTURE

THE COLLAPSE OF MEDIÆVAL IMPERIALISM

The attractiveness of universal rule — Boniface VIII and his Bull "Unam Sanctam" — The ruin of the Papal supremacy — The Avignon schism — Pierre DuBois and French overlordship — Augustine Trionfo — The soul of the Middle Ages — The paradoxes of the period — The range and character of Mediæval interests — The scholastic philosophy and its exponents — Augustinian and classical influences — The monastic orders, Innocent III, and St. Francis of Assisi —The losses and gains of Monasticism — Toleration known but persecution chosen by Church and Empire — Their renewed wars for supremacy — The triumph of Innocent IV — Dante, Marsiglio and Wyclif — The substance of "De Monarchia," "Defensor Pacis," "De Ecclesia," and 'De Officio Regis " — The summons to the modern world.

It was doubtless exceedingly attractive to many Christians of Mediævalism that there should be but one world governance, so long as it was that of Christ. And if a theocracy were only possible which enabled His two vicegerents, as Pope and Emperor, to insure the well-being of mankind, few would have questioned its right to rule. The conflict between these vicegerents did not arise from the principles involved in their sovereignty, but from the application of the principles. The Holy Roman Empire, moreover, did not actually expire after the downfall of the Hohenstaufen dynasty. It had a name, and lived on for six hundred years more till it became an antiquarian relic scarcely more venerable than ridiculous, which Voltaire characterized in its last phase, as "neither holy, nor Roman, nor an Empire." Its tenure was prolonged, in part, by the belief that it was an instrument of the Divine Order, but chiefly by its connection with the German principalities.[1]

[1] Cf. Viscount Bryce: "The Holy Roman Empire," Ch. XIII.

The rejoicings of the Holy See over the ruin of the Imperial House were destined to be short lived. France and England became increasingly restive; and, in Philip the Fair of the former Kingdom, Pope Boniface VIII [2] faced a decided supporter of Gallican clericalism, who summoned the States General to nationalize the French Church by subordinating it to the Crown. Philip's best weapon was the law, not the sword. Expert legal authorities like Pierre Flotte; and Guillaume de Nogaret, who was "learned, astute, and daring beyond the thoughts of others," stood at Philip's right hand. His kingdom was no longer the loose confederation of duchies and provinces of Hildebrand's day, always jealous of each other, often at war, and owning a merely nominal obedience to the monarch in Paris, but a far more centralized and self-conscious State. Normandy, which was long an alien province on the northern flank, had finally been detached from England. In the South, the dangers that might have arisen from the independence of Toulouse had been ended by the Albigensian wars. The enthusiasm of its citizens for the political entity of France, first and always, was aroused by their sanguine speculations about her future. The hour had come in which she should organize in better forms the strength and splendor that once had belonged to the now dying Empire. France was vaguely related to that Empire; her fair provinces of Burgundy, Besançon and Lyons were still its fiefs. But her leading spirits were practically severed from it, and busily engaged in saluting the rising sun of Nationalism. To this we shall return later.

The haughty decrees of the Holy See gave France the opening she desired. The Papal Bull "Unam Sanctam," published on November 18, 1302, reasserted the Gregorian

[2] Benedetto Gaetani, who took on the pontifical throne the name of Boniface VIII, was a nephew through his mother of Pope Alexander IV. He distinguished himself as a student at Paris, especially in law; had a brilliant mind, gracious and prepossessing manners, and a warm admiration for the religions of antiquity. He was learned, wise, subtle, but worldly and rich. He was seventy-seven years old when he became Pope. He was the master of a faultless Latin style.

idea of world-dominion for the Pontificate. In the words of this document: "there is now only one head, not two heads, as if it were a monster." The two swords that St. Peter offered to Christ, and which hitherto had been assigned respectively to the imperial and papal jurisdictions, were claimed by Boniface as the exclusive possession of the Church. He argued that St. Peter was commanded to put up the sword in the sheath, that is, within the keeping of the Church. The Bull ended with an assertion echoing the sentiments of Aquinas, "that it is altogether necessary to salvation for every human being to be subject to the Roman Pontiff." Its immediate outcome was the ruin of papal supremacy. Philip retaliated by dispatching Nogaret to Italy to kidnap the Pope and take him to Lyons. The attempt failed, but the aged and broken Boniface died within a fortnight, and his successor, Benedict XI, reigned but a few months. The Holy See was now forcibly transferred to Avignon, where it became to all intents and purposes a fief of the French monarchy. The Pontiff, Bertrand de Gouth, who had been Archbishop of Bordeaux, and as such, a subject of the English monarch, was yet Philip's creature, elected at his biddance, and crowned as Clement V at Lyons. For a short time Europe seemed to pass under French domination, and its partisans urged that the French king should be appointed to receive the homage of his fellow monarchs who held to the Pope, the King of England included. There is no need to enlarge upon the further consequence of these outrageous measures. The seventy years of "Babylonish Captivity" at Avignon were the beginning of a new chapter in the relation of Church and State, and of the end of the Papacy's spiritual leadership of Western Europe.[3] The Christian nations were rent asunder, deprived of their court of last resort, and precedents made for the sixteenth century revolt.

France used plausible pretexts to assume the older forms

[3] Cf. Henry Osborn Taylor: "Thought and Expression in the Sixteenth Century," Vol. I. p. 75.

of imperial supremacy, with herself as its nucleus, and the Papacy as a French dependency. Her abuse of an authority to which she was not entitled and had never been accustomed was to be anticipated. The Papal Court at Avignon became a "forge of lies and a sink of iniquity." The Order of the Knights Templar, founded in 1118, in connection with the Crusades, and prominent as a redoubtable but corrupt agency of the Papacy, was condemned by the Bull "Vox in Excelso," dated April 3, 1312; and on March 18, 1314, its Grand Master, Jacques de Molay, was burned at the stake. As he stood in the flames which cast their crimson glare over the surrounding buildings of the Isle de la Cite and across the waters of the Seine, in a loud voice he summoned Pope Clement V and Philip to meet him at the bar of God. Within forty days Clement obeyed the call, and Philip within the year. The king who died at Fontainebleau on the 29th of November 1314, was an able ruler who advanced nearly every interest of France, but as a man, he was unscrupulous and treacherous. He, more than any other, more even than Luther or Calvin, gave to papal supremacy its fatal wound. Nor was the disgrace it had inflicted upon the Hohenstaufens forgotten or forgiven in Germany, where it had its sequel two hundred years later.

While Europe lay in the shadow of French overlordship, its chauvinists were vocal about the new nationalism. Pierre DuBois,[4] a lawyer of Normandy, published in 1309 a well-written and cogent treatise which should be mentioned. The author, a firm adherent of that advanced thinker, Siger de Brabant, was by no means an obscurantist, but rather a mediæval progressive who pronounced against the usurpations of ecclesiastical tyranny. DuBois pleaded for universal peace; for a Court of Appeals for Christendom; for the deliverance of the Holy Land from the Moslem; for the strong monarchy of competent princes, who should not be at the

[4] The best information about DuBois is found in "Owen's College Historical Essays," Ch. VI.

bidding of rebellious vassals, but free to maintain the welfare of their subjects. Educational reforms and the need of graduated schools were also stressed by him. What could be better for Europe, he urged, in terms usually characteristic of extreme patriotism, than its subjection to the French monarchy? "Rome, Tuscany, the coasts and mountains, Sicily, England, Aragon and all other countries" that had formed Constantine's Empire and the patrimony of the Papacy, should be handed over to the French king. The Pope should be adequately pensioned, and the ancient rule supplanted by that of France. Such in brief, were the proposals of this Gallican lawyer. But his dreams and those of his countrymen were ended by the disastrous Hundred Years War. The close of the fourteenth century found the Holy See in the throes of the Great Schism. The Holy Roman Empire was equally bereft of its former power, and France no longer capable, if she had ever been, of world dominion. The rise of various nations, each determined to live as it pleased, was the prevailing feature of the time.

The comparative demolition of the papal claims provoked vigorous remonstrances from their apologists, in whom Hildebrand's influence was still paramount. The best known of these, Augustine Trionfo,wrote a tractate on papal privileges that raised them to the highest pitch.[5] Spiritual and temporal rule belonged exclusively to the successors of St. Peter. Even were the Pope a wicked man, his reign was none the less of God, and neither Emperors nor laymen had any rights so far as he was concerned. His power far exceeded that of temporal princes; his court was the august tribunal of the world. The existence of secular states was only justified by the fact that spiritual priesthood presided over them. In ways of which these statements are typical, Trionfo expounded the doctrine of Hildebrand in his letter to Bishop Hermann of Metz, that "civil power was the invention of

[5] For Trionfo, the reader is referred to R. L. Poole: "Illustrations of the History of Mediæval Thought," p. 253 ff.

worldly men, ignorant of God, and prompted by the devil." Yet such ultramontanism was not altogether wanting in concessions to what would now be termed democracy. Provided the State was willing to recognize the lordship of the Church, she, in turn, was willing to yield a great deal to popular sentiment. The clericalism of that age would have utterly denied the divine right of kings, a Reformation doctrine which appeared later as counterpart to the claim of the Papacy to the power of deposition. Hildebrand himself had sanctioned the theory of Manegold, a priest of Lautenbach in Alsace, that monarchy is not a name of nature but a title of office; and, therefore, that as soon as the monarch acted the tyrant he was liable to deposition. "If anyone should be engaged for a fair wage to tend swine," said this wholesome priest, "and he found means not to tend but to steal them, would not one remove him from his charge?" For St. Thomas, who has appeared in these lectures and will do so again, the powers that be were ordained of God, with the reservation that God acted through the Church. He sought to check the overweening demands of royalty by advocating an elective rather than a hereditary monarchy. Indeed, the ablest of the Scholastics would not concede the title of prince to those who did not govern according to virtue and eternal right. His chief contribution to the conception of Church and State was a well-reasoned discourse in which he contended that the State was not the outcome of human transgressions, but of the social instincts native to human beings. With this argument as his premise, he arrived at political conclusions in keeping with the dignity of his mind and the nobility of his disposition. The best modern theories of popular sovereignty have little of value to add to the substance of St. Thomas' teachings, and his works can always be consulted by present day thinkers with real advantage.

II

The thirteenth century, which contained the brilliancy, variety, beauty, the very soul of the mediæval world, came to its close in the thirty-fourth year of Dante's life. He was by far its foremost personalty; the citizen who placed his civic passion at the disposal of the Empire; the poet who vividly depicted the wisdom and the folly of the Catholic and Feudal Estates of the Middle Ages; the prophet between whose lines of homage for the past one reads its death sentence. It was a dubious because it was a transitional period. The old order changed, gave place to the new, and its sublimest hymn, "Dies Iræ," was in some respects the Florentine seer's requiem over the end of a luminous day. His contemporaries eagerly desired either what had been or should be; few of them were of the present, many were of the past or for the future. The masters of knowledge, as well as the mediocre but ambitious rulers who endangered their own interests, looked after or before, and longed for what was not. It was the misused trial time of Europe and Christianity. Statesmen ande cclesiastics, scholars and humanists, warriors and fanatics, great ladies and courtiers, appeared in the phantasmagoria of its life. Strong personalities emerged, typical of the proud spirit of the era, but too many forgot that they who would lead their age must first learn its duties. In their struggles for aggrandizement, Popes and Emperors mutually destroyed one another. The gradual amendment of society, the advance of moral ideas, their maintenance against material forces, the prevalence of rational persuasion over military violence, lost headway with the close of the thirteenth century. Their rapid decline after this date excites regret even at our remote hour. Yet the rise and fall of the public welfare confirms Lord Acton's statement that history's course is "our deliverer not only from the undue significance of other times, but from the undue influence of our own, from the tyranny of environment and the pressure of the air we breathe." [6] It exposes ancient errors and crimes that persistently recur; it cultivates considerate discretion, and the capacity for the wise management of public affairs; it shows that the chief values of any period are frequently found in its fluctuations.

Assuredly the Mediæval period was filled with bewildering paradoxes and contradictions. The largest ideas and the pettiest conceits consorted in many of the leading characters. They were given to fine gestures which they were often at a loss to sustain. Its political and religious federalism was dissolved by internal treasons, and the disunion which ensued produced both good and evil. The good has been exaggerated and its gains unduly magnified; yet one cannot avoid the opinion that they far exceed the losses. The nature and range of its intellectual pursuits were largely determined by the literature of antiquity. The core of its theology was directly connected with the hopes and fears of Judgment Day. Its highly conjectural eschatology bestrode nearly every conception of life here and hereafter. Its forms of thought were those of Aristotle. Its religious aspirations, if they had but few prophets who gave them wings, were never separated from men and women in whom the eternities dwelt. A ceaseless flood of allegorical and symbolic interpretations increased the power of the Church over the people. Saints, doctors and dreamers lived in the mystical realm, and lavished their ingenuities on its fancies. Nearly everything pertaining to life and death was within the compass of the religious medieval mind. It knew no half-way measures: all souls were either near to Heaven itself or on the verge of an abyss of woe. They had fellowship with God, with Christ, with the Blessed Virgin, with the saints and angels in glory everlasting. But the devil and his legions were also vivid to them as ever present and ominous agents of their undoing. The visions of women like Hildegard of Bingen represented generally received beliefs and dogmas, which sprang from the

[6] "Lectures on Modern History," p. 33.

intellect rather than the heart of Mediævalism. Its trances, ecstasies, excursions into the invisible, and occult revelations of trivial details were the reactions of an imagination susceptible to common beliefs. The senses subserved these ghostly experiences, and often gave them an uncouth realism. Odorous winds from Paradise, horrible stenches from Perdition, jubilations of the redeemed, agonizings of the damned, took on the semblance of physical perceptions. The Mediævalists cannot be charged, as we are, with believing too little; but though they often believed too much, and made prostrated emotionalism do duty for faith, they went to considerable pains to amplify what they believed, and to make it express the popular mind.[7]

The Universities were dominated by the Scholastics whose philosophy gave coherence to religious sentiment, to the manners and morals of the people, and to their ways of thinking. This philosophy was expounded, among others, by St. Bonaventura, by Albertus Magnus, by his pupil St. Thomas, and by Roger Bacon. St. Bonaventura related Scholasticism to the ideas of the twelfth century; Albertus Magnus occupied an intermediate position; St. Thomas is still the guide and mentor of the Roman Catholic Church. From his death in 1274 he became supreme in Christian Theology until the rise of modern thought. All acknowledged St. Augustine as their theological master, and shared the universal belief that the Bible was an infallible Book, the interpretation of which was established by the authorized tradition of the Church. Every other branch of knowledge was subordinated to theology as the queen of the sciences.

In some respects Bacon was the most fascinating thinker of Mediævalism. There was no lack of monotony in his career. His premonitions of later and organized learning enabled him to detect some truths he did not fully apprehend, and overshadowed some theological presuppositions he never disavowed. The separation between what he sincerely felt

[7] Cf. Henry Osborn Taylor: "The Mediæval Mind," Vol. I. p. 458 ff.

and what he dimly foresaw, caused his life to be an intellectual tragedy. He was always suspect, always under surveillance, often hindered by Pontiffs and bishops, obnoxious to his own order of the Franciscans. The output of his amazing industry increases our regard for a much misunderstood scholar, whose greatness was not mentioned until long after his beclouded hour had passed. Once dead, he seemed to be buried forever, and has only been unearthed in our time from the neglect and obloquy heaped upon his memory. The prevailing metaphysic received its consummate treatment, however, from St. Thomas, whose breadth of intellect and sympathy was governed by his sense of responsibility to God and man. The relations between all things in heaven and earth were interpreted by him in what, for his age, was a thoroughly satisfactory system of religious philosophy.

Duns Scotus has been described as the pinnacle set upon this system. Probably his was its most acute mind, with a critical sharpness all too likely to leave opposing opinions ragged and torn. He could analyze better than he could synthesize, and he would not have been what he was had he not lived after St. Thomas. But the main feature of Duns Scotus' writings is their destructive criticism. He practically annihilated reasonableness and based everything upon the unrelated Will of God. Faith, for him, was a leap into the dark. By his hostility toward its rational side he undermined Scholasticism, and paved the way for the Renaissance, and for the new outlook of Descartes. It was not a far cry from Duns Scotus and his Realism, which ascribed an actual objective existence to general ideas, to the Nominalism or Conceptualism of William of Ockham, which denied that Realism. In Ockham's denial, and in the substitute theories which he propounded, the signs of Scholasticism's decay can be discerned. His work had upon it those autumnal tints which presaged the approaching winter. The philosophy that had for centuries upheld the Mediæval Order and coördinated its character and rule, was at last fading away. Its labyrinthine windings offer one an intriguing theme that takes us too far afield from the purpose of these lectures. But occasional references to its main ideas can hardly be avoided in any intelligent treatment of the Middle Ages. Nor should its interrelations with very different and subsequent systems of thought be ignored by present day scholarship. It imparted numerous spiritual meanings of life and pressed home upon men the consciousness of their common needs and their common civilization. Its exponents determined the doctrines of Church and State, and in doing this, they followed an unrelaxing regimen which has not been surpassed by ancient or modern thinkers. Their skill in argumentation and scrupulously logical processes were a first rate intellectual drill which left its impress upon the mentality of after ages. It cleared the way for the careful precision required by the deductive method, and taught those who employed it the need of correct observation and of patience in experiment. From this viewpoint the Scholastics may be regarded as the pioneers of the natural sciences that have since revolutionized the material world.

The monastic orders to which they usually belonged were another falling buttress of Mediævalism. These also deserve a fullness of investigation which can only be made by their separate consideration. We have to be content here with scanty references to an institution which profoundly influenced the doctrine and polity of the Church for nearly a thousand years. The regular clergy, as the monks were called, because they lived according to a predetermined rule, have been accused of well-nigh all crimes and vices. But in their prime they imbued with human elements the theology handed down from the Fathers, and emotionalized its dry and musty articles to good effect. The heart of the living Christ resumed its beating of compassion for mankind in the original recluses and friars. What human beings love or hate was attached to its highest objectives by the purest monastic devotion. I shall reiterate nothing concerning the numerous advantages which the system conferred upon city slums and rural solitudes. It suffices to say that Monasticism enlarged men's capacity for immortality by instructing them in the care of their souls as well as their bodies. The religious motives and habits generated in the earlier monasteries became a model of life for millions, and exemplary recluses frequently fulfilled them so admirably as to belie man's reputation for frailty.[8]

The art of the Middle Ages, their manuscript libraries and ecclesiastical architecture, have so plainly told the monastic story at its height that it is perhaps better read in Fra Angelico's paintings or St. Alban's stately abbey, than even from the printed page.[9] Yet we should not forget the devotional literature of the cloister, which contains numerous examples of Christian excellence and exhortations to Christian holiness. In an age when men and women were notoriously buoyant sinners or sorely stricken penitents, they were apt to look upon the monk as the symmetrical saint. Lusts that were often uncontrolled by any semblance of reason ceased at the gateway of the monastery. Within its grateful refuge everything was tranquil on the surface, and wearied souls fled to its shelter from an arid and exhausting world. There temptations which had hitherto given them no respite were to be conquered. But their torments could not always be subdued; and as the centuries came and went, human nature reasserted itself, and dragged down Monasticism to a naturalistic level. Chastity, poverty and obedience did not surrender without a hard fight, and frequently a victorious one. Yet once the degeneration began it was hastened by the absence in monastic life of the outlets or restraints of normal life. The pious introspection which had become morbid, the service which had been transferred from others to self, were unchecked by that intercourse with secular society which necessitates a degree of altruism. Consequently the records of Monasti-

[8] Cf. Henry Osborn Taylor: "The Mediæval Mind," Vol. I. p. 357 ff. Also G. G. Coulton: "Five Centuries of Religion," Vol. I. Ch. I on "The Significance of Monasticism."

[9] Cf. Peter Taylor Forsyth: "Christ on Parnassus," pp. 98–191.

cism are those of repeated reforms or renewals. Its leaders nearly always appear as pleaders for the path which wayward regulars had forsaken. Communal virtues and aims were praised; the social instincts were invoked in behalf of a stricter observance of the monastic rule. Those who instituted new Orders with a severer discipline were often quick to resent the control of the higher clergy. Several of their movements began, like that of Wesley in the eighteenth century, as more or less unconscious protests against ossified parochial systems; and like him, the monasteries had to encounter the resistance of their mitered antagonists.

III

It was characteristic of Innocent III, perhaps the greatest of the Pontiffs, that he rose above this prejudice when he commissioned the holiest and most famous friar of Mediævalism. This Pope's reception of St. Francis was in keeping with nearly all we know of both men. Frederic Harrison declares that those who would understand the Middle Ages must study the lengthy and crowded Pontificate of Innocent. In commanding genius, in greatness of nature, in audacity of design, he has few rivals in the fourteen centuries of Roman Pontiffs, and few superiors in any age on any throne in the world. "His eighteen years of rule, from 1198 to 1216, were one long effort, for the moment successful, and in part deserving success, to enforce on the kings and peoples of Europe a higher morality, respect for the spiritual mission of the Church, and a sense of their common civilization." [10] Not even Hildebrand vied with Innocent as a discerner and ruler of the souls of men. It was this gift of reading and exploring the hidden springs of human conduct which enabled him to give to his office its maximum development. He never used it to better purpose than when with an eagle eye he saw, beneath the unpromising exterior of

[10] Frederic Harrison: "The Meaning of History," p. 157 ff.

his youthful suppliant, a ray of hope for the spiritualities of his world-domain. Accordingly, Innocent sent St. Francis forth after the manner in which our Lord had dispatched His disciples; and the adventure was justified by the beatific splendor which he shed upon it. Of all regulars of the period he has impressed himself most deeply and lastingly upon Christendom, even exceeding in this respect St. Bernard of Clairvaux. The title bestowed on him, "the grand climacteric of Mediæval Faith," well became a personal sanctity which rose above its description.

He assembled his followers, pledged them to the vows of his Fraternity, and journeyed with them throughout Europe, preaching the Evangel of Divine Love and human redemption. His message was not embarrassed by the arduous circumstances that confronted it. The everlasting and the universal dwelt in him, and radiated from him and his utterances to all ranks and conditions. He was a living testimony to the truth that "charity never faileth." Without marked intellectual gifts, averse to scholarly pursuits, as simple in mind as he was single in heart, St. Francis is reverenced as one of the noblest embodiments of Christian consecration since the Apostolic age. Although nothing appealed to his mentality alone, and whatever was unsuited to his way of life repelled rather than attracted him, he solved the problem for which the learned and the wise of this world have seldom, if ever, found a solution, by becoming a dedicated spirit, overflowing with grace and benediction. For him all the virtues were sacrosanct, and their acquirement lay in imitating his Lord. To follow Christ was to find the goal of eternal bliss; to obey Him insured a joyous freedom. His brethren in the enterprise were as he was; together they stood out against the background of uncertainties and dangers everywhere abroad, "blameless and harmless, children of God without blemish in the midst of a crooked and perverse generation." [11] Beneath their ministry of the Word a hallow-

[11] Philippians II. 15.

ing tenderness subdued the adamantine temper of the age. For a brief moment it seemed as though "the Kingdom in which dwelleth righteousness " had indeed come. The hardships attending their evangelization of the nations were transformed into delights by the romantic gladness of the more spiritual Franciscans. They sought the poor, the forsaken, the morally destitute, and became one with them that they might upraise them. To this end they explored the rookeries outside the walls of mediæval towns and cities, and entered the hovels of rustic hamlets, addressing their miserable occupants in words they could understand, and winning them to a cleaner and more spiritual life.[12] Such evangelists as they proved to be, sharing all naked needs and facing all hazards, are the immediate gifts of the Spirit of God. Their apologetic values surpass those of the Schools. They admonish skeptical intellectuals in every age that:

> "On our heels a fresh perfection treads,
> A power more strong in beauty."

After the first glow of the Revival had subsided in those depravities of the fourteenth century which quenched its brightness, it was gratefully recalled by believing souls. Its influence survived the loud tumults of the sixteenth century, and remain to this day as a witness to the innate authority of the Gospel of Jesus Christ over the human soul. The fame of St. Francis has recently overshadowed that of St. Bernard, whose demands upon himself and upon his brethren at Clairvaux were extraordinary. He was almost the last first class theologian produced by the older orders; a saint whose eloquence moved the hearts of princes and peoples alike. "The Abbot Bernard," wrote Eude de Deuil, "hid a robust soul under a frail and seemingly dying body. He went about like the wind, preaching everywhere." The King of

[12] Cf. Henry Osborn Taylor: "The Mediæval Mind," Vol. I. p. 431 ff. "Life of St. Francis of Assisi," by Paul Sabatier; G. K. Chesterton: "St; Francis of Assisi."

France attended some of his itineraries. The orator's clothes were torn off him and made into crosses. [13]

One should do justice to Monasticism and to its founders, and portray them as Cromwell insisted he should be painted; "with the warts." As an international fraternity it was a "mixed magnitude," with opposing characteristics that forbid rapid generalization. The debt which Christianity owes it, as we have seen, is great enough, though not so great as some have claimed. There was generally a regrettable distance between the monk and his rule. It gave the State and the Church such guiding spirits as Lanfranc and Anselm. The great Cistercian, Franciscan and Dominican movements and revivals stirred up the Cenobitic sea for a time. But Popes and Councils tried in vain to keep it from re-stagnation. Dr. Coulton comments that "the true monk lived a noble life, but it was not really Christ's life." Principal Workman speaks of the age-long errors: for instance, that the monks were great builders of churches, or that all dwelt in dark monastic cells, or that they founded our universities and established our schools; which have begun to give way to more accurate knowledge. Nearly every European State has legislated against the monks, and again and again the Church had openly to reprimand the later friars. Their religious conceptions no longer commend themselves to the ethical judgments of mankind. The secret of their downfall was that human nature being what it is, the monastic system could not have been other than it eventually became. The shipwreck of so many good intentions, and the destruction of numerous social and religious ties, were sad but inevitable consequences. Frivolity instead of zeal, gluttony instead of abstinence, greed instead of alms-giving, malice instead of charity, boasting instead of meekness, eventually devoured the noble heart of original Monasticism, and destroyed the zeal of the earlier Orders. Invectives, satires, expostulations, alike from friend and foe, bear witness with camera-like candor to the intrigues

[13] Cf. F. Funck Brentano: "The Middle Ages," p. 248.

and evils that corrupted later Monasticism, and its rivals, the later Friars. An intense public animosity sometimes found vent in these exposures. Almost the first place to be attacked in a city riot was the monastery. Its occupants were often at daggers drawn with the populace and the nobility. The secular clergy resented the wealth and aloofness of the regulars. So the institutions which once had been rich with blessing for the individual and for society were now viewed with widespread and implacable hostility. The reasonable defense of the system is that, taken as a whole, it did infinitely more good than evil. To assert either that it was entirely beneficial or entirely harmful is a controversial trick. Here the matter may be left, with the added comment that the waning of Monasticism predicted the collapse of Mediæval Imperialism. [14]

There is no particular reason why we should enlarge upon the current superstitions with which Monasticism was identified. Veneration of relics, image worship and the like, were no worse than some practices that afflict our generation. In fact, the modern cults are often more intolerable because they are more irrational and degrading than those of the Middle Ages. It is to the point, however, to observe that the myths typical of the period often captured its ablest minds, and occasionally fashioned human character upon more tractable lines. Not a few of the Dominicans rose above them, and steeped their preaching in an intellectualism derived from Augustinian theology, which may be favorably compared with that of modern divines. The spiritual jurisdiction which lent itself to casuistry, "that baleful shadow which clings so closely to nearly all great religious movements,"

[14] Cf. "The London Spectator," April 28, 1923, pp. 712–713; Also G. G. Coulton: "Five Centuries of Religion," Vol, I. "St. Bernard, His Predecessors and Successors"; Principal Herbert B. Workman: "Evolution of the Monastic Ideal" (a masterly work); Cardinal Gasquet: "Henry VIII and the Dissolution of the Monasteries," and his "English Monastic Life"; Mr. Heimbucher: "Die Orden und Kongregationen der Katholische Kirche," André Lagarde: "The Latin Church in the Middle Ages," Chapters III and XI.

was offset by the logical discourses of these members of the second great Monastic Order. Its founder, St. Dominic, soon became aware of the futility of persecution for heresy, and attacked it, not so much as the result of wilful depravity but as the source of speculative error. We do not now seriously think that heresy is to be ascribed to immorality of life. "Even the official mouthpiece of established beliefs now usually represent a bad heart as only one among other possible causes of unbelief. It divides the curse with ignorance, intellectual shallowness, the unfortunate influence of plausible heresiarchs, and other alternative roots of evil."[15] But while the Papacy was making its last rally to weld Europe into spiritual unity by means of the Crusades, and the Mendicant Friars were assisting the effort, heresy-hunting began afresh, and has run an intermittent course until now.

The great name of Innocent III is stained by its connection with the establishment of the Inquisition, which was in itself another token of the nearing collapse of Mediæval Imperialism.[16] That persecution for the sake of religious conformity is always unwise because it is damnably wicked, is perhaps a trite remark. What is not so trite is the statement that the persecutor himself stands on the verge of his own destruction. The killing of schismatics, sectaries, Jews and heretical groups, and the confiscation of their goods, only served to advertise their peculiar views and their fortitude. The Marian martyrdoms made England unquestionably Protestant for four hundred years, and the "smell of the burnings" in Scotland brought about the same result in that nation. Such infamous outrages were sure to react against those responsible for their perpetration. Nor could they be defended on the ground of ignorance, still less that of necessity. Toleration was as well understood then as it is now, but it was purposely repudiated by Roman

[15] Viscount Morley: "On Compromise," p. 159.
[16] Cf. H. C. Lea: "A History of the Inquisition in the Middle Ages."

Catholics and Protestants, in behalf of a monarchical supremacy or an ecclesiastical unity upon which they themselves were never agreed.

The Church that could descend to the abominable practices of the Holy Office was certainly speeding toward failure. The State that could license these practices was sooner or later bound to succumb. Three distinct movements began to undermine their citadels of terror, and afterwards took historic shape in Puritanism, Mysticism, and Skepticism. Meanwhile the Waldenses, Albigenses, anti-Ritualists, Manichæans, Quietists, as well as the Flagellants and other groups of various sorts, were as the straws which showed which way the stream of mediæval life and thought was flowing. In them, as in the Wyclifians and the Hussites, were some primal sources of the overturning which had been impossible in the twelfth century, and was unavoidable in the sixteenth. The unification of society that could not be achieved by the might of Hildebrand, Alexander III or Innocent III, was a hopeless task for succeeding Popes who were but a parody on those princes. Their quarrels with the Empire lingered on until the fatal arrogance of Boniface VIII precipitated what Dante describes as "the mockery, the vinegar, the gall, of a new crucifixion of the Vicar of Christ." At the time he wrote these words the Holy See was smothered in ignominy at Avignon. But the handwriting on the walls of Christendom had been there since the failure of the Crusades and the rise of the Ottoman Power.

When there was a peaceful interlude between Gregory IX and Frederic II, the greatest of the Hohenstaufens, it was nothing more than outward amity concealing inward distrust. Frederic was a wary and dangerous antagonist of the Pontificate. "Extraordinarily varied and many-sided," he "reflected every aspect of his time, and responded to every impulse." Full of the joy of life, of art, of friendship, the Emperor's nature, though it sometimes chilled his retainers, more often warmed and won them. By contrast with him, the figures of the three Pontiffs whom he overcame seemed "cold, narrow, unlovable, and even inhuman." His sudden death on December 13, 1250, gave imperial affairs another complexion. His son Conrad IV succeeded him, and died in May, 1254. Yet he reigned long enough for Innocent IV, who was a far better diplomatist than Conrad, to outwit him at every turn. The Pontiff's astute methods savored of deceit, and reduced the German Church to a mere "agency of temporal welfare, producing a deep resentment not only among the German laity, but among the finer minds of the clergy." Innocent did not have the nobility of soul of his namesake Innocent III, nor the moral strength of Honorius III, nor the fiery vehemence of Gregory IX. Nevertheless, he trampled down opposition and enthroned the spiritual over the temporal authority. His worldly wisdom, self-control, knowledge of the canon law, and financial prudence served his immediate purpose by enabling him to humiliate the Empire. But he left the Pontificate heavily encumbered with those obligations which low politics have always bequeathed to the Church.

IV

The seeds of divergencies and insurrection sown by the talented but wily Innocent soon began to germinate. The strife between Guelfs and Ghibellines, apparently quelled by him, really entered upon its final and most disastrous phase. The Guelfs became victorious after the battle of Campaldino in 1289, and the prospects of their secure control of Florence were bright until 1300, when this party was split into two rival sections, known as the "Whites" and the "Blacks," and distinguished by their respective allegiances to the Republic and the Pope. By a coup d'état the Black Guelfs won over the papal emissary who had been sent to make peace between the two factions, with the result that the leaders of the "Whites," including their foremost champion Dante, were exiled. For a while Dante renounced his ancestral party, and identified himself with the Ghibellines, but he found that they viewed the Empire as a means to secure their own party supremacy. He therefore abandoned them, and henceforth lived without any party affiliations, becoming as it were a party in himself.[17] While in exile he wrote his "De Monarchia," in which he laid down in scholastic syllogisms his ideal of a universal empire founded on justice, without any element of faction. Dante's hatred of endless internecine wars which threatened the unity and peace of his country, caused him to raise a soul-piercing cry for some power strong enough to quell the tempest. This power was not to be found in the Papacy, but in the Empire. Only when the Emperor became the sole shepherd of the one civic flock would mankind secure freedom and peace.

After the scholastic fashion, he developed in three books his three principles; that universal monarchy was necessary for society; that this imperium belonged to the Roman people; that its authority was derived immediately from God and not from the Pope as His Vicar. In an indignant outburst he impeached the misuses of her wealth by the Church. "The patrimony of the poor" had been squandered by its spiritual overseers, while the private estates of their own kinsfolk were suddenly enriched. As a citizen Dante shared the prevalent view that Church and State were an entity, in which Pope and Emperor should behave as brothers holding joint authority; with the proviso that supremacy belonged to the civic rule.[18] Hence he contended that there must be one Federal State, with a single head, and that both the State and its ruler must be Christian. "Man," he said, "had need of two guides for his life, as he had a twofold end in life; whereof one is the Supreme Pontiff, to lead mankind to eternal life according to the things revealed to us; and the other is the Emperor, to guide mankind to happiness in the world, in ac-

[17] Cf. "Paradiso," Canto XVII, 68–69.
[18] Cf. J. N. Figgis: "Churches in the Modern State," p. 190 ff.

cordance with the teaching of philosophy." Cæsar must be reverent toward St. Peter, but "the authority of temporal monarchy comes down with no intermediate will from the fountain of universal authority."[19]

The controversy between the Pope and the Emperor bore upon the relative position of each to the other. But the breach could have been healed had the disputants conceded that the two thrones were equally balanced, and alike derived from God as the source of all law. Dante prayed for a monarchy of the world: a reign of tranquility, righteousness and Christian fraternity. Those who five centuries later invoked his great name as the earliest prophet of their creed, strove after an idea that never crossed his mind. He was not seeking the national unification of Italy, but of Europe, and through Europe of the world; to be achieved by the exclusion of the Papacy from secular government, and the supremacy of that government in all temporal matters, beneath the ægis of the Emperorship.[20] Justice required a supreme ruler, himself above the prejudice and animosity of parties, impervious to the solicitations of ambitions; since his dominions were commensurate with Christendom, and his highest political aspirations were completely satisfied.

The reader who has opportunity to scan Dante's pages probably will turn with impatience from imperialistic theories whose absoluteness is only matched by their historic unreality. He will marvel at the fantastic mediæval logic that attempted to prove that Christ was born under the Roman Empire, "in the fulness of times," because He was persuaded of its justice; while by dying under the sentence of that Empire He sanctioned its sway over the whole human race. Such a reader will marvel most of all at the chapter in which Dante set forth the miracles whereby God had indorsed the authority of the Empire. The fall of the shields of Numa, the fable of the geese of the Capitol, the hailstorm after Cannæ, and

[19] "De Monarchia," Book III. Ch. XVI.
[20] Cf. Viscount Bryce: "The Holy Roman Empire," Ch. XVI.

similar fictions, were gravely quoted as irrefutable proofs of the Divine intervention in favor of Rome. And he will probably recall that within a few years after the poet's glorification, this very Empire, under Lewis of Bavaria and his successors, sank to its lowest depths of feebleness and corruption. But Dante's impassioned tributes should not be altogether disqualified by our standards of history or appeals to facts. Despite his romancings, the remorseless chill of his detachment of view pervaded many of his judgments. Ever and anon the touch of his almost infallible authority is felt; of a nature whose supernal gifts can only be compared with those of Shakespeare. Thus, as Viscount Bryce has shown, with reference to the date at which it was written, Dante's eulogy proved "an epitaph instead of a prophecy." No abstract splendors of theory, no idealized descriptions, no compressed energy of diction, could conceal from later onlookers that the mediæval concept was dead; that the once boasted imperialism of Charles the Great had become scarcely more than an honored name. Its diploma of sovereignty was, in the telling phrase of Gregorovius, but "a document smothered in dust, on which were inscribed claims to universal supremacy." No small factor in the verdict was the clearness with which the poet's genius was compelled to testify against his dearest wishes as a patriot. His ideal insisted on looking backward instead of forward. As a partisan he would not admit that no earthly throne forever remains; no altar always stand secure. Nevertheless, the prophetic depths within Dante perforce assented to this truth.

For us to point out these unavoidable changes is not to covet them. On the contrary, there was a very desirable possibility for good in the Imperial Federalism which Dante envisaged. But the betterment and stability of human society could not be secured by a system which had already misused its opportunity, and was fast disappearing. It is only fair to add that the poet's dream was not entirely monopolized by a vanishing past. For us the chief importance of

"De Monarchia" consists in its ennoblement of the political rule which held the reversion of the future. The work translated the presidency of the world Commonwealth from Church to State. Its ideal temporal monarch, "rex mundi et Dei minister," was but Hildebrand's ideal Pontiff with a difference. The secular realm became the concrete embodiment of the Divine Order in society, and also the revelation of the operation of the Divine Spirit in man. As Gregorovius justly remarks, there lay at the bottom of "Dante's enthusiasm for the Roman Empire, a deep love of historic humanity, the life of which, in all its revelations, is conceived as a revelation of the Divine Spirit, having no lower claims than those of the Church." To that life and its relations, every organization, however sacred, must be serviceable. Herein the poet has proved to be, as in all else he wrote besides "De Monarchia," a great prophet of the future. In spite of its abstractions and unrealities, by reason of its denunciation of clerical tyranny, and still more because of its emphasis on the values of secular life, the work laid solid foundations upon which forthcoming statesmen could build.

The resounding lines of the "Æneid," which inspired Dante's theory of the imperial rule:

> "Tu regere imperio populos, Romane, memento,—
> Hae tibi erunt artes,—pacisque imponere morem,
> Parcere subjectis, et debellare superbos," [21]

were destined to find their accomplishment, not by seeking the living among the dead, but by the evolution of the near future. In July, 1338, Germany awoke to the consciousness of the unendurable suzerainty which the Empire had acquired over her. At Rhense, a hamlet on the Rhine, five miles from Coblenz, the German electors renounced in the name of the nations the claims of the Papacy to ratify or reject their nomination as imperial electors. This separation of the twin partners in the dualism of Empire and Church was

[21] Book VI. 851–3.

the beginning of the greater severance of the German intellect from the Holy See. At the same time, in Italy, the adventurer, Cola di Rienzi, seized and exploited the then novel idea of revolt. The insurrectionist was something more than a "tragic actor in the tattered purple of antiquity." His significance is attributable to his discovery that the salvation of Italy was neither of Guelf nor of Ghibelline, but must proceed from Italy herself. Though in later years Rienzi disgraced his purpose, and though five centuries had yet to elapse before it could be attained, its author, despite his extravagances, is worthy of mention for having advocated the idea of justifiable revolution.

V

Marsiglio of Padua, the gifted and fearless apologist of the Ghibellines, was another interesting if impracticable thinker whose writings marked the rapid dissolution of the mediæval dominion. His epochal work, "Defensor Pacis," erred in the opposite direction from that of Dante by projecting upon society advanced theories which were not even understood, much less appreciated, until modern times. Born of a burgher family in Padua in 1270, Marsiglio's restless disposition drove him from the study of medicine to the profession of arms. In 1321 he resided at Paris as a pupil of William of Ockham. In March of the following year, while rector of the University there, he issued regulations under its seal. The theologians of Paris afterwards made a declaration in 1375 that neither Marsiglio nor his friend, John of Jandun, ever graduated in theology, even as bachelors. Yet they seem to have begun the course. At a later date Marsiglio took orders as a secular cleric. Though an ally of the Spiritual Franciscans, he did not enter their ranks. By occupation it would appear that eventually he practiced as a physician. These fragmentary references to a roaming scholar's career are not strictly necessary to our quest, since it was not as a physician nor as a scholastic theologian that Marsiglio made his reputation, but as a publicist and politician. He showed his bent at an early date by writing in 1313 on the wellworn theme of the transference of the Empire. On June 24, 1324, with the help of John of Jandun, he finished his masterpiece "Defensor Pacis" within the almost incredible space of two months. Two years later the two men, who were dubbed by the Pope as "beasts from the abyss of Satan," joined themselves to Lewis of Bavaria at Nuremburg.

At the court of Lewis, Marsiglio became the leader of a band of daring visionaries who defied the Holy See, and backed the Emperor in his contest for secular supremacy. Ockham is reported to have said to Lewis, when in 1328 he fled to his court at Pisa: "Do thou defend me with thy sword; I will defend thee with my pen." Both master and pupil kept their promise. In treatise after treatise they attacked the nature of the papal rule, denied its assertions, ridiculed the reigning Pontiff, whom they called "priest John of Cahors," and pronounced him a guilty heretic already virtually deposed. The Pope retorted by upbraiding Lewis for his patronage of such refractory wretches. Since his reproaches had no effect, on October 23, 1327, he condemned the book "Defensor Pacis," and on May 30, 1329, ordered steps to be taken against its author. These measures were followed by a more formal condemnation in the Papal Bull "Cum Processum," issued in 1330.

The work thus launched in a hurricane of villification is the most original and suggestive political treatise of Mediævalism. Its importance is revealed by the number of its manuscript copies, at least twenty of which still exist in various libraries of Europe. It begins, as the title indicates, in the praise of peace, and with a recital of the intolerable hurts that come of strife. From the prelude Marsiglio naturally passes to "open the sophism of this said singular cause of discord which threateneth to all realms and communities no little harm." The first section or volume discusses in Aristotelian forms the origin and principles of government. After the usual mediæval manner, as seen in Hildebrand and other contemporary authorities, the author relates the effects of Adam's Fall upon political administration. In digression, one may note that Marsiglio, a typical Italian, defines a city "as a perfect community having in itself all things necessary to the sufficiency of life, and ordained not only for man to live in, but principally to live *well* in." From this proposition he deduces that in such a city bondage is illogical, "for that thing which is thrall or bond cannot be sufficient in itself." Sovereignty therefore pertains to the whole body of citizens, and freeman should agree to this end. For the purpose of action, "the rule of a king is perhaps the more perfect," but the king, as the people's officer, must be directly elected by them. He abjured divine right and the hereditary principle as outside the pale of reason. In this he followed the argument of another hardy speculator to whom reference has been made, Manegold of Lautenbach in Alsace. The elected monarch was responsible to his subjects, whose instrument he was, and by whom he could be deposed if he thwarted the national will. In his conception of human equality, a fundamental of Christianity altogether lacking in many authors of the age, Marsiglio was only pushing to their logical conclusion the premises of modern politics. The marrow of Jeffersonian doctrine was contained in the writings of this obscure and nomadic partisan of the fourteenth century.

In his second volume he submitted the nature and claims of the priesthood to a no less microscopic and startling examination. He began by defining the Church as the entire body of Christian men; "the university (universitas) and congregation of all faithful believers and callers upon the name of Jesus Christ; which is the most true and proper signification." The idea that the Church was founded upon or restricted to the sacerdotal order was summarily excluded. The sole business of the priest was to preach the Faith and administer the Sacraments. "There is," he owned, "another certain authority belonging to the priest, that is, whereby bread and wine is transubstantiated or turned into the substance of Christ's blessed body at the oration of the priest." But this authority was solely spiritual, and the priest's rights should be limited accordingly. Excommunication, for instance, the most dreaded weapon of the clerical arm, could only be decreed by the entire congregation to which the erring member belonged. In all but their religious functions the clergy were to be treated as members of the civil society, save only that their offenses should be punished with greater severity because they could not plead ignorance of the laws. Marsiglio seconded Jerome in maintaining that bishop and presbyter were convertible terms. More advanced than these views was his assertion that heresy should go unpenalized in this world, except in so far as it proved inimical to the State; and even then its repression should be confined to the civil jurisdiction.

The result of his reasonings reduced Church government to a matter of expediency. Though theoretically all priests were equal, the Papacy, he held, was a convenient symbol of the unity of the Church and an historic center for her work. None the less, however, did he set aside the trustworthiness of papal historicity, stating that it was doubtful if St. Peter had ever been Bishop of Rome; nor was he in any way superior to the other apostles, nor did he communicate any spiritual gifts to his successors. The Decretals were not necessary to salvation, since these "according to truth are nothing else but certain ordinances, constitutions or decrees . . . which Christian men are not bound . . . to obey." The origin of the Holy See was traced by him with rare critical insight to the influence of the Roman Empire and to the Donation of Constantine, the genuineness of which he did not dispute. The power of the keys is "the science of knowledge, discerning the good from the evil." They opened and closed the doors of pardon to the penitent, but the turnkey was not the judge. Without the contrition of the sinner, priestly absolution was of no avail, since it was God alone who cleansed men inwardly. The Papacy had no temporal sovereignty, nor should priests meddle with secular judgments. As servants and ministers of Christ, let them be patterned after His precept and example, Who deliberately refused the dignity of a monarchy, and said, "My Kingdom is not of this world." With Marsiglio, as with Calvin, the State and the Church became practically one. But it was the State which must summon all clergy, high and low, even the Pope himself, to its bar; and their number and allotment were to be determined by its pleasure. Patronage belonged to it, and should, as a rule, be exercised by the free action of parishes and churches. Ecclesiastical property was to be vested in the State, which could at any time secularize superfluities to other uses, a claim that Christ acknowledged when He paid tribute to Cæsar.

The most impressive of Marsiglio's ecclesiastical contentions was his plea for a General Council, to be composed of clericals and laymen alike, acting as the Supreme Court of the Church Universal; and as the Parliament of federated nations in matters temporal or spiritual, adjudicating Catholic belief and practice. This was, in truth, nothing less than that representative assembly of united Christendom for which many enlightened citizens are now asking. Its interpretation of creeds should in all cases be solely based upon the Bible as the source of Faith and Order. The Popes must be bound by its decisions, and it alone should pronounce excommunication upon rulers or their subjects.

It is quite comprehensible that to the Holy See Marsiglio was a heretic of heretics. But the Empire which he had defended had need to beware of an independent and fearless advocate, many of whose arguments were made not merely in behalf of imperial sovereignty, but in the interests of the people as against the pretensions of absolutism. "What do you find there," he asks, speaking of the Papacy, "but a swarm of simoniacs from every quarter? What but the clamor of pettifoggers, the insults of calumny, the abuse of honorable men? There justice to the innocent falls to the ground or is so long delayed unless they can buy it for a price that finally, worn out with endless struggle, they are compelled to give up even just and deserving claims. For there man-made laws are loudly proclaimed; the laws of God are silent or rarely heard. There are hatched conspiracies and plots for invading the territories of Christian peoples and snatching them from their lawful guardians. But for the winning of souls there is neither care nor counsel." [22] His animadversions upon the clergy were no less caustic. There had been a time when doubtful questions could be settled by them. "Now, however, on account of the corruption of the Church administration, the greater part of the priests and bishops are but little versed in sacred Scriptures, so that the temporalities of benefices are gained by greedy and litigious office seekers, through servility, or importunity, or bribery, or physical violence. And, before God and the company of the faithful, I have known numbers of priests, abbots, and other Church dignitaries of such low quality that they could not even speak grammatically. And what is worse, I have known and seen a man less than twenty years of age, and almost completely ignorant of the divine law, entrusted with the office of bishop in a great and important city, when he not only lacked priestly ordination, but had not passed through the diaconate or subdiaconate." [23]

These presentations, which were far in advance of the era, received two centuries later a strong impetus at the Reformation; and, later still, in the following century, were the bone of contention between English Independency and the Stuart dynasty. But it is only in our day that men are beginning to recognize what Marsiglio foresaw: that the Church of the future must be a layman's Church, not in the sense of discarding the division of clerics and laymen, or that of labor

[22] E. Emerton: "The Defensor Pacis of Marsiglio of Padua," p. 66.
[23] E. Emerton: "The Defensor Pacis of Marsiglio of Padua," p. 53.

between teacher and taught, but in placing all members of the Church on an equal basis of spiritual liberty, privilege, and responsibility. Marsiglio's political radicalism secured for him the rabid detestation of the hierarchy which had already branded the mildest of constitutionalists, Simon de Montfort, as "that pestilent man." When to this radicalism were added Marsiglio's revolutionary proposals against Church authority, his cup of iniquity was filled to overflowing.

He was a visionary only in the sense in which all predictive spirits are such. Of necessity the seer is before his age, and the vindication of his utterance may be indefinitely postponed. Yet no contemporary thinker had a clearer gaze than this mediæval modernist, or saw more deeply into the future toward which a stubborn world reluctantly moved. In his principles, as Dr. Poole observes, statesmen of today find little to alter; they have had but to develop and fill in their outlines.[24] Much that was valuable in the political and ecclesiastical writing of Wycliff had already been expressed more succinctly and with greater force in the writings of Marsiglio. He possessed in a preëminent degree that lucidity of his race which enabled him to expound and apply with prescience the ideals that now regulate civilized States. The bolts forged in his ardent mind clove asunder the doctrine of divine right, and seriously disturbed the temporal claims of the Papacy. His wise and accurate estimate of Holy Scripture preceded that of Wyclif, Luther and Calvin. In his remonstrance against the exclusion of the laity from official positions in the Church, he anticipated the stroke of temerity by which Wesley made Methodism a world-power. His insistence upon the autonomy of local congregations signalized him as the forerunner of Independency. A matured judgment upon the author of "Defensor Pacis" entitles him to the honors of a herald of beneficial movements, with which other and more familiar names have been associated at the expense of his own.

[24] Cf. R. L. Poole: "Illustrations of the History of Mediæval Thought."

Marsiglio was, however, far from being without influence upon his age. About the close of 1374, his work was translated from Latin "into French or an idiom such as meets the approval of the Emperor and other earthly potentates." In September, 1375, an unfriendly inquiry was instituted concerning the translation. The members of the Theological Faculty of Paris were convened, and individually questioned whether they knew or had suspicion who had committed the offense, but the inquisition seems to have been in vain. Meanwhile Marsiglio's masterly formulation of the idea of a supreme Church parliament won a widening acceptance. However much he may have disliked some of its conclusions, the learned Gerson, the leader of the conciliar party at Constance, praised the "Defensor Pacis" as "mirabiliter bene fundatus"; a eulogy that helps to explain the ease with which its conciliar theory gained ground. A copy of the work fell into the hands of that sturdy opponent of prevalent abuses, Dr. Thomas Gascoigne of Oxford, who gave it to Lincoln College. In 1529 it was placed on the list of prohibited works, but this act did not prevent its translation into English six years later by one William Marshall, an enthusiastic reformer who served as one of Thomas Cromwell's agents. In his definition of the limits of ecclesiastical authority and his assertion of the native dignity of the individual believer, Marsiglio's ideas still await complete realization. Nevertheless, for breadth and verity of speculation he stood solitary, and superior to the thinkers and writers of his age. The truths which he alone brought into view afterwards had to be rediscovered at immense cost by political philosophers of modern times, who were scarcely aware of his existence.

VI

Wyclif's contribution to the collapse of Mediæval Imperialism, and his conception of Church and State must not be passed over, if only because of their national results in Bohemia, where John Huss adopted almost word for word the Englishman's "De Ecclesia" as the original of his publications. I have discussed the Evangelical Doctor's relations to his time elsewhere, and they do not concern us here except as they cast light upon the issues before us.[25] His declaration that the Church militant consisted solely of the predestinated, and so could contain none but the elect, was his chief contribution to the problem. No man, not even a Pope, knew whether he was blessed or reprobate. The secret of the eternal separation between the saved and the lost was with the God who decreed it. No earthly institution, not even the Church, but a heavenly fiat, became the center of His redemptive design; a fiat existent in His timeless present with Whom was neither past nor future. This scholastic construction, too artificial and inflexible for use or benefit, had no actual connection with human life, nor with the facts of which its idealism fell foul. The same major fault is visible in Wyclif's doctrine of the State, which can be ascertained from his "De Officio Regis," a companion work to "De Ecclesia," and afterwards recast and enlarged as the eighth volume of his great "Summa."[26] He there stated that his object was to treat of the military caste, as in "De Ecclesia" he had treated of the clerical; and specifically to show what the kingly office was, and what were its relations to the sacerdotal power. His starting point, furnished by his opponents, lay in their plea that as a civil dominion is a perfection, it must belong to the most perfect part of the Church. His reply, disentangled from needless digressions, allegorical wrestings of Scripture and feudal terminologies, was, that since the kingly office derived immediately from God, it was independent of the Church and the Papacy. This divine origin was recognized by Christ in the Adoration of the Magi, and by the teaching of the New Testament in reference to monarchy.

[25] Cf. The Author's "The Three Religious Leaders of Oxford," pp. 15–170.

[26] "De Officio Regis," has been printed by the Wyclif Society and is edited by A. W. Pollard, under the date 1887.

The Monarch was God's vicar as the Pope was Christ's vicar, and as God's vicar he was obligated to exhibit heavenly justice in all his actions.

Wyclif was addicted to fanciful portrayals of the king as embodying the divinity, and the priest the humanity of Christ: a mediæval notion due to the statements of St. Augustine, Ambrosiaster and Cathulfus that "the king has the image of God, as the bishop has that of Christ." This idea he amplified to mean that the king represented the glorified and reigning Lord, the priest the suffering and submissive Jesus. The one was the image of the will, the other of the love of Deity. The real significance of the priest, whose office was the more perfect and honorable, was in his sanctity and humility. Farther removed from the world, he was therefore greater than the king. To confirm this view Wyclif twisted the Decretal of Innocent III in a way that would have outraged that Pontiff. Outward or "sensible honor" was to be rendered more freely to kings than to priests, for though the Pope was spiritually above the Monarch, the Monarch was temporarily above the Pope. Both enjoyed authority from God, but that of the king was prior to that of the priest. "Adam," said St. Augustine, "was the first king and Cain the first priest." The priestly consecration of the king conferred no superior powers upon his consecrators. Corrupt kings, though possessing veritable lordship, must be recognized as appointed by God, just as froward priests were esteemed for the sake of their office, or as the image of their Creator was honored even in the damned. But if wicked kings injured God's cause, they should be withstood to the death: an advice that Wyclif at once qualified by emphasizing the non-resistance of our Lord and His martyrs.

In the second chapter of "De Officio Regis" he distinguished at length between the consideration due to office and that due to merit, and insisted that no cleric should receive credit because of his connection with lay dignities. The futile pursuit of worldly rewards and emoluments was habitual in "scholastic camps," where the worst that could be was seen in priests by profession, who were proud militarists in practice. To forbid these clerics to marry, while granting them the tenure and income of lay offices, was to strain out a gnat and swallow a camel. The third chapter related in some detail the duties of the king. He should be a man of integrity and wisdom, versed in the holy oracles, with prudent counsellors and domestic chaplains who were infinitely more than mere table companions. He must realize that good government was best secured by a few just laws which should never be abrogated save for the most cogent reasons. As God's vicar he was to rule in humility, submissive to the Eternal Righteousness, and mindful that justice was the brightest of the virtues. He must see to it that the clergy lived on their tithes and private alms, and were deprived of the temporalities which they had acquired contrary to Scriptural command. With the ill-gotten wealth thus disgorged, capable ministers "might be hired for lay service." To the objection that things consecrated could not be taken from the altar, Wyclif replied that it was no violation to correct or improve their use. In the fourth chapter, he describes the extent of the royal prerogative, and insisted upon its jurisdiction over the clergy. The loyalty of the subject should never involve him in "sins of consent," which were of five different kinds, alike damnable in a secular prince, and still more so in a cleric. As particulars he named the cases of monarchs who refused to withdraw temporalities from the clergy, and also of those who connived at simony.

In the fifth chapter, Wyclif dealt with the king's submission to law; reasoning that law was divine and therefore obligatory upon all men. Our Lord Himself conformed to it, and His conduct should lead the king to do likewise, as an example of consistency and obedience to his people. He concluded the chapter with a disquisition on the essentials and limits of the obedience required, substantially identifying it with humility. In civil rule even Pilate was entitled to receive the obedience of Christ.[27] But as regards spiritual things, men should obey the veriest pauper, if he were a better man, rather than a corrupt Pontiff or Cæsar. One element in true obedience was its freedom. Hence the discipline of the secular clergy was more worthy than that of the regulars. But in all obedience to the law rules laid down by Christ were the deciding factor. Papal Bulls and minor clerical proscriptions were of moment only as they harmonized with His Divine Will, and it was more perilous to resist God than to resist the Pope. Wyclif's strategical position was thus left unprotected from sheer individualism, and the entire drift of this chapter has been construed by his enemies as an attack upon legitimate authority. In the sixth chapter he developed his theory in a fashion satisfactory to despots. Since the sin of any one person weakened the State, all sins should be probed by the king, from whom episcopal government itself was derived. His right to correct the secular clergy at the instigation of his clerical ministers had been fully acknowledged by the resort of Urban VI to the secular arm to crush the anti-pope. The higher the rank of the offending ecclesiastic, the more necessary became the king's power of punishment. The claim of "Christ's pretending vicar" to control monarchs was pure blasphemy; for the sole support of papal authority was in its purely spiritual nature.

Parliamentary language was never Wyclif's strong point, and he did nothing to improve in this matter the pronouncedly bad manners of his foes. When the Abbot of Chertsey would have abolished the authority of secular princes over the clergy, the Reformer railed upon him in a vigorous but vulgar tirade. Scattered throughout his discourses were forced comparisons, irrelevant references and numerous digressions, the meanings of which are more or less obscure. Occasionally his indomitable spirit flashed out, as in the request that some foreign born clericals should be made

[27] By obedience Wyclif simply meant recognition of existing facts and circumstances. Passive resistance to them was dictated by internal principles.

to take the oath of allegiance on entering England. He also asserted that the monarch must not allow the lands of his knighthood to be assigned to the dead hand. He observed that if Pontiffs had deposed Emperors, Emperors had more often deposed Pontiffs, and that "England is not bound to obey any Pope except so far as obedience can be deduced from Scriptures." In his later works he tirelessly inveighed against the doctrine that Monasticism was a more complete exhibition of Christianity than its ordinary forms. Nor would he allow that priesthood inhered in the clergy. The inflamed question of patronage was decided by him as belonging wholly to the laity, and he denounced Pope John XXII for his reservation of English benefices and sees. The political side of his propaganda appeared in his appeal to the monarch to order yearly visitations of the clergy by ministers of State, who should investigate the conditions of the respective dioceses, and summon provincial Church Councils to remedy notorious abuses. Every parish must be occupied by scholarly and devout curates whose income ought to depend upon their efficiency. And the extension, defense and betterment of the theological faculty of the Church was an imperative obligation of the Crown.

Herein, as elsewhere, we see how representative Wyclif was of that national self-consciousness which presaged the coming England of an insistent and exclusive patriotism. Aware that education was indispensable to the good of the State, he pleaded for learned doctors and trained pastors, and would have made a clearance of the swarms of legalists who packed the higher courts of the Church. That they smarted under his attacks, and were prejudiced by them, was evident when in later years he came before them for trial as a heretic. But in his zeal for change he stammered out many things he did not fully understand, and showed at critical junctures the bewilderment of a brave soul lost in the twilight zone. Thus, while protesting against the reckless use of excommunication by the clergy, he asserted that the removal of heretics was the duty of the State, solemnly enjoined upon it by "God's law." Evidently he failed to perceive, as did the Presbyterians of a later period, that under this ruling he could not consistently claim exemption from persecution for his own followers. Besides, when did persecutors of any time fail to justify their cruelty by appeals to "God's law?" Incidentally for him, but not for us, he discounted extreme pacificism. Wars waged in "the cause of the Church or for the honor of Christ," were righteously undertaken. Yet he stigmatized the maxim that force must be repelled by force as an argument of his pet abomination, antichrist. To deduce otherwise, he averred, was Mohammedan and not Christian logic. He also complained that "the most powerful horses of Christ's chariot" forsook the royal road to peace "to save Pharoah." His noble declarations that conquest was usually wrong, and that the employment of mercenaries, ignorant of the causes for which they fought, was altogether vile, are as pleasing to us as they might have been distasteful to the Plantagenet princes who endeavored, at the staggering expense of one hundred years of conflict, famine and pestilence, to exercise dominion over both France and England. Remove cupidity and ambition, said this great iconoclast who had seen the disasters of needless war, and its outbreaks would cease.

Wyclif's exaltation of monarchy, although essentially a reaction against the Roman Curia, sounds strange and unreal to the modern ear. Nor is the strangeness diminished when we note that his theory drove him to speak with some puerility of the deceased Black Prince as especially devoted to the Trinity. His tendency to assert the untrammeled supremacy of the King in State and Church left nothing for a rapacious monarch like Henry VIII to imagine. His plea that all clerical endowments should be confiscated for the spiritual advantage of the Church would have gained the hearty assent of that monarch's unspeakably greedy nobles; whereas they could afford to ignore his *caveat* that the poor ought to be beneficiaries of the confiscation. Once they were allowed to appropriate properties to which they had not a vestige of right, they used them strictly for themselves alone.

The keynote of his doctrine, that whatever was of importance to national welfare came within the reigning monarch's jurisdiction, was simply open absolutism. What more could the Tudors or their lords and leeches want for their work of absorption, than Wyclif's overture to assess all Church funds and holdings, or his rash statement that it was lawful to pull down a Church to build a fortress and to melt chalices to pay soldiers? As a matter of fact, most of the monastic spoils which Henry's sycophants and flatterers did not bag were squandered on the defense of Calais. How Thomas Cromwell and the barons who fattened on sacrilege would have exulted in Wyclif's statement that the folly of pious ancestors who had endowed the Church should be corrected! These gross and selfish plunderers would have assented, with a grimace, to his qualifications that what really mattered was not gold or silver, but the pure worship of God. The robbers of the English Guilds inflicted upon the nation's social life the greatest depredation of the Reformation era. It may have been that in defense of their thefts they quoted Wyclif's excoriation of the Guilds because of their masses for the dead. In truth, this was the reason put forward by those who first destroyed them, and then pocketed their wealth.

The Reformer really advocated the divine right of kings, especially against the priesthood. Like Luther, two hundred years afterward, what he took from Popes he gave to princes. It was useless for him to insist that "all the king's work should be copied from the justice of God." For Richard II, Henry VII, his despicable son, and every similarly disposed despot since them, this glittering generality would have been no more than an invitation to conscienceless autocracy. There is not a vestige of proof that contemporary rulers heeded Wyclif's pious admonition to be merciful in their use of unlicensed power. On the contrary, there is abundant evidence that, although they did not recognize his main propositions, they acted upon them. Yet in spite of his unguarded utterances about the obedience due to the Crown, Wyclif had little sympathy with the non-resistance theory of the Reformation, so sedulously preached by seventeenth century divines. By a scholastic paradox, which he endeavored to ratify from the writings of Grosseteste, he maintained that sometimes the truest obedience lay in resistance. If you are inclined to censure his intellectual vagaries, recall that, like Hildebrand, he too attempted the impossible. He was intent upon the king's supremacy as against that of the Papacy, and upon the preservation of popular rights against all supremacy. History afterwards showed how necessary it was to redress the balance of the monarchical power which he favored, by the execution of Charles I, the banishment of his son James, and also by the substitution of ministerial for monarchial responsibility. Yet could Wyclif have predicted these epoch-making events, he would have been above our plane of inquiry. It is in his claim that no institution, whatsoever its excellent qualities, was immune from dissolution, that we should recognize and revere his heroical efforts in behalf of progress. He stood almost alone among the thinkers of his day for the unity of the realm and against the special privileges of clericalism in matters of law. In these respects, at any rate, he ceased to agitate against evils at the peril of worse evils, and became prophetical.

With this hasty treatment of Wyclif our review of mediæval concepts and of their results can perhaps appropriately end. When problems of Church and State were afterwards debated by Luther, Calvin and other sixteenth century leaders, two decisive factors had intervened. The Reformation and its progeny in Nationalism had displaced the ideas and policies of Roman supremacy. The wealth of the New World in the West, and the trade routes that opened up the homes and empires of the human race in the far East, gave to vigorous and aggressive Commonwealths an unprecedented self-sufficiency. With their ascent to power the dreams of a world State ended. Colossal figures like Hildebrand, Innocent III and Charles the Great sank into the statuesque repose of history. The political theories and ecclesiastical ideals of Dante and Wyclif and of their opponents, though not of Marsiglio, assumed an archaic aspect. The hymns of St. Thomas Aquinas, of St. Bonaventura, of Thomas of Celano, gradually acquired the quaint flavor which accentuates their quality. Legends of the Arthurian cycle became more legendary still. The songs of gay Troubadours lost their vivacious charm. Yet I do not envy the individual who exults in the downfall of so much majesty and strength, or who fails to see in it a solemn warning for the period in which we live. For we too have known vile and blood-stained monarchs, lying leaders, treacherous diplomatists, peoples insatiate for vengeance, or for power and territory. The devotion that built the Universities and Cathedrals; the spirit that inspired the early Friars and the Dantean epic, are scarcely outdone by the best aspirations of our mechanistic age. Although it has a zeal which is more accordant with knowledge, and has achieved more useful, if not more permanent ends, we who belong to it cannot study, without grave memories and reflections, the collapse of Mediævalism and its meanings for the modern era.

EIGHTH LECTURE

THE RISE OF NATIONALISM

" . . . . Prognostics told
Man's near approach; so in man's self arise
August anticipations, symbols, types
Of a dim splendor ever on before
In that eternal circle life pursues.
For men begin to pass their nature's bound,
And find new hopes and cares which fast supplant
Their proper joys and griefs; they grow too great
For narrow creeds of right and wrong, which fade
Before the unmeasured thirst for good: while peace
Rises within them ever more and more.
Such men are even now upon the earth,
Serene amid the half-formed creatures round
Who should be saved by them and joined with them."

ROBERT BROWNING: *Paracelsus,* Part V.

EIGHTH LECTURE

THE RISE OF NATIONALISM

The need of an Eirenicon between Roman Catholics and Protestants — Interregnum between Hildebrand and Luther — Grosseteste, Bishop of Lincoln — Religious sources of the Sixteenth Century Revolt — Luther at the Diet of Worms — Defeat and abdication of Charles V — The decline of Protestant freedom — The supplanting of reformers by princes and legalists — Calvin's intervention — The influence of the Renaissance — Erasmus, Colet and More — The Bible as the Rock of free nations — Puritanism in Great Britain, Europe and America — The Wars of Nationalism — The separatism of Protestantism and its recovery of the reasoning mind — The age of revolution — State worship and its Nemesis — The higher discipline and obedience.

WESTERN civilization has manifold faults and vices, and one compensating virtue. It is capable of change and therefore of progress; it moves because it lives; it reorganizes its forces and accepts their new forms; it is courageous enough to go through life's adventure. The rise of modern Nationalism is perhaps the largest verifiable proof of these assertions. As a historic movement it is bound up with Protestantism, which, in turn, had its original source, not in Church or State, but in the hearts and consciences of individual men. Both Nationalism and Protestantism are comparatively young in the world, and their past or present relations should receive that flexibility of treatment which best suits their youth. Such treatment is seldom given them by their ardent defenders. However sincere and amenable, they are apt to express a belief in their principles which is not always warranted by past experience. Since persons seldom outgrow their inherited ideas or special callings, they may be depended upon to deduce what they desire, not from facts, but from a tangle of generalities. In these habits they resemble the detective Bernadet in one of Jules Claretie's stories, who supposed a picture reflected in the murdered victim's eye was the actual assassin himself, and narrowly escaped responsibility for a serious miscarriage of justice. So the people who imagine that the Reformation was a sudden revolt against decadent Mediævalism, which was miraculously led by the son of a German peasant, and had no connection with what went before it, miss the true interpretation of a world-shaping event.

Protestant partisans formerly accounted for the Lutheran upheaval by painting the previous régime absolutely black; nothing was grey or neutral, and this, despite the fact that had its flagrancies been so intolerable, they would have insured their own extermination. The Church of the age was caricatured. "A superficial account of the traffic in indulgences, and a rough and ready assumption which even Köstlin makes that the darkness was greatest just before the dawn," were the crude overtures to a revolt that shook all Christian States. Their difficulty was that they proved too much, for conditions were no better and no worse immediately before the revolt than they had been for centuries, and German complaints of papal tyranny go back to Hildegard.[1] On the other hand, the idea of National Churches as the parents of Nationalism has often been misrepresented by those papal partisans who seldom, if ever, judged it by a fair comparison with its alternative. They ignored the pivotal truth that the concept of a Church, universal in organization but autocratic in government, had failed because of its inability to make room for the two most powerful forces in the modern world — those of freedom and of patriotism. These forces have their defects. They need the instruction and the discipline which it is the duty of the Church to impart. But they must not be airily dismissed from the sixteenth and preceding centuries by those who attempt to nullify history in

[1] Cf. "Encyclopædia Britannica," (Eleventh Edition), Vol. XXIII, p. 4 ff.

ascribing to Mediævalism a fictitious ecclesiastical or imperial rectitude.

The student who does not know the best which has been thought and said by unbiased authorities on such issues is also fairly sure to set an undue value upon some conventional ideas of the Reformation period. These ideas need a thorough revision because of their mischief making extravagance. They excite hate and calumny; create religious prejudice, and sadden every informed lover of his fellow men. Nor will the separations and jealousies that weaken Christianity be removed until the apparently exhaustless credulity of factionists is abandoned by common consent. If, then, we are to deal justly with an era in which many noble loves were inspired, and many cheated loves were turned to utter loathing, not a few popular conceptions about it will have to be sanitated. Chronicles that unduly embellish its events must be used discriminatingly. Men who own allegiance to one Lord must cease to speak and write as though they had nothing but animosities to gratify, or selfish interests to advance. The healing of the Church and the settling of the world depend upon a more eirenic disposition in the two great branches of Western Christianity. The commendable aspirations of Nationalism, the moral ideals that should be supported, the dreams of betterment by our finer spirits, and the practical needs which political leaders almost despair of meeting, cannot be materially helped by a contentious Christianity. If its Gospel is to become more social, collective and international; if it is to embrace, as never before, the whole life of mankind, emphatically it must be inspired by the love which St. Paul prayed "may abound yet more and more in knowledge and all discernment; . . . being filled with the fruits of righteousness, which are through Jesus Christ, unto the glory and praise of God " [2]

In this temper we would now proceed to survey briefly the formative elements of the modern Church and State,

[2] Philippians I. 9 ff.

which were active from the reign of Hildebrand to the birth of Luther in 1483. Life was anything but stagnant during that period. Its associations were seldom a fixed quantity, and their changes were traceable to the fact that some rulers were as pilots asleep in the storm, while others seemed able to still it for a space. As we have seen already, the supremacy of the Holy See was formerly advocated by many of the best minds of the interregnum. Convinced that the safety of the world and of the Church lay in her connection with Rome, they endeavored to guard her against secular interferences with her freedom or her reform. Among those thus convinced was Robert Grosseteste, Bishop of Lincoln, Chancellor of Oxford, and one of the foremost Englishmen of his own or of any other day. As energetic as Luther, Grosseteste went beyond him in statesmanship, and often attained an elevation of conduct inaccessible to reason alone. The genuineness of his "sharp epistle" to Master Innocent, the representative of Pope Innocent IV in England, cannot be seriously questioned. A manuscript copy of the correspondence is kept at Corpus Christi College, Cambridge. Its fierce blast against the imposing pretensions of the Holy See was heard again in Grosseteste's Memorandum, presented at Lyons in 1250.

This public-spirited Bishop has been described by Matthew of Paris as "the chastiser of prelates, the corrector of monks, the director of priests, the trainer of clerks, the supporter of scholars, the preacher of the people, the persecutor of the unchaste, the diligent student of the Scriptures, the open confuter of the Popes, the hammerer and despiser of the Romans." [3] The description excites anticipations which the reading of the Memorandum satisfies. It praised Catholicism, but also suggested Nationalism, and while asserting the true function and necessity of the Holy See, defined the limits of its authority. The reigning Pontiff was censured for creating a needless crisis in the Church, and the theory of Anglican

[3] Cf. A. L. Smith: "Church and State in the Middle Ages," p. 102.

independence was foreshadowed against papal tactlessness and violence. But Grosseteste's rebukes and warnings passed almost unheeded at a moment when many enormous wrongs crippled society. The spiritual prospects of Europe darkened as the great Prelate came to the close of his life. He died predicting doom for the Catholicism which he had loved too deeply for his own peace, and upon which his wisdom and piety seemed to have been wasted. His complaints, and those of contemporaries, were the tidal movements of an otherwise stagnant sea which preceded the inundation that two hundred years later swallowed up the last vestiges of Mediæval Imperialism.

One is curious to know what were the ideas of the laymen, priests, merchants, guildsmen and peasants of Grosseteste's age. In the mass they seem to have been indifferent to the quarrels of their temporal and spiritual overseers. Prayers were said, crops were sown and reaped, homes kept up, and the daily round of duty done by men and women whose religion was an admixture of simple trust, sound sense, primitive notions and emotional impulses.[4] They often set a peaceful example to those militant superiors who fought to the last for their philosophic or political theories. The reception they gave to the earlier Franciscans showed with what readiness the plain people heard a purer Gospel. But since for two hundred years few of them knew whether the Vicar of Christ lived in Italy or France, the comfort and strength of their faith were denied them; and the denial proved exceedingly detrimental to papal authority. To damage the essentials of a national religion is always a serious offense. To damage those essentials among the mediæval peoples, whose vices and virtues were in closest proximity, within whom were the ageless contentions of barbarism and civilized living, made the offense malignant.

Here and there the customary opposites of the period as-

[4] Cf. G. G. Coulton: "The Plain Man's Religion in the Middle Ages," in "The Hibbert Journal," April, 1916. p. 592 ff.

serted themselves, and opinions were advanced which showed that all was not so well with the Church as her defenders claimed. The supposed harmony and solidity of pre-Reformation society were not without their accusers; its "wanton disruption" is not to be ascribed solely to the "inexplicable Luther." For if the two centuries before he appeared were often mired in a morass of corruptions, they were also certainly stirred by "prologues to the omen coming on." It was the period of Savonarola as well as of Machiavelli; of declining interest in creeds, and of a heightening realization of the truths above all creeds. The Revival of Learning belonged to it, and so did a shameless recrudescence of follies and superstitions. It saw the discovery of the New World, and also the persecutions of the Holy Office; the conquest of the Moors in Spain, and also the triumph of Islam at Gallipoli; the first great Catholic Missions to heathen peoples, and also the renewal of cultured paganism in high ecclesiastics. In it the growth of thought and action suffered from the past; the future struggled to escape from the present. These oppositions generated in turn the conditions in which rebellion could not only prosper, but be warmly indorsed by one half the monarchs of Europe.

II

Although individuals, and often large groups, even given regions, had rejected the Roman authority, yet until the burning of the Canon Law by Luther, no temporal prince had publicly forsaken the international Church-State of which the Pontiff was the Head. After the Reformer's act, kings and their agents who accepted it furthered its results. They declared that the temporal power which had been ordained of God for "the chastisement of the wicked and the protection of the good" should now be permitted to exercise its functions "unhampered throughout the whole Christian body without respect to persons." Its subjection to the papal rule was ended with a suddenness which revealed the bitter resentment the rule had engendered. Such was the final outcome of the conflict between the Empire and the Papacy, and the Protestant Revolt is to be understood in the light of that conflict. The mediæval relations between Church and Empire, the abuses that impaired them, the friction to which Popes like Innocent IV, Boniface VIII and John XXII added their full share, the absolutist theories of rulers that have since dug the graves of empires, were alike parts of the process which made Nationalism the political ideal of modern Europe and America.[5]

The separation of the State from churchly control was given a free hand, for which the differences between Eastern and Western Christianity, not yet discussed here, furnished a historic precedent. After the declining Roman Empire found it necessary to have two capitals, Byzantium and Rome, the varying tendencies of their respective subjects took shape in a division between the Eastern and Western Churches. The division did not arise from any real schism in the Faith, but from opposing conceptions of civil authority which were accentuated by diversities of language and of modes of thought. "The State continued to exist in the East after it had fallen in the West. The Church went with it, and continued to present the Faith in the old forms with which the Eastern peoples were familiar. In the West, where the old State had disappeared, the Church stepped into its place, and maintained the appearance of a religious Commonwealth, whose civil affairs were administered by local rulers. . . . Its innovations were rejected as unlawful by the more settled and conservative East. The consequent separation destroyed the idea of one Church united in outward organization. There was still one Church, united essentially in one Faith, and setting it forth in the world; but it differed about the mode of government and the method of teaching."[6] It

[5] Cf. "Encyclopædia Britannica," (Eleventh Edition), Vol. XXIII. p. 4 ff.
[6] Bishop Mandell Creighton: "The Church and the Nation," p. 209 f.

is interesting to note that Russia, where the Eastern Church gained national dignity, preserved the Byzantine tradition that in all matters outside the sphere of dogma the ecclesiastical was subordinate to the civil power. There were lapses from this position, however, and to prevent their recurrence Peter the Great wiped out the Patriarchate for the time being, and entrusted the administration of the Church to a Synod entirely dependent upon the imperial government.[7]

The most vigorous protests obviously remain negative if they only show how deeply embedded men and institutions are in their erroneous methods and policies. From this viewpoint, the mere mobilization of Church and State in some new forms does not present the constructive side of the Reformation. True, the Church had long ceased to be Catholic before Luther renounced the Roman supremacy, and her Eastern branch was always an indirect reminder of the neglected rights of Councils and of nations. But without those spiritual principles by which all human movements live, the sixteenth century revolt could scarcely have survived. Leaders soon cease to lead, rallying cries are soon hushed, procrustean moralities soon resume their limitations, unless a united purpose, as strong in reason as it is in righteousness, animates reforms and reformers. Nothing purely secular stands alone; it is either built into the divine dwellingplace of the spirit, or fated to perish.

Those permanent elements of every age, which are its intellectual, ethical and religious forces, lived in "the honest monk" whom Cardinal Cajetan summoned before him, but summarily dismissed as "a beast with deep-set eyes, and strange speculations in his head." It has been said that there was method in Luther's seeming madness, because he made his onslaught on the Pope and the Curia when it coincided with the political ambitions of the northern nations. But though his earlier legal studies had prepared him to sympathize with the German Church and Empire against Roman

[7] Cf. Walter F. Adeney: "The Greek and Eastern Churches," p. 355 ff

aggressions, for some years before he nailed his famous theses to the Church doors at Wittenberg, external matters of any kind were banished from him by his spiritual perplexities. He sought in Holy Scripture a solution of the engrossing problem of man's personal salvation. So far back as 1511 he had visited Rome in the course of his quest, but he found little in the Holy City's ritualistic pomp and spiritual poverty to assist him in ascertaining how the individual can be just before his Maker. On his return to the University at Wittenberg, where he became a Doctor of Biblical Theology, he began to preach "Justification by Faith" throughout Saxony.

This preaching, novel to an age deprived of evangelical instruction, collided head on with the entrenched system and its sacerdotal castes. Tetzel, a Dominican monk, who had been commissioned by Pope Leo X to travel throughout Germany selling indulgences in the form of stamped tickets at the rate of a few ducats for the graver sins, furnished the occasion for Luther's defiance. But its real source lay in his recent and more personal and immediate experiences of religion. To them we must look, and to the writings of St. Paul, for the origin of German Protestantism. Had the Reformer not pondered over his own inward difficulties, he would never have spoken as he did; had he not absorbed the teaching of the letters to the Romans and the Galatians, he would scarcely have known what to say. Once more those who belittle theological controversy should recall that in its crucible modern Nationalism was fused. For good or ill, its unforeseen consequences sprang from Luther's interpretation of that Pauline doctrine which had been shaped for Christian purposes by the legal ideas of Rome.

Luther's truce with the Holy See was skillfully arranged by Cardinal Miltitz, only to be broken by Dr. Eck, who challenged the rebel to a public disputation on Indulgences at Leipzig. It could have been no more than a transient peace unless he surrendered the doctrine of "Justification by Faith," and this he would not do. Consequently he had to encounter

Charles V at Worms in April, 1521. This young prince ruled a twofold domain which included Spain and Portugal on the one side; and on the other, Austria, Burgundy and the Netherlands. As against the strength of his Empire, which appeared more imposing than it actually was, Luther had only the assurance of his personal belief and his conscience, and the support of his German friends. Naturally enough, Charles was intent on religious unity as the basis of political unity, and he announced that to stay the plague of these heretical opinions, he would peril "kingdoms, treasures and friends; body and blood, and life and soul." Emperor and Pope, sworn foes in nearly everything else, were united against the rising rebellion that centered in the new Nationalism. On the very day when the imperial edict against Luther was to be signed, May 8, 1521, a private treaty was concluded between Charles and Leo X, in which the latter agreed to help the Emperor to drive his brilliant rival, Francis I, King of France, out of Milan and Genoa.[8] Henry VIII of England, another monarch then in the prime of life, who added little to the credit or tranquility of the age, rushed into print to vanquish the daring schismatic, and was decked by Leo with the proud title, "Defender of the Faith;" a distinction which Henry's subsequent behavior did very little to adorn.[9] What could have sustained Luther against these potentates, despite the help he received from Frederick of Saxony and like-minded men, had he not been fortified by the power higher than that of earth, which finally turns the scale for truth and justice against fearful odds?

Following a series of negotiations and skirmishes, in 1555 the Diet of Augsburg formally enacted the religious settlement which is still the basis of the German policy. It was a compromise between the defeated Charles and his Protes-

[8] For a comprehensive discussion of these episodes see A. Taylor Innes: "Church and State," p. 111 ff.

[9] Cf. "Henry VIII" by James Gairdner in "The Cambridge Modern History," Vol. II. Chapter XIII; Preserved Smith: "The Age of the Reformation," Chapter VI.

tant foes, which stipulated that the supreme Civil Power in each nation must choose whether the State religion should be Roman or Lutheran. Thus the obscure monk whom Leo hastily derided humilated Pope and Emperor. Charles now resigned his burdensome regalities and retired to the lovely retreat at Yuste. There, after muddling the fortunes of half a dozen countries, he spent the last two years of his life in making clocks. He never ceased to regret that he had not violated the safe conduct which brought the Reformer to Worms, for he imagined he could have rescued the Church from schism by repeating in Luther's case the infamous betrayal of Huss at Constance.

None could plunge into the tumult and deviltry of Europe's soul, as Luther did, and hope to escape its contagion. "Nor must it be forgotten that no great leader ever flung about wild words in such a reckless way." [10] This was evidenced by his conduct during the Peasants' War in 1525, waged by them to throw off an oppressive feudal yoke from which there was no appeal save by force. At first Luther proposed arbitration, but when his proposal fell through, and the trouble spread, his innate conservatism reasserted itself. He denounced the insurrection with disgraceful vehemence, and urged the suppression of the helpless peasants whom their rulers slaughtered wholesale. The Anabaptists also aroused his indignation, though they but extended his favorite principle of individualism; and many of them only asked for the liberty of conscience which had been asserted by Luther himself in his conflict with the papal authorities. The leaders of the sect ran to fanatical extremes in their plea that the believer's inner light was his sole guide, requiring neither divine revelation nor human inventions for its maintenance;

[10] Cf. T. M. Lindsay: "A History of the Reformation," Vol. I, p. 326 ff; A. C. McGiffert: "Martin Luther, the Man and His Work"; Preserved Smith: "The Life and Letters of Martin Luther"; "The Cambridge Modern History," Vol. II. "The Reformation," Chapters IV., V., VI.; Preserved Smith: "The Age of the Reformation," Chapter II.; H. O. Taylor: "Thought and Expression in the Sixteenth Century," Vol. I. Chapters VIII. and IX.

and Romanists and Lutherans combined against these schismatics as enemies of order. One of their chief offenses was the precept that no Christian should accept political office, or use the sword, or engage in armed conflict. The merciless treatment dealt out to them showed that the older purer motives of the Lutheran Reformation were exhausted, and that a new orientation had robbed it of much moral energy. A general reaction against liberty had set in; toleration was tabooed; and oppressive practices were established which existed until very recently in German rule.

III

At first Luther declared that Christians had the right to test every theory for themselves, and to believe in all matters as their experience of God's forgiving love suggested. Later, he had so far retreated as to say that Zwingli, who strongly resisted State interference in Church affairs, was no Christian. He advised force against unsound doctrine. Preachers who opposed him were to be displaced, and heretics punished for their profanity. The Church was made the helot of the State in his intolerant claim that the latter must judge who were heretical; a subjection, be it noted, that the Holy See never made.[11] The prophet of religious reform had become the agent of political power. Freedom of conscience and Church independence were his watchwords from 1521 to 1525. After this date he invoked the secular arm against the Papists, and urged that the sword had been committed to princes that they might penalize the ungodly. The Elector Frederick reminded the irate Reformer of his previous teaching that believers should rely solely upon the Sacred Word. But he and his associates, separated from Western Christianity, and from the bulk of their fellow countrymen, became the instruments of German princes, and paid for their support with servility and truckling. Even Melanchthon, without whose colder genius Luther could not have received the support of

[11] Cf. Lord Acton: "History of Freedom," p. 155 ff.

the Universities, admitted that the decrees of the Lutheran Church were merely platonic utterances until ratified by political rulers. The weakness of Lutheranism lay in the fact that it adopted as its motto, "Cujus regio," thus constituting the political basis of the State the basis of religion, and making the religion of any province dependent upon the prince. This has practically been the basis of German history. Indeed, the exaggeration of the State, which has always been the weakness of Germany, manifested itself as far back as the Reformation, and was the actual cause of so many internal divisions. Toleration became a political matter from the first, but owing to the theory of the State, it scarcely existed until its lesson was driven in by the Thirty Years' War.

Nevertheless the principles of the Augsburg Confession of 1530, and of other Protestant Confessions embodying similar views of Church and State, were landmarks in the history of Nationalism which could not be removed. The one from which I quote was drafted by Melanchthon under Luther's personal direction: "Concerning civil affairs, our churches teach that civil ordinances, when they are lawful, are good works of God, and that it is right for Christians to take the magistrate's office. . . . Christians, therefore must of necessity obey their governors and laws, save only when they command to sin, for then they must obey God rather than men. . . . We are compelled, therefore, for the satisfaction of men's consciences, to set forth the distinction between the ecclesiastical power and the power of the sword. We have no doubt, that both of them because of God's commandment, are dutifully to be reverenced and honored, as God's greatest blessings on this earth. But our view as to the distinction is this: The power of the keys, or the power of bishops, is, according to the gospels, a power or commission from God of preaching the gospel, of remitting and retaining sins, and of administering the sacraments. . . . Seeing, then, that the ecclesiastical power deals with things eternal, and is exercised only by the ministry of the word, it does not interfere with (*non impedit*) the administration of civil affairs, any more than does the art of singing. For the administration of civil affairs has to deal with other matters than the gospel deals with. The magistrate does not defend men's minds, but their bodies, and other corporeal things, against manifest injuries; and he coerces men by the sword and by corporal pains, in order to uphold civil justice and peace. Wherefore the ecclesiastical and civil powers are not to be confounded. The ecclesiastical has its own command to preach the gospel and to administer the sacraments. Let it not intrude into the office of another than itself; let it not transfer the kingdoms of this world; let it not abrogate the magistrate's laws; let it not withdraw from them lawful obedience; let it not hinder judicial decisions touching any civil ordinances or contracts; let it not prescribe laws to the magistrates as to the form of the Commonwealth. In this way do our teachers distinguish the functions of either power, while they exhort men to hold both in honor, and to acknowledge both as the gift and blessing of God." [12]

Although this, the first Protestant definition of the separated provinces of Church and State, clearly defined their independent yet coördinate functions, its careful reading arouses mingled feelings. The advance it made in liberal ideas was really a return to those of the early Church, and of the mediæval period before Hildebrand's Pontificate. It relinquished in theory the prosecution of heretics by the State, but it was without a hint of the wider toleration which nearly all churches have been reluctant to admit. In it are the germs of that deified Nationalism which is now everywhere suspect, and which has made other thinkers besides Coleridge differentiate a national Church from a Christian Church. There is nothing, as Dr. Richard Roberts remarks, in the principle of nationality to make it intrinsically exclusive.[13]

[12] Cf. A. Taylor Innes: "Church and State," p. 128 f.
[13] "The Church and the Commonwealth," p. 61 f.

On the contrary, there in no reason why it should not become an integral unit in the coöperative catholicity of an undivided Church. But the identification of the spiritual interests of Protestantism with those of secular Monarchs and their ministers was subversive of its catholicity, and degraded it to the level of a worldly corporation. It lacked that spirit in which rivalries are harmonized, and therefore could not avoid the burdens of material policy. That Luther had his qualms about this possible outcome is shown by his treatise, "On the Secular State and How Far Obedience is Due to It," in which he insisted that "God cannot and will not allow any one but Himself to rule the soul," and that when the temporal authority encroaches upon the spiritual domain it is impotent. The Emperor governs body, gold and good; the heart is reserved to the control of its Creator. But the Reformer made concessions to political expedience which confirmed the previous determination of the German princes to hang and burn for heresy, and to disregard minority rights.

Lord Acton asserts that by regarding the protection of orthodoxy as their principal business, they put out of sight the more immediate duties of government, and caused the political objects of the State to disappear behind its religious ends. The sacred ichor of pontifical blood began to run in their veins. Their government was judged, in the eyes of Protestants, by its fidelity to the Protestant Church. "If it fulfilled these requirements, no other complaints against it could be entertained. A tyrannical prince could not be resisted if he was orthodox; a just prince could be dethroned if he failed in the more essential condition of faith. In this way Protestantism became favorable at once to despotism and to revolution, and was ever ready to sacrifice good government to its own interests. It subverted monarchies, and, at the same time, denounced those who, for political causes, sought their subversion; but though the monarchies it subverted were sometimes tyrannical, and the seditions it prevented sometimes revolutionary, the order it defended or sought to establish was never legitimate and free, for it was always invested with the function of religious proselytism, and with the obligation of removing every traditional, social, or political right or power which could oppose the discharge of that essential duty." [14]

The religious values of the Reformation were materially reduced by the conduct of its divines at Augsburg. They ceased to be the shepherds of the people. The energy and moderation with which they had proposed reforms that were afterwards demonstrated as necessary by the Council of Trent, seemed to desert them in the task of governing the insurgent Churches. If the institutions of the fifteenth century were no longer adequate for the life of the Spirit, those of the sixteenth likewise began to reveal their inadequacy. A disproportionate intellectual and political progress was procured at the cost of spiritual progress. Prophets and reformers made way for legalists and publicists; vital issues were deferred to the material prosperity of the State. Hence in the sentiment of Nationalism which it evoked there was nothing original. It was one of the main tenets of Luther's Reformation, out of which old history and new ideas produced Nationalism's dominating force. Viscount Morley indicts it for its "oppression, intolerable economic disorder, governmental failure, senseless wars, senseless ambition, and the misery that was their baleful fruit." Nationality "first inflamed visionaries, then it grew potent with the multitudes, who thought the foreigner the author of their wretchedness. Thus Nationality went through all the stages. From instinct it became idea; from idea abstract principle; then fervid prepossession; ending where it is today, in dogma, whether accepted or evaded." [15] If Canossa warns us against the evils of unlicensed Imperialism, surely the annals of the last four centuries warn us against the evils of unlicensed Nationalism. Both theories of government displaced the bal-

[14] "History of Freedom," p. 181.
[15] "Politics and History," p. 46 f.

ance between the visible and the invisible realms; and, by so doing, jeopardized the entire structure of society.

Luther saved his movement by sacrificing one of its chief contentions. Calvin, as we have already said, took command of its bewildered forces, and directed them in behalf of Protestant Nationalism. There was need of his intervention, for Anabaptist and Zwinglian doctrines, and those who assumed arms in their defense, might have disorganized Protestantism at the start but for his masterly counter strokes. His theory of the State, which has been mentioned in an earlier lecture, implied rather than defined its relation with the Church. The theocratic conception of government which prompted all his ideas was republican rather than democratic in nature, for Calvin himself was not disposed to trust the multitudes.[16] Although princes and nobles came to his assistance, he depended chiefly upon the middle classes: the burghers, merchants, yeomen and artisans of the larger cities and towns which were usually the centers of municipal freedom, and of the rights of the growing State. History shows that one class is continually merging into another and inheriting its power and its apprehensions. So, as the world goes, there will probably be a middle class of some sort in all social formations.[17] But this concession should not debar us from recognizing that the particular middle class which imbibed Calvinism, from the seventeenth century to the present time, has perhaps accomplished more for Democracy than either the aristocracies or the proletariat.

IV

The twilight dawn of Protestantism could not have broken, nor would it have broadened into the noon of Nationalism, save for the Renaissance which began approximately in 1485. From an inclusive viewpoint, the Reformation, whether Lu-

[16] " Cf. Viscount Bryce: " Modern Democracies," Vol. I. p. 84 ff.
[17] Cf. John Corbin: " The Return of the Middle Class."

theran, Genevan or Anglican in kind, was only another aspect of the Renaissance. But "without Christianity, the Renaissance itself would have been impossible."[18] Speculations that seldom passed from literary into actual history attended the Revival of Learning. Yet behind their discontent and intellectual ingenuity were settled purposes for social regeneration, that have profoundly influenced the nations of northern Europe and America. The benefits of democratic Nationalism in those nations have been the prelude to present individual self-determination.

So the cycle is completed between the fifteenth century and our own; and not a few thinkers wonder whether we can reasonably expect a second Renaissance as the ultimate sequel of the first. Be this as it shall prove, we cannot do justice here to a movement of general exaltation like that of the Renaissance proper. It achieved advances in every sphere which in their turn made possible the modern world of politics, literature, art, science and learning. The abstractions of the Scholastics, and the religious mysteries of the Church palled upon the Humanists of the fifteenth and sixteenth centuries. In Italy, and later in France, they magnified the pre-Christian past, and gave prominence to its philosophical and artistic forms. Theology became the Cinderella of the classics; the study of Greek in Plato and in the New Testament discounted dogma and instilled a practical or a critical attitude. In England the native dislike for speculation has since given rise to a new short catechism: "What is mind?" "No Matter." "What is Matter?" "Never Mind." Men returned to ancient ways by restoring to the Bible its apostolic honor. Their love of religion, as well as of intellectual liberty, made them eager to place popular versions of the Scriptures in the hands of the people. They coveted truth more than they coveted art, and were intent upon a civilized freedom as the source of culture and social progress.

These were the salient characteristics of the New Learning

[18] Miguel de Unamuno: "The Tragic Sense of Life," p. 112.

which had vital relations with the rise of nations. Its painters, architects, romancers, poets; its splendid or decrepit dreamers; its immoral braveries, bombastic rhetoric and pagan proclivities, do not directly concern us. It was the ethical and not the æsthetic strength of the Renaissance that helped to destroy the ancient seats of political power, and to transfer their sovereignty to the Northern peoples. Erasmus showed the movement's excellence when he resolved to bring the documents of historic Christianity into line with those of classic authors, and to make a beginning with the Greek text of the New Testament, and a new Latin translation of it, in parallel columns. This work he proposed to call the "Novum Instrumentum," and such it was in many and beneficial ways. Mark Pattison asserts that, "it contributed to the *liberation of the human mind* from the thraldom of the clergy more than all the uproar and rage of Luther's many pamphlets. . . . It revealed the fact that the Vulgate, the Bible of the Church, was not only a second-hand document, but, in many places an erroneous document. A shock was thus given to the credit of the clergy in the province of literature, equal to that given in the provinces of science by the astronomical discoveries of the seventeenth century." [19] In the preface to his translation Erasmus wrote: "I wish that even the weakest women should read the Gospel — should read the Epistles of Paul. And I wish these were translated into all languages, so that they might be read and understood, not only by Scots and Irishmen, but also by Turks and Saracens. It may be that they might be ridiculed by many, but some would take them to heart. I long that the husbandman should sing portions of them to himself as he follows the plough, that the weaver should hum them to the tune of his shuttle, that the traveller should beguile with their stories the tedium of his journey." [20]

Some writers insist that what is wanted to deliver modern

[19] Cf. "London Times Literary Supplement," November 23, 1922, p. 754.
[20] Cf. T. M. Lindsay: "A History of the Reformation," Vol. I. p. 174.

States from their present distresses is not values but explanations, not aspirations and good wishes, but a larger control of human conditions. Others inform us that these conditions are already fully subject to human control, and speak as though the constituents of a reasonable life were always the same and always available. They contend, in the Socratic manner, that the lesson of life has been learned by the wise, and needs but to be taught by them to the obstinate and the ignorant. But the history of Nationalism testifies that the moral significance of society is made by its spiritual readjustments. This is plainly seen in the movements of the sixteenth century. They were not sheltered in safe harbors. The tempestuous elements which always surround human life were then lashed to fury. At intervals the hurricane seemed to drive Humanists, Catholics and Protestants, none knew whither. The great anchorage of the Reformation Age was in the Bible. No individual or party intent on change helped men and women to outride the storm as did this ancient literature. It connected their pressing necessities with its multiform sources of relief, including within its ministry every problem and aspect of human existence.

Monarchs who exercised by "divine right" an unquestioned authority hitherto acceded to none save Popes and Emperors, and statesmen who endeavored to reconcile that "right" with the public welfare, alike resorted to the Bible for their support. Rival Popes during the Avignon Schism, and reformers and traditionalists of the sixteenth century, constituted the Book their final Court of Appeal. Claims for freedom of speculation made by Catholics or Protestants, Jesuits or Puritans, against rulers of a creed different than their own, were allowed or disallowed on Scriptural grounds. Not only the sale of indulgences or the oppressions and immoralities of the clergy, but the wrongs wrought by princes and pastors of the Reformed Faith were liable to impeachments framed upon the word of Prophets and Apostles. The growing individualism of the industrial and merchant classes, which displeased the fuedalistic class, was judged by Scriptural teachings. Unendurable governmental machines were smashed by patriots who quoted the Bible as their warrant for war upon tyrants. It stood in the wide breach made by the removal of the papal federalism of the Middle Ages. Upon it the builders of nations erected their defenses, and by its standards they were approved or condemned.

Sociologists tell us that the historical tendency to organize the human race into political States is actuated by blood, by tradition, and in a general sense, by culture. Doubtless these are among the causes of Nationalism, but its safety and continuance were derived from the Sacred Oracles. Where they were honored, States rose to a higher plane of civilization; where they were little known, States sank to a lower plane. The subordinate nations, which, in a vaguer definition, consisted in an external government of different peoples, without community of habit or belief, were advantaged by the principles such government obtained from the Bible. Britons, Colonial Americans and Hollanders might have lost their acquired territories but for its counsel and guidance. Whatever the condition of heterogeneous racial elements under one rule may be today, unquestionably their political, economic and moral interests have been purified by Biblical doctrines.

Language is one of the chief cohesive forces of Nationalism which the Bible has ennobled. Indeed, its translations are usually the greatest monuments of the speech of civilized States. That of Luther rejuvenated the German people through their language. The Evangelicalism traceable to Wyclif's translation of the whole Bible which he was the first to make into English, though stamped out in his own land, took Bohemia by storm. The King James Version of 1611 has gained deserved supremacy in the English language, and in the English-speaking realm of letters. Its sayings are bone of our bone, flesh of our flesh, woven into the moral fibre of our domestic and national being. John Richard

Green, in his well known tribute to its sway over Puritanism, speaks of the Book as the light and guide of all Englishmen: the source of their ideals, customs, religious and secular beliefs, and of every mode of their self-expression. Their religious experiences, like those of the Scots, the Dutch, the Swiss, the Huguenot French, and the Scandinavian nations, owed their strength and fire to the deliverance effected in them by the Bible. It enjoyed a limited monarchy before the sixteenth century, after which it rose to universal empire in Protestant Europe and America. Current theories of Church and State were dictated by its precepts; politics became its reaction. For one problem which it created, it solved a thousand; for one defeat it incurred, it gained numberless victories. Nationalism, in its gradual ascent toward democracy, has to admit that at every stage the sacred writers of the Orient have been the pathfinders for their more adventurous brothers of the West. They opened the magic casements looking toward the East of which Bunyan dreamed. Their "measured beat of passion in restraint," musical rhythm, picturesque imagery and limitless freedom of moral and religious utterance, are venerated by every patriotic heart and international mind. Their writings are still what they have been for three thousand years: the strength and honor of free nations.[21]

As coercion subsided and intelligence and conscience grew, men who were no longer ignorant of history repaired to Scripture for its explanation. Despondent ones, oppressed by the consciousness of a decay in which each generation seemed inferior to the last, got comfort and hope from its assurance that humanity's future was blessed. By its spirit, even more than by its words, imperishable truths and principles were impressed afresh upon successive periods. New experiments in government and education; new methods for

[21] Cf. W. F. Moulton: "The History of the English Bible"; Ernst von Dobschütz: "The Influence of the Bible on Civilization"; Julius F. Seebach: "The Book of Free Men"; E. W. Work: "The Bible in English Literature."

changing climates of thought and sentiment, were based upon the Divine Revelation which remained a fixity in man's constant flux. Why then should we have to bewail its loss of prestige and authority? For though it is still highly esteemed by numberless Christians, and by devout scholars who have set its light upon a golden candlestick, the masses either give it lip service, or habitually neglect it. Ten States of our Federal Union have shut it out of their public schools; nineteen are silent about its use in them; six require that a portion shall be read daily; six more permit its reading, and the issue is in doubt in Michigan and California. Other English-speaking and continental countries report a similar neglect. The self-deceptions of a democracy which needs direction quite as much as it needs impulse are one explanation of this indifference toward the Book which has been the rock of civilized Nationalism. Another explanation is found in the injurious defenses of its friends, who impose upon it dogmatic ideas it does not require, and which its spirit repudiates. I do not have to further discuss their superfluous additions to its plain text, to its rich varieties of meaning, and its divine humanness. For where men who revere it have misunderstood its inner meanings they could not rob it of its authority. No imaginary ideas about it for the sake of gratified emotions can hide the illumination which streams from its pages: an illumination too real for traditionalists or liberals either to obscure or to forsake.

V

The end is not yet; for the unexhausted significance of the Bible is one of the main reliances of future democracy. Other experiments have to be made in government; other controversies between States will arise; other congested peoples will go on pilgrimages. Whether reason and goodwill, or prejudice and suspicion are to have right of way in their making or unmaking is temporarily uncertain; though we believe it to be finally sure. Meanwhile, it is very easy to be too sure of the forms of higher things at the very moment when their realities are ebbing away. If they preserve these realities they will have to return to the Bible.

But these propositions open much serious and complex debate which is not to our present purpose, except as we detect in them the religious facts and needs they either contain or imply. The deviations of nationalistic politics, the records of peace or war, the work of servants of the State, do not immediately concern us, save as they were also serviceable to the cause of God. We seek the essentials of His Divine Order, which Christianity embodies, the Church represents, and the Bible expresses. We seek them, aware, I trust, that they are now environed by a materialism with which the Bible refuses to bargain, and to which the real welfare of Nationalism is unalterably opposed. At present its political machineries and impersonal things should be devoted to an international expansion in behalf of world amity and concord, which no State can undertake without patience, wisdom, courage, the vision of faith, and that love of mankind which many waters cannot quench. These gifts and graces are purely personal and spiritual. By their aid the Bible was written and modern nations were made free; nothing good has been rightly apprehended apart from them. The better day of democracy may come when it cultivates them again; forsakes a vulgar and sensational literature for the teaching of Biblical realities; abolishes its false gods of self-will and pride for the worship of the one true God; and finds the explanation and the practice of good government, not in mere politics, but in the foreordinations of His Will.

The Renaissance, the Reformation, the various translations of the Bible, Luther's virile personality, and Calvin's formidable intellectualism, were the chief formative factors of modern Nationalism. That of Scotland was derived from Geneva through John Knox; that of England came by the circuitous route of a characteristic independence, intensified by the isolation of the English people, and the resolution of the Plantagenet and Tudor monarchs to govern without outside interference. In Scotland the transition of the State to what eventually proved to be a harmonious and vigorous Nationalism was deferred for a time by the uniting of her ancient northern realm with that of England. But Presbyterian doctrines, the poetry of Burns, the novels of Scott, and the intellectual and commercial integrity of the Scotch people soon gave them an eminence which no modern nation surpasses. Their services to the British Empire and to our Republic have been out of all proportion to the size of their country, or the number of its inhabitants. In England, Nationalism's later courses were so wisely pursued after the revolt of the American Colonies, that they led to the establishment of a series of Commonwealths and of Crown provinces which outvie in extent the former empires of the world. The administration of these vast domains is the model of its kind. Its contributions to civilization and to the general welfare of the race cannot be easily estimated.

Behind all formative factors of sixteenth century Nationalism, however, was that felt lack of system which followed the collapse of Mediævalism. In the ensuing chaos two contrary laws solicited men's obedience. The one was the law of tribalism, obliging them to be always under arms and prepared for battle; the other, the law of peace, urging thrift and industry for the sake of social wellbeing. Founders and reformers of nations discovered that old antagonisms revived in their new associations; that, as Nietzsche said, "Where the State begins, Humanity ends." Torn by factions, unable to agree on anything except to disagree, threatened by foreign foes, deprived of the politico-ecclesiastical system which had been the guardian of their recent past, busy in constructing States at a time when official arrogance, unscrupulous acquisition and oppression were rife, the makers of earlier Nationalism were often compelled to fight, not for conquest but for existence. The Ottoman Turk took his toll of revenge for the earlier Crusades. Religious wars arose between national Churches or between the various sects that divided them. The City of God that was supposed to include the whole of Christendom was supplanted by "a number of Israels, each ruled by its own successor of David." Catholicism remained loyal to the Papacy; it would neither abolish the throne of St. Peter, nor in any way reduce its claims, since to have done so would have de-Romanized it forever. For believers in Rome the economic status of Protestant States was negligible when compared with the ageless precedence of the Eternal City, and with the supremacy of the Pontiff as God's vicegerent over an Eternal Society.

The Holy See no longer openly pronounced against the State as of diabolic origin, but it plotted against it and disparaged its claims. For the sake of ecclesiastical interests it championed the persecutions of Philip II of Spain in Holland, and his designs against the rising naval strength of Elizabethan England. Latinized to provincialism, the Curia seemed unable to understand that after the abdication of Charles V, Nationalism had the game in its own hand, provided it could compose its interminable squabbles. For it was not the great Emperor alone; it was the Empire that had abdicated. No such hegemony as his could now operate in Europe; and when Philip's "Invincible Armada" was dashed to pieces against the storm-bound coasts of Great Britain and Ireland, the predominance of the new order was assured. Since then it has had a blood-stained history. The Thirty Years' War forced Germany into a condition of neutrality and weakness that lasted till the second half of the nineteenth century. The campaigns of Marlborough, of Louis XIV, of Napoleon I, of Italy against Austria, of France against Germany; and the civil wars in England, in the South American Republics, and in the United States, caused those endless sufferings and piled up those enormous public debts that stifled social reforms for three centuries.

A few of these conflicts arose out of interests that seemed

to have no other possible settlement than that of the sword. As we have seen, its benevolent use seems paradoxical, yet it cannot be gainsaid that physical force has extended the scope of civilization, and inaugurated its reign in communities where barbarism was once supreme. The United States, Canada, Australia, New Zealand and South Africa were formerly occupied by non-progressive aborigines whom their white conquerors frequently treated with unpardonable brutality. Yet in the sequel some freedom was won, some fusions were made, some questions decided rightly. The fair minded historian must therefore concede that the militant forces of Nationalism, though often greedy and lawless, were not always as utterly non-religious as some hold them to have been. They had a religion of their own: one of valor, and not without its fascinations. It moved men's souls because it was based, not on falsehoods but on half-truths. It seemed to them to be the salt that saved the world from putrefaction. Against the slackness of selfish individualism it set the citizen's supreme duty to the State. But it is with the future of war as a brutal and useless appendage to human society, rather than with its past, that we have to do; and even that past, in the main, witnesses against it as the outbreak of an atavistic bestiality which must be exterminated, or it will exterminate nations.

No account of Nationalism would be sufficient for us which did not emphasize the impetus given to it by the Puritanism of Holland, England, Scotland and America. The chief difference between these diversified groups of one religious persuasion, and the Roman Catholics or Anglicans who opposed them, was related to the visible Church, in which only those who fulfilled their obligations to ecclesiastical lordship were regarded as citizens of the Commonwealth. The one party contended that believers reached Christ through the Church, the other that they reached the Church through Christ. So far there was truth on both sides. But when, as Dr. Oman puts it, the further contention was made by Catholicism that the legally privileged clergy did not have to belong to the community of believers at all, but were of a superior realm, the assumptions of ecclesiasticism reached their ultimate.[22] Although the separations were begun in the religious world, they reached their fuller dimensions in that of politics. Not all was different that seemed to be so on the surface. When the Puritan affirmed that man could never be right in his human relations until he was right in his divine relations, and the Pilgrim affirmed that the civil magistrate should not control religious affairs, they were nearer to their Roman Catholic brethren than is commonly supposed. Both were agreed upon the paramountcy of the Eternal Will in human society, but they did not agree, and are not yet agreed, upon the authorized vehicles of that Will.

The modern conception of religion as an individual concern was then, except in the case of the Pilgrims, as foreign to Protestant as to Catholic churchmen. They accepted the implications of political nationality as fixed principles, and even stimulated national temper and ideas that were destructive of Catholicity. It never seems to have occurred to them that there were moral facts in the ideal of a Universal Divine Society which had to be reckoned with, or that the failure to be really Catholic was a failure to be really Christian.[23] Churchmanship for all parties, except the sectarians of Plymouth Colony, was a matter of citizenship, and this idea has thriven until our own day. "No man," said Richard Hooker, "is a member of the Commonwealth who is not also a member of the Church of England"; and the original settlers of Virginia heartily agreed with him. As late as 1792 Burke wrote: "An alliance between Church and State in a Christian Commonwealth is an idle opinion. For in that Commonwealth Church and State are one and the same thing." His view suggested one of the first literary

[22] Cf. John Oman: "The Problem of Faith and Freedom," p. 353 f.
[23] Cf Richard Roberts: "The Church and the Commonwealth," p. 63.

efforts of Gladstone, whose treatise upon it earned Macaulay's salutation of the Victorian Liberal Premier as the "rising hope of the stern and unbending Tories."

VI

During the seventeenth and eighteenth centuries, governing authority of every kind came under fire from many quarters. Another age of revolution had set in as the further result of the Reformation. A quickened public conscience attacked Protestantism and Catholicism. The philosophy of "natural rights" bore down upon the inequalities and tyrannies of States. Presently the whole religious and political organism which has been briefly outlined here was indicted for its faults and vices with an intellectual and moral efficiency that would have rejoiced Mediæval doctors. Nearly every ascertainable principle of rule and method of administration was arraigned by competent advocates who demanded a larger measure of individual and social liberty. This disturbance took active form in the American Revolution, and culminated in that of France at the close of the eighteenth century. But it had already received its initial impulse from the Encyclopædists of the latter nation, who in turn derived their staple ideas from the Scotch metaphysicians. It has been prolific both of conflicts and of progress. Democratic States trace their constitutionalism to the general movement in question. It had its altruistic as well as its selfish aspects, its estimable and intimate connections with lawful freedom and broadening political equality. But it also gave rise to the egoism which characterizes modern society.

Yet it was not in substance, as some writers have said, a historic effort to elevate the individual above the mass. It is more accurately described as an attempt to penetrate behind all existing laws, forms and institutions to their real life and meaning. The peril of the process lay, as it still lies, in its emphasis on personality, and its insufficient conception of community life.[24] Nevertheless, as a reaction against the fatuous complacency with the existing order, it did good work, and is doing it today as a preparatory cause of social and industrial advance. Our world feels conscious that it has the individual on its heart and hands as never before.

Some modern theories of Nationalism that bid fair to sweep away every other authority, except that of the State, usurp the vital spiritual liberty of the past two thousand years which originated in Christianity. Nationalists of an advanced sort wink at immoral action if, as they imagine, the State profits by it. Thus, one of the leading daily journals of America, which gravely informs its readers that it is "the greatest newspaper in the world," prints upon its editorial page the oft quoted sentiment, "My country, right or wrong." According to this emotional outburst there is more than one moral order for the moral universe, in which Nationalism enjoys exemptions which nothing else can claim. To say that our moral criticism of the State must rest on identically ethical grounds with that of the individual offends a species of State worship. What are the principles of the Decalogue or of the Sermon on the Mount, when compared with the demands of national prosperity and expansion? Moreover, the citizen is dragged into the immoralities of the State. If in its organized selfishness it falsifies, then all patriots must become liars; if it steals, they must become thieves. The inconsistency of this position has been noted by Lord Acton: "By proclaiming the abolition of privileges, it (the State) emancipates the subjects of every such authority in order to transfer them exclusively to its own. It recognizes liberty only in the individual, because it is only in the individual that liberty can be separated from authority, and the right of conditional obedience deprived of the security of a limited command."[25] Under obedience to a majority

[24] Cf. John Oman: "Grace and Personality," p. 52 ff.
[25] "History of Freedom," p. 151.

rule, as the alternative for aristocracies and monarchies of the patriarchal order, an irresistible power is substituted for an idolatrous principle. I have said enough to show that the passage of the State from absolutism to constitutionalism has not been calm and uninterrupted. The Scylla of tyranny and the Charybdis of anarchy are never far away from human organizations so long as sin, selfishness and greed prevail in human nature; nor is there any prevention of these conditions outside noble religious and political beliefs.

Let me repeat that governments, whether national or municipal, absolutist or democratic, can neither be successfully organized nor maintained on any other basis than the honesty and integrity of the individual citizen; and these virtues have to be assumed in order to carry on their administration. Occasional contradictions of their assumption are harsh reminders that no rule, however free, is ever freed from righteousness; and that when it endeavors to escape the control of Supreme Righteousness it becomes a tyranny. Men's salvation from political servitude is only achieved by their unfaltering adherence to right and repudiation of wrong. That they are alive to the issue is shown by constitutional amendments, swollen codes of legislation, carefully contrived charters, recipes for civic virtue, and theories most numerous in democratic States, that would substitute very different political methods for those now in use. These devices may be good, bad or indifferent, but all are empirical; subject to the fact that there is no human way to prevent peoples from entertaining erroneous views, nor from cherishing evil designs. They can be reduced to a condition bordering on immoral insanity by misrepresentations as to facts, as was the case with Germany and other nations during the late war;[26] or again, through having the blank of ignorance filled in by passion and prejudice, to the exclusion of inquiry and reflection. Public opinion may thus be driven to find expression in abnormal, egotistical and dangerous ways.

[26] Cf. Herbert H. Asquith: "The Genesis of the War."

Men's sense of civilization may be temporarily overcome by the instincts of primitivism. Both are under the human skin, and the last is the first in point of time. Its physical and psychic elements have occupied the cells of the human body from the remotest ages, and do not intend to be dispossessed. So long, therefore, as public opinion in free States controls their national and international intercourse and action, they will require religious control. Even a little prosperity often proves too much for their mental equilibrium; a little adversity or opposition arouses their unwarranted anger.

Notwithstanding these contingencies, political freedom is vital in democratic Nationalism; and we are not likely to exchange its doctrines for those of repressive systems. But it can hardly be said to be the last phase of Nationalism. Its history shows that in the exceedingly difficult and delicate art of State government, dealing as it does with refractory human beings, it is always best to practice just and humane policies. That history also shows that it is unwise to suppose such policies are finalities in themselves. Facts are more important in this connection than constitutional or legislative documents; and actual experience invariably goes beyond their provisions. The conclusion is that no marked progress will be made by means of the finest political instruments, unless they are sustained by an enlightened public conscience, and enforced by the compulsions of a higher law. Hence Nationalism has no problems which are not moral and religious in nature; and this being so, the qualities of the people are the sole means for the resolving of their confused purposes, habits and beliefs, into a commonalty of right living.

Historians who tell us what Christianity has done to forward this kind of living are often better critics of its worth than controversial clerics who only think of what it is or is not. For historians are at least aware that while other religious beliefs have created an intense and vigorous Nationalism in Egypt, Judæa and the Hellenic nations, the Church of God alone has undertaken the absorption of all races into one Fraternity, combining a stringent ethical discipline with the ameliorations of universal good will. It is also true that Protestantism, as a late form of Christianity, has given first rank in the family of nations to those peoples who accepted its teachings. Cardinal Newman's objection that the material benefits of Protestantism are but an illusory good, assuredly not worth its spiritual cost, evades the point by arbitrarily separating the sacred from the secular in human affairs.[27] It cannot be denied that States whose intelligence and morality have commanded the respect and allegiance of Catholics and Protestants, were usually founded upon the principles evolved out of the conflicts of Mediævalism with the modern spirit. Yet Protestantism, as we have seen, did not invariably insist upon civil and religious freedom, nor always make concessions to the right of private judgment. The advanced positions taken by St. Thomas and Marsiglio were not steadfastly held by the Reformation leaders. They appeared for tyranny as well as for liberty, seized monarchies which remained absolute, and republics which remained as free as they were before. Modern States retained the penal codes against heresy, and decreed that every schism should be punished but their own. Too often Protestantism handed over to civil magistrates the autocratic power it had wrested from ecclesiastics. The superflous baggage which it brought out of the house of bondage hampered it for a prolonged period. Many of its political and theological ideas continued their subservience to archaic beliefs and methods of inquiry.

Despite these drawbacks, its encouragement of learning produced the sense of rationality: of a Creation ruled by reason, not by thaumaturgy. The romanticism of the Mediævalists had well nigh outlawed the intellectual facul-

[27] Cf. "Lectures on Certain Difficulties felt by Anglicans in submitting to the Catholic Church," Lecture VIII.

ties which Protestantism recovered and stimulated to good effect. To it, therefore, must be attributed the scientific discoveries of the modern period. Their results, like a clean but corroding acid, have dissolved the curious imaginations of a bygone world, and helped men to discern real and infinitely greater marvels in God's Universe, by teaching them to believe in the sanctity of correct and straighforward thinking. Protestantism has grave defects: it is often too separative, hard, metallic, materialized. But it furnished a counter irritant for the emotionalism which formerly arrested progress, and sometimes approached idiocy. The full stream of its power was diverted from life's arts and elegancies, fancies and delights, to the practical management of human affairs. It bred those magistrates who led in the formation of great though isolated States, and who were chary of a federalism which neither Hildebrand nor Innocent III could render efficient. The English-speaking nations, composed as they are of Roman Catholics and Protestants alike, are nearly always quoted as the prime examples of Protestant statesmanship. For though members of both Churches participated in their making, Protestant principles prevailed in it. Prussia has been contrasted with Austria as a despotism in a desert, without egress to the sea, which nevertheless surpassed its southern and far more fortunately situated and richer rival in finance, education, intelligence and administrative capacity. After Sadowa, Catholic Austria had to surrender her historic hegemony of the German nations to Protestant Prussia. At Sedan the same result banished the last remnants of the Napoleonic legend as a political force in Europe. After these victories the praises of Prussia were chanted by millions of Protestants whose children now sing to a very different tune. They were in no sense religious triumphs, nor did freedom receive advantage from them. They were the triumphs of a paganized Nationalism masquerading behind a Deity invented for its own fell purpose, and for which the world has had to pay full dearly.

Pursue the comparison elsewhere, between the Swiss Cantons of Berne and Valais, Sweden and Sicily, Holland and Spain, and you will find, I think, that the advantages of Protestant, or largely Protestant nations, are traceable to a religious creed which expresses itself in statesmanship, in economics, in inventions, in manufactures. It assumes the risks of progress, and carries with it the resolution to know and apply all knowledge that can be gained. It refuses to distrust the creative forces of intellectual freedom as inimical to religious faith, and they have amply repaid its confidence in them. Even its theology, which excites no special admiration among some scholars or wealthy worldlings, is closely related to their prosperity. Its contacts with the secular and political realms are the more impressive because of the contrasts I have mentioned. These contrasts have arisen during and since the sixteenth century; they have recast the maps of the world, and changed the headquarters of its governments. What was the England of the Tudors, or the Holland of William the Silent, or the Brandenburg of the Hohenzollerns when Luther's thunderings broke the repose of Church and Empire? Or what again became of the Spanish possessions in the New World after the Protestant mariners of the sixteenth and seventeenth centuries gained the freedom of the seas?

According to Nationalism's prevailing creed, the moral is, that if you want a powerful State, thoroughly modern, with the latest scientific equipment, fresh ideas and enduring government, it must be a free State in which the Church is also free, and does not prohibit the expanding life of the Commonwealth, nor regard an ecclesiastical frontier as the sacred enclosure of intellectual stagnation. But there are numberless Roman Catholic citizens who readily assent to these proposals, and, in asserting them, Protestants must beware of vanity. They, too, are liable to borrow their principles from a lower but more convenient level than that of the New Testament; and their failures are palpable to the critics who are always at their heels. When tempted to boast of Nationalism's historic connection with their Churches, it is well for Protestants to recall the sinister side of the shield of victory.

VII

A few far-sighted poets and thinkers perceived at the moment what is now patent to everybody, that if Nationalism meant the suppression of everything that opposed it, it ceased to be beneficent, became destructive, and wound up in a materialized imperialism. This is exactly what happened in the case of Prussia, and will happen again if State absolutism, such as Prussia fastened on Germany, is repeated elsewhere. The era of her *Weltpolitik* as the logical outcome of unrestrained Nationalism did not begin until 1900. It was Bismarck who in 1871 gave it leeway in his creation of the German Empire, which he left intact and to all appearances impregnable.[28] Herbert H. Asquith says that Bismarck was probably the most consummate master of the strategy of the political chessboard in history. Yet though the insane measures that led to the World War would never have been sanctioned by him, he has a place in the pedigree of its authors. It was his objective idealism which moulded Germany's character, her thought and her political ambitions. Taking every possible advantage of other nations, with some of whose rulers ineptitude in statesmanship had become an inveterate habit, he forged the bonds of German unity, to use his own phrase, "in blood and iron." Further, in his own speech, "to do this I set one man against another, and again and again I broke them." Jealous, irritable, candid in his confessions of duplicity and fraud, averse to the mistiness which some mistake for wisdom, Jovian in outline and of achievement, he lived long enough to regret some results of his gigantic undertakings, and to predict the unavoidable conflict which destroyed the Empire he had reared.

[28] William Kay Wallace: "The Trend of History," p. 301 ff.

I have no desire to inflict upon you the story, well known in its broad outlines, of the Machiavellian duplicities and frauds of the pre-war period, except to say that no more disgraceful period ever ended in a worse catastrophe. Insidious weapons of diplomacy, seductions of journalism, suggestions aimed at misleading the masses, were all too common in other European nations besides Germany and Austria. They poisoned personal character as well as national and international relations, and inflamed Protestants to kill Protestants, and Catholics to kill Catholics. All religious boundaries broke down when the nationalized imperialistic flood came. These events, fresh in the memory of mankind, explain the distrust of Nationalism's aspirations which many justly feel. With them, its apotheosis has left it reprobate. For if the State could properly disregard natural rights and treat them as nonexistent, then it could logically take the same attitude toward all other elements of the moral law. This is precisely the view of Burgess, who asserts that the State is the only authority competent to decide whether or not its proposed action constitutes a violation of morality: "the best interpreter of the laws of God and reason, and the human organ least likely to do wrong; hence one must hold to the principle that the State can do no wrong." [29] Its actual wrong-doing leaves men terrorized at the thought of repetition. They now understand that before States can fly to force they must cut loose from right and freedom. Then very quickly all criteria of right and wrong, or of freedom; and all standards of public interest and humanitarianism, become as a dissolving dream. Thus the claim of the State to an unlimited supremacy not only ignores religion and the Church; it shuts off intervention while it cuts the throat of morality.

This is the post-war scenery that oppresses many millions of hearts at home and abroad. Some who patronize or ridicule their fears for the spiritual fabric of society have bad moments

[29] Cf. John A. Ryan and Moorhouse F. X. Millar: "The State and the Church," p. 201.

of their own. They are haunted by the ghosts of Socialism, and unsparingly denounce its agitators who even in their defeat so often win the day. The capitalistic system which has built up Nationalism is plied with abuse, obloquy and defiance. The rude jostlings of forces that nothing but a united religious faith can direct aright threaten to grind civilization to powder. Street corner orators are the flying wing of an army of essayists, editors, publicists and industrialists, which promises us another and a better Reformation: a Renaissance that shall be for all peoples, and not for the literary, artistic, or the ruling classes alone. The proletariat has put itself ahead even of the people in communistic Russia. Only those who engage in manual toil, and are without productive property, are entitled to political privileges. They are the nation; and educated or wealthy people, employers or owners of property, are aliens to a man. So according to Nationalism's final pretensions, when on the rampage in Communism, its sword cuts both ways. In its latest form it assassinates traditional ideals only to turn on liberal ideals, and is as ready to suppress the latter as the former. The inconsistencies of separatism are more painfully evident now than when it meant revolt against a stupendous world Church, united in theory, in will, in practice, in rule, and also in the support of an overweighted and maladministered organization. But when separatism carries the war into Africa, and breeds dissensions in nations themselves, setting religious and political authorities by the ears, and loosening the structure of Church and State, you can be certain that unification will come to its own.

Against this view, extreme dissidents urge that agitation for the sake of improvement is the chief mission of the Church. She exists to pull down in order that she may set up again, to lose herself in the ennoblement of society. So long as she has a discerning vision of the actual verities of life, and a firm hand for using them, who, being a genuine son of Protestantism, laments the sacrifice of her being? Yet there are limits to such sacrifice, or it would degenerate into suicide, as there are limits to liberty, or it would run to despotism. There is not much real freedom in our self-contradictions, nor in the vagaries of private judgment which we cannot check. Protestantism has organized great States, but it has yet to organize a universal Church which can save States from mutual destruction. Its failure to furnish a catholic center for contending sects; to silence disloyalty and even malevolence in its own ranks, and to absorb excrescent cults has to be sadly acknowledged. The failure cannot be quoted in praise of freedom, since it arises from the insolence of individualism. But if our ancestral faith, while throwing off the subtleties and errors of the past, has taken on staggering burdens of its own, it has also produced free men and women, together with their finest political organizations. And if it does not justify the utmost praise of its eulogists, neither does it deserve the utmost blame of its opponents. The facts of its history cannot be spirited away by verbal legerdemain. They are the ineffaceable records that Time inscribes on the front of majestic States to commemorate the Reformers of the Mediæval Church.

We do not have to agree, therefore, that the alternatives are all State in Protestantism and all Church in Catholicism. Both Communions participate in State consciousness and in Church consciousness. The point is, which blends them best and makes the best use of both conjointly? Roman Catholicism and Protestantism are alike versed in secular politics, and laymen often feel the pull of their Faith in civic affairs. I shall not undertake to judge between them, although Dean Inge insists that where clerical Catholicism preponderates it is an injury to good citizenship. Yet he also insists that the old idea of the Church as "the nation under its spiritual aspect, is surely the right one;" in which case these who agree with him have a very disordered household to set to rights. He admits that the idea "is impracticable at present partly because the spiritual Roman Empire, with its claims to supernational or extranational obedience, still survives — a relic of the dead world-empire still vigorous in the midst of modern nationalism; and partly because the Church has split up into smaller corporations, none of which is capable of acting as the complete embodiment of the religion of the nation, while many prefer to stand outside all religious organizations." We are tempted to ask what keeps the relic of a dead empire alive? It shows no sign of impending death, and it must possess a marked propensity for life to hold it under such difficulties. It may also be added that there is an obedience, whatever qualification it demands, which is due to God and not to man, nor to any human associations. The Dean seems to wish that the State could be placed under the protection of religion existing as a moral institution, recognized by all citizens as the agent of their highest possible life. Then "we might hope to see a great improvement in the lamentably low standard of international morality, and a diminution in the sordid corruption, class-bribery and intrigue which made up the life of democratic politics." [30]

These observations indicate that the State is no longer for the modern man what it was for the ancient Greek: solitary, unique, sacred; the sole repository of human hopes and fears. He has to do with the Church, organized from the beginning as a universal body. There has never been a similar organization of civil society, or one that was intended to exist in such independence of all other earthly institutions. It succeeded to the place of former empires and gave inception to the modern State. Perhaps, as Troeltsch is confident, a "Church-directed civilization" is no longer possible. Yet a Church determined to combat spiritual evils with spiritual weapons, opposing to the world's standards of values those which she has received from her living Lord, is quite possible. Assuredly, the actual Church we serve cannot for-

[30] W. R. Inge: "Religion and the State" in "The Hibbert Journal," July 1920, p. 657.

ever coöperate in a guilty partnership of limited liability with political bodies that are organized apart from God.

The conclusion for believers in the New Testament Faith and in the ethic of prophetic Israel is, that Nationalism is a necessary but mediating institution between tribalism and a further Christian development of human association, which corresponds more closely with the ideals of Jesus Christ. To dismiss these statements as absurd does not confute them. Nationalism itself was ushered in, after Imperialism played out its part, with a chorus of contempt from the great and the powerful. And Nationalism now clutches us so rigidly that we can scarcely imagine a recent age when Frenchmen who could not speak English ruled England, and Germans ruled in Continental Europe over a diversity of peoples, and Popes of a varied lineage ruled Christendom's many races. Mediæval Federalism appeared to be firmly established; its policies were by no means always despicable; on the contrary, many were quite as wise as those of modern nations. Its government, like contemporary Gothic cathedrals, followed the principle of adjusted thrusts: every department was braced upon another, and all rested on a common foundation. Nevertheless, its responsible chieftains pulled down the pillars of their own temple, and human progress took a bold and startling urge forward. Do not be surprised, therefore, if Nationalism, imitating every previous system, slowly yields to changes that no political or racial obstinacy can avert. It has had the good will of the virtuous and the brave; their domestic habits have been its stay; the best breeds of mankind have fought for it; the most sagacious statesmen have administered its legislation, and held the scales of its justice with an even hand. Temperament, climate, territory and selective colonization have favored it in Europe and America. It is still so immense a factor that many deem it presumptuous even to call it to account.[31]

[31] Cf. Philip Marshal Brown: "International Society, Its Nature and Interests," Ch. XIII on "Imponderables," p. 150 ff.

Yet many patriotic men and women reluctantly scrutinize some of its effects. They ask if Christianity, taking pattern from the scientific associations and movements of the age, and from organizations which exist for social propaganda, cannot find a like federation and expansion for Nationalism. Then it may become the living soul of the internationalism of peace and justice which the Old Testament predicts, and for which we are commanded to preach the Gospel of Jesus Christ among all nations. The answer must be deferred to the next and concluding lecture.

NINTH LECTURE

THE CHALLENGE TO PROTESTANTISM

"I should have wished to show you that the same deliberate rejection of the moral code which smoothed the paths of absolute monarchy and of oligarchy, signalized the advent of the democratic claim to unlimited power — that one of its leading champions avowed the design of corrupting the moral sense of men, in order to destroy the influence of religion, and a famous apostle of enlightenment and toleration wished that the last king might be strangled with the entrails of the last priest. I would have tried to explain the connection between the doctrine of Adam Smith, that labor is the original source of all wealth, and the conclusion that the producers of wealth virtually compose the nation, by which Sieyès subverted historic France; and to show that Rousseau's definition of the social compact as a voluntary association of equal partners conducted Marat, by short and unavoidable stages, to declare that the poorer classes were absolved, by the law of self-preservation, from the conditions of a contract which awarded to them misery and death; that they were at war with society, and had a right to all they could get by exterminating the rich, and their inflexible theory of equality . . . has been associated with envy and hatred and bloodshed, and is now the most dangerous enemy lurking in our path."

LORD ACTON: *The History of Freedom*, pp. 57–58.

NINTH LECTURE

THE CHALLENGE TO PROTESTANTISM

Review of preceding lectures — Admonitions of the past and challenges of the present — No partnership between Church and State — Politics and Principles — Lights and Shadows of the World — The imperative duty of Protestantism for world peace — A coalition of Protestantism for the readjustment of Christendom — Education and Democracy — Education and Religion — The need for a mutual understanding between Roman Catholicism and Protestantism — Saints found in both sections of the Western Church — The responsibility of Protestantism in the face of atheistical Socialism and the Moslem advance — The need of a unified Church consciousness in Protestantism — The charges against sectarianism — The call for leadership — The adequate solution.

We come to the last of these lectures aware that they have only touched the fringe of the theme they are supposed to expound. We have seen how often freedom was either unknown, or adopted as a last resort when men had grown weary of despotism. Because they could not live by compulsion, they were bound to release themselves and their institutions from the clutch of the dead. Their selfish as distinguished from their benevolent uses of power have been noted. Forms of philosophical reaction against more liberal conceptions of government have been mentioned. Theories that identified the citizen with the State, or that merged his individuality in the State's political aggrandizement, are herein related. How ecclesiastics endeavored to subject all human associations to the Church, or temporal princes sought to enforce their policies upon her, is woven into this fragmentary story. It could not deal with these complicated issues in fullness of principle or of detail. Many vital things have been necessarily omitted; many crises arose in the evolution of modern society to which no reference is made. Yet if what is narrated promotes the living unity which generates its own loyalties in Christian men and nations, the chief aim of the lectures will have been gained.

Though a momentous epoch closed with the late war, and opinions and beliefs once deemed unassailable then perished, the world which needs them no more still needs the instruction of the past. Protestantism hears the challenge of its Apostolic, Patristic, and Mediæval periods; charged with admonition and encouragement for Church and State. As our knowledge of those periods is marshaled, and what they teach better understood, their influence grows upon our faith and thought. When troubled by the present indifference toward organized religion, we are reminded of the strange oblivion in which early Christianity was buried by Pagan scholars and historians. Bishop Lightfoot asks how a movement so rich in moral phenomena could have escaped Seneca's notice; how one so productive of transforming personalities could have been unheeded by Plutarch? "How is it again, that Marcus Aurelius, the philosophical emperor, dismisses 'the Christians' in his writings with one brief scornful allusion, though he had been flooded with apologies and memorials in their behalf, and though they had served in the very army which he commanded in person?" [1] The answer would be more difficult than it is, did we not apprehend, first, that the wisdom of men is frequently foolishness with God, and again, that reticence is sometimes the sole defense of skepticism, confronted by what is, to it, an inexplicable spiritual progress. The finest example of such progress belongs to that Apostolic Age whose life and power it is the avowed mission of Christianity to perpetuate. Should the Churches of the Reformed Faith be tempted to forget this mission, they may well recall the fate of the Communions to which the letters of the New Testament were originally addressed. Although they were first in

[1] Bishop Lightfoot: "Commentary: St. Paul's Epistle to the Philippians," Introduction, pp. 27–29.

the service and fellowship of Jesus Christ, nearly all have ceased to exist. Their extinction warns us of His determination that every branch shall be grafted into the true Vine, and be filled with its living juices.

Protestantism, like Apostolic Christianity, was born into a world of peril and promise. It has flourished in outward strength and gained ascendency in the foremost nations of our day. Nevertheless, it may exist on compromise only to disappear. Unless it devotes itself afresh to the life of the Risen Lord, which is the true life alike of individuals and of nations, it cannot hope to escape the doom that fell upon the Churches in Asia Minor. Neither theological orthodoxy nor correct ecclesiastical codes avail without that inward state of the soul which is the source of divine wisdom and sacrificial effort.

The challenge of the Patristic and Mediæval periods, if less authoritative, is hardly less peremptory than that of the Apostolic period. Their needless disparagement ill becomes those who would rightly interpret our religious problems. Fathers, Pontiffs, Schoolmen, Monastics, Prelates and Cannonists follow on in the processional ranks of eighteen hundred years, bearing gifts for us as their fellow servants in Christ. Each outstanding figure among them is momentarily lit by the pale lamp of historic knowledge. Here a great preacher passes in review; there a martyr for the Master whom he loved; yonder a brave thinker who fared forth into new seas of thought. All are helpful to us concerning the meaning and the use of liberty; its organic connection with the higher freedom of the Spirit, its embodiment in Christianity, and its applications to every age and condition. Their intellectual pedigree was mixed, and many of their ideas and plans came to naught by the Will of God. But they withstood the opposition of far-reaching and foul traditions, and established the Gospel in an alienated world, not only as a doctrine, but as an institution.[2]

Mediæval Christianity reiterates its challenge to Protes-

[2] Cf. Henry Osborn Taylor: "Freedom of the Mind in History."

tantism, because it absolutely refused to be a disembodied religion. Monasticism apart, its delight was with the masses, to whom it made itself vividly real. It did not covet ethereal regions beyond human good and evil, from which it looked down upon them with the impartiality of the sun which shines upon the just and the unjust. It identified itself with the citizen, and with his temporal and spiritual obligations. Although the realization of its ideals was backward, the difficult task of selecting its basic principles was well to the front. In their practice these principles combined Church and State, giving Christendom a resemblance to the Kingdom of God on earth, which its internal disparities often flatly contradicted. But the constant aim of the statesmen of the Middle Ages was to maintain an efficient rule and protection for society. By this aim they should be judged, and not by their insistence upon the precedence of the Church. Her supremacy did not obsess them, nor did it represent the undivided result of their thinking, since Church and State in their conception were a solidarity. They were astute and competent men, awake to their responsibility for the safety of mankind; politicians not easily gulled, who did not live by policy alone. Their attempt to build civilization upon a religious foundation conditioned every habit of their minds, and made them both merciless and magnanimous. They had a keen sense of human depravity: of its rebellion against righteousness, its private incontinence and public lawlessness. They saw it, as our century has had to see it, with the mask off, armed, ferocious, severed from moral restraint. They knew that nations were very far away from Plato's dream, in which he compared them with a virtuous being of valor, wisdom and temperance.

The sacerdotalism which alienates Protestantism from the Mediævalists was a natural expression of their worship. Its doctrines bound families and peoples in religious oneness, and defended them from the further encroachments of wickedness and despair. Priestism had priority because those to whom it ministered desired symbolism and not discussion. Learned and simple had an inborn taste for what was artistic or even grotesque in religion. Nowhere did their social instinct assert itself so strongly as before the Mass, which placed an equal value on every soul. It gratifies some Protestants to hear that "prophets emancipate the faith which priests enslave;" but the axiom would have had no meaning for their Mediæval brethren. Even now, it is one of those half-truths which is itself untrue. The prevalence of sacerdotalism in every era is not explained by such glittering generalities. Be it also remembered that the Middle Ages had their prophets, few in number, perhaps, but regnant in faith, who left less for modern prophets to forecast than some of us imagine; and with them, poets too, whose product, though small, was choice. A chaotic period does not need a prophetic so much as a fortressed religion, which shelters men and women from surrounding distraction and tumult. Such a period was then in passage. Its priests took the chains their selected prophets had forged, and used them for the discipline of the Divine Society. It had to be made conscious of its own past, which heralded its hope and confidence for the future. So long as believers must achieve a new being in Jesus Christ, and interminable stretches of degraded humanity have to be raised to the level which He demands, the priest will continue to be the hierophant of sacred mysteries. Christ Himself is the Eternal Priest; the Church is His *Alter Ego;* and all Christians have a royal priesthood in Him. The abuses of sacerdotalism met with swift and condign punishment. But for a millennium before the Reformation, the peoples of Europe adored the saving omnipotence which they believed was enthroned in the Eucharist and in the Church.[3]

This was the wonderful achievement of the period that we must not underrate. Its challenge rings resonantly across the intervening centuries. It says to Protestants: "Bring

[3] Cf. G. G. Coulton: "Five Centuries of Religion," p. 100 ff.; "Anglican Essays," essay on "Communion or Mass," by W. L. Paige-Cox (editor). p. 139 ff.

forth fruit as we did. If you have a purer and a more reasonable faith than ours, demonstrate it to mankind. Let St. Louis be the pattern of princes and St. Francis of saints; St. Bernard the prototype of preachers; and the works of St. Thomas the stimulus of a new Christian philosophy. Exterminate the militarism that threatens the ruin of the race, as we subdued the wrath of predacious monarchs and barons. Rebuke the shifts of deceitful diplomacy, as we rebuked some lies that vexed our international peace. Rescue your fellow Christians of the Near East from the misrule of Islam, as we rescued those of the Danube Valley. Guard the nations we first evangelized from going down into the pit. Convert the Moslems of Africa, and the Brahmans and Buddhists of Asia, as we converted the tribes of Northern Europe. Show your proud world of many inventions that it is subject to that Divine Order, belief in which we instilled into the consciousness of our more difficult and blundering world."

The present age likewise challenges those Protestants who are too much participants in its affairs to understand their import. The secular State, for which the Reformation was largely responsible, is at a low ebb in ethics; nor can it continue to revolve on statecraft alone. Its moral destitution is illustrated by a conversation which Sir J. Rennell Rodd had in the eighties of the last century with a famous diplomat who had been used for immoral purposes relative to international politics. This official was sensible of the unsavory reputation of his employment, and when rallied by Rodd about his unsociability he replied suggestively: "The service of the State has spoiled me as a human being." [4] The confession reveals a condition as abject as any that obtained in Mediævalism, and one which has been fairly general in temporal hierarchies to which the public was en-

[4] "Social and Diplomatic Memories," pp. 115–116. Sir Francis Bacon, centuries before, had written as follows: "Men in great place are thrice servants; servants of the sovereign or State, servants of fame, and servants of business; so as they have no freedom, neither in their persons, nor in their action, nor in their times."

slaved. Even in Australia and America, countries to which men had looked for the climax of freedom and of industrial prosperity, the ideals of the State have faltered.[5] Alfred Deakin, a gifted publicist of the Antipodes, speaks of Liberalism there as "a spent force." Politicians played with its name and glorified its shadows. Principles were really extinct; civil rule was abandoned to cliques and coteries; to the reign of accident or of domineering ability.[6] Cries and catchwords, selfishness and shams, cant and materialism, have made havoc of the virtues of democracy. There is all too little real love of ideas, of history, or of literature among well-paid and reasonably leisured artisans and members of the commercial classes. Their shrewdness in business is noticeable; their mediocrity outside business is equally noticeable.

Christianity, not politics, assuredly not the kind of politics to which Sir J. Rennell Rodd referred, is the life of the State. The false lights and exiguous standards of internationalism are highly detrimental to civilization. But how to abolish them, and put sound principles of human intercourse in their place, is the problem of churches and of nations. Arrangements between the theoretical catholicity of the Church and the real provincialism of the State are either tentative or ineffective. Yet what must not be in these arrangements can be stated as preparatory for what should be. The exceptional privileges of the Church as a temporal power are no longer tolerated by free peoples. Whatever earthly authority belongs to her has to be won in the loftier regions of moral suasion and assent. She may ask for guarantees that her spiritual functions shall not be hampered by restrictive political measures. But compliance with this request is at the option of the State, and no guarantees can violate in the slightest degree the principle of equal laws for

[5] Cf. John Simpson Penman: "The Irresistible Movement of Democracy," p. 164 ff.
[6] Cf. his "Biography" by Walter Murdoch, p. 174 ff.

all. This I say, as a friend of all Churches and as a firm believer in their present indispensability and future unity. I say it also as a believer in that true freedom for the soul and circumstances of every individual and nation, which is the very breath of the Christian Evangel, and of the Hebrew Prophecies. What is more, in a world where distance decreases daily, where ideas circulate with miraculous speed, and men's nearness increases correspondingly, State and Church can have no wicked partnerships, and that world not know of them. An elevated sense of churchmanship, which forbids complicity with the State in anything inimical to Christianity, is our crying need. The multitudes may be as wayward and untrustworthy about moral issues as Calvin was inclined to think they were. But the Protestantism that is eventually to mould their beliefs, and retain their trust, must not act at the mere solicitation of the State, nor from popular desire, but from a far fuller and nobler realization of God's Will for the Church and for humanity as a whole.

II

Nearly every great conflict that has trampled down mankind was preceded by an era of materialism in which that Will apparently was submerged. Christians as well as non-Christians forgot, for the time being, that politics are the concern of this world, but principles a manifestation of that which is to come. The best possibilities of politics are realized in practice; the truth sought in principles is final and eternal. There can be no lasting political good that does not proceed from principles which express the Divine intention for human society. Those principles proceed in turn from the realm of spiritual verities of which the Church is the visible embodiment. Every legitimate connection, therefore, that she sustains to the State is one of moral sincerity and religious inspiration. She lives that the State may live more abundantly in justice, peace and brotherhood.

How have these principles and ideals fared during the last half-century? The present condition of Europe, to say nothing of other continents, furnishes a convincing but saddening answer to the question.

During that period extreme violence of thought and action frequently prevailed in the Balkan States, in Turkey, in the Austro-Hungarian Empire, and in Central Europe generally. The drill sergeant outdid the scholar and the cleric. The coarse, second-rate sentiments of junkers, bureaucrats, chauvinistic officials and journalists menaced the good will of nations. Few great thinkers or prophets received a thousandth part of the attention given to the ravings of militarism. Invocations to battle, and the triumph of the sword as the passport to all that honorably befits nations, were the stock tenets of nationalistic barbarism. Even the poetry and the drama of our yesterdays are full of hacking and hewing; of gold-braided uniforms, blood and gunpowder. They are grossly brutal, painfully monotonous, without a ray of human interest or sympathy to lighten the black shadows of their adoration of physical force. To butcher the foe is a heavenly enterprise, sanctioned by churchmen who repealed the Sermon on the Mount for the sake of State conquest and State worship. These travesties upon Christianity registered the actual situation in Europe. Her fate, and that of half of the world besides, lay in the hands of a dozen men more suited to the tastes of Tamerlane than to civilized rule. They had their day; then the seething volcano exploded, and now they have their night, which should be a long one. For us the weightiest conclusions are: first, that an international condition which could permit so stupendous a crime against the race was the negation of God; and, second, that it is the inescapable obligation of Christians, and of all sane and moralized people, to prevent a repetition of the crime.

Right triumphed, but there were no spoils for the victors. They cannot annex, still less can they destroy the defeated nations, nor can they make them pay the huge indemnities for irreparable damage done. In the reaction of conflict, some of the allied Powers exalt the warlike propensities they once execrated, and several of them have more men under arms than they had in the spring of 1914. The atmosphere of moral steadfastness no longer envelopes Continental Europe. Wise and patient statesmen, unhurried, yet not in retreat, and never merely opportunist, seem to have vanished from the higher councils of mankind. Even while the Washington Conference for the reduction of naval armaments was in session, the race for war supremacy began afresh, and bids fair to commandeer the air for the destructive forces now partly excluded from the sea. France recently had one hundred and forty squadrons of nine planes, each ready for combat duty. Whereupon Great Britain authorized an annual sum of twenty-five million dollars for three years to offset France, and she promptly retaliated by providing for two hundred and twenty squadrons. Italy, Russia and the United States are the latest entrants in this competition of death, against which the American veterans of the World War have made an official protest. Enough has been said for our purpose, and what is said is designedly understated, lest the impressions made should be misleading. What an appalling revelation of Nationalism's intrinsic deviltries these facts make, and one which moves every Christian heart with mingled compassion and indignation! From the lands named, Americans derived their religion, language, cultural ideas, literature and law. None can witness the present helplessness and degradation of Europe without emotion. Her industries are crippled, her trade is restricted, her productive ability is seriously impaired for at least a century to come, and her hopes of social betterment are similarly postponed. In some of her States dull apathy in the midst of decadence, or a senile acquiescence with ignominious conditions, shows how near to dissolution they are. Neither the best nor the worst can be readily depicted, and as a consequence they cannot be easily appreciated. In reflecting upon the desolations of godless Nationalism, one wonders what Hildebrand would say, could he gaze today on the Continent he once dominated? What would be his verdict upon the policies that have brought it to the verge of ruin?

The imperative duty of Protestantism is world peace. If it will not tolerate such a jurisdiction as Hildebrand's, which is certainly the case, then in God's Name, let it suggest a more efficient jurisdiction of its own. There can be no moral or spiritual growth in nations till the causes of war are abolished by a united Christian consciousness. All Churches should organize and act for this end. They are in honor bound to proceed against the "peace of violence" which is based upon armaments. It is their duty to ask for the withdrawal of armies of occupation and of absurd claims and impossible indemnities. They should require the political authorities of their respective nations to define and codify international law; and by its means make covenants which substitute arbitration for combat in the disputes of Christian nations. Peace and war are primarily states of mind, and until now, peace has been prostituted for the continuance of war. The disruption of Europe's economic life is only symptomatic of her ethical disruption. Here churchmen have their sphere of action, which they ought unhesitatingly to appropriate. The task of world reconstruction is laid upon civilization at large, but its heavy end rests upon those historic Churches which have bred great nations and fostered their sense of superiority. They are now in the rather enviable position of choosing their own future. Should they undertake to restore to decent and righteous behavior the States they largely created, Protestantism will, in my judgment, enter upon an era of vigorous health which it has never yet known. As things are, it must follow the restorative policy, cost what it may, or lose its moral control over human society. One does not have to indulge either the needless fears which defeat good sense, or the wild conjectures which outrun possibility. But a careful consideration of the latent and active forces of Protestantism convinces me that it can and should coalesce for the readjustment of Christendom.

III

Coalition of this kind is suspected by political Protestants who imagine that nearly all civic benefits began with the Reformation. As we have hinted, the results of that Movement had their shady side. The defederalization of Europe left much good in question, and much evil entrenched. After the dramatic disappearance of Mediæval Imperialism, a sensible separation of vital interests deeply affected both Church and State. The distrust of a world society was not stayed for centuries, and the wars of nations kept pace with that distrust. The England of George I was very little larger in population than that of Edward II; the subjects of Henry VIII were no more intelligent nor humane than those of Edward I; the Parliament of Henry was probably the most servile in the history of the Island Kingdom. On the Continent the segregated provinces of the Mediterranean and of the Rhine Valley experienced reversals, from which the latter regions had not recovered when Napoleon I crushed Prussia at Jena.

Nationalism has also an upper side which presents to men the highest freedom of Christianity. This freedom could not be the source of personal and social righteousness, or of the justice that deals with nations as it does with individuals, were it not untrammeled. It is the liberty of the sons of God, which they enjoy in heart, reason and conscience through faith in Christ. No lower forms of authority should be allowed to usurp its sway over the entire life of Christian citizenship. For Protestants, the principles, not the forms of political government are the vital matter. As they view the Church, she is interested, not in monarchy or republicanism as such, but in their application of those principles. The rights and obligations she upholds are sacred and inviolable, and cannot be changed nor compromised by the dictates of political democracies, any more than by the decrees of despots. Here, as I see it, the Protestantism which accepts the challenge of the New Testament Faith must always resist theories that insist on the sovereignty of the democratic State as the organ of the Popular Will. May that Will always conform to righteous standards. But when it does not, the Christian's course is clear. The decisions of Democracy have not reversed, nor will they ever reverse, the decision of Christ's disciples that His Church alone determines the nature and the application of her own religious convictions and beliefs.[7]

The radiations of His Soul in her membership today cast new light upon this question, specifically as it relates to internationalism. The ultimate goal of nations is that Christianized Brotherhood which means nothing less than a fit habitation for human beings on earth. It matters not what forms the internationalism shall assume, nor what are the proximate affections and objects of Protestants. Their final aim, and that of all believers, is found in the prayer: "Thy Kingdom come." Since it must come, why should the Reformed Churches not hasten its coming, and desist from useless attempts to reconcile the irreconcilable elements of human society with that Kingdom? The people at large have not lost sight of this paramount issue. They narrowly observe our attitude toward it, and their support can be obtained for those Churches which move against the iniquities of unlicensed Nationalism with all possible fervor. This duty belongs to them, nor can it be devolved upon statesmen and diplomatists. They may negotiate successfully with other countries; know what to do, and when not to do it. These are delicate arts that require a special train-

[7] Cf. William Adams Brown: "Imperialistic Religion and the Religion of Democracy," p. 136 ff.

ing as much as law or surgery. But the Church, as such, knows no foreign countries; her field is the world; she exists to pull down barriers, to foster in men and nations the fraternity which banishes their alien tendencies. The very word foreign is a reflection upon the catholicity of her Evangel. Can she meet this test? Can she absorb patriotism into a suprapatriotism? Can her love for any land relate its good to that of all mankind; and restrain its selfishness so that it shall not injure mankind? This is the crucial question for Protestantism in the twentieth century.

Economic and other domestic problems are open to these reasonings. Too often the logic of industrial disputes is applied without regard to the truer social conscience. Public welfare is so constantly usurped by the quarrels of corporations, employers and employees, that when wars cease, we are almost worse confounded in peace. As we have already seen, the Reformed Faith is usually associated with commercial States and their industrial pursuits. When those who conduct them hide behind legislation in which there is too much scope for wealthy malefactors or unscrupulous laborites, the practice disgusts the public, and shows that law can be one thing and justice another. The enforcement of legal rights at the expense of natural rights must not be countenanced by the Churches. But until the Federal Council was instituted, they were hindered by their lack of an efficient organization, and could not contend with those who,

> "Trusting to crowded factory and mart
> And proud discoveries of the intellect,
> Heed not the pillage of man's ancient heart."

The latest and one of the best verdicts of Christianity and Judaism combined against social injustice is, that "bad morals can never be good economics." Valuable in itself, this truth is even more valuable because it shows the possibilities for social justice contained in concerted action, and also the changed bearing of the church upon industrial controversies. But bad morals will persist to the undoing of good economics unless unified Christian action proves too strong for them. Should Protestantism, alive to the danger, direct its onpressing energies against open wrongs, it can, with the help of all believers in justice, clear the economic jungle of its beasts of prey. Yet the jungle will not be transformed into the Lord's garden, where toil is welcome, until His winds have breathed upon it the life from above. The new social order is not to be ushered in by blows, nor hewn out after the fashion of the sword, nor tempered on anvils of steel. Those who shall introduce it, Jew or Gentile, Catholic or Protestant, must stand Godward and together, interpreting its requirements with the vision of faith, with "the patience of passion," with "the signet of love for a seal."

Further, the divisions we have noted between classes and nations are largely caused by the fundamental separation between the temporal and the eternal. So long as men avidly desire the perishable, arbitrary divisions will perists in society. Nowhere is this maladjustment more palpable than in public education, which, next to religion, is the making or unmaking of individuals and of States. The American citizen demands mastery over his local circumstances, and any knowledge which does not readily lend itself to that mastery is likely to be discounted by him. It is also the settled policy of our Republic that religious knowledge, which involves religious control, must be excluded from the public schools, and that such control furnishes the constitutional basis for its exclusion. The democratization of America's citizenship, we are informed, is essential to its peace and welfare. Its self-government centers around political ideas upon which rightminded men and women are supposed to agree. The Constitution, the State, and its common mind are thus closely related to public education. But since men differ about nothing else as they do about religion, it cannot be taught in any institution supported by general taxation.

This doctrine derives its strength quite as much from sectarian disputes as from political necessities. Those who encourage sectarianism must share the onus, if it be such, for the secular system of education which many of them deplore. I need not say that the service rendered to the State by the public school is beyond praise. It has assimilated countless numbers of foreign born and native Americans, and imbued the rank and file of our countrymen with some of the best tenets of citizenship. As an institution it has boundless significance, and a record of well-nigh unparalleled devotion to the public good, which endear it to the heart of the nation. Until the last ten years adverse criticism of it was resented as bordering on sedition.

Today a challenge which Protestantism cannot ignore comes from educational quarters. Many supporters of the public school ask if the concessions made by institutional religion to the democratic theory of education promote the benefit of either. They wonder if the soul of all improvement is not still in the improvement of the soul. If the fear of God is the beginning of wisdom, and the love of Him is the crown of wisdom, what truer orientation can be given to education than these emotions supply? Moreover, if religion separates people, certainly neither education nor politics solidify them. The solidarity of the nation is spiritual, not intellectual, nor political. It belongs to the soul of the Republic, where a civic love that surpasses knowledge must be enshrined. Yet sectional, sectarian and religious prejudices have seldom been more lusty and agressive than they are at the present time. Not since the Civil War have citizens banded against each other in matters of blood and belief as they do today, and this, notwithstanding the prevalence of secular education. One of the weightiest arguments against its continuance is presented by some of its ardent supporters. Despite their attachment to the public school as the premier institution for democratization, these partisans live and act apart to perpetuate discord and hatred.

Others who have received untold benefits from the State antagonize its methods of government. Secularists in education to a man, and resentful of any attempts to introduce religion into the public school, they nevertheless berate what they call Anglo-Saxon domination, and predict the eclipse of some of its best traditions. Men and women whose ancestors did not succeed in self-government in the lands from which they came, here remain apart in heart, if not in appearance. Unused to freedom, not always justly treated, suspicious of law, opposed to all religion, and inclined to belittle its influence in our political history, they associate democratic liberty with the absence of spiritual discipline. Another group of secularists in education makes a sorry showing in citizenship. Not community spirit, but crass individualism is their ideal. To get on whoever falls off; to shift responsibility from themselves to the State; to place a premium on commercial success; to procure the maximum of self-indulgence at the minimum of personal risk, are their distinctive traits. Since the types I have sketched are increasing, especially in large cities; and the secular policy which they uphold does not provide a sufficient ethic for the State, it is the deliberate judgment of numerous Americans, whose patriotism cannot be questioned, that the policy should be modified.[8]

IV

The relaxation of the religious bond in the United States is a further challenge to Protestantism. Its Gospel, from the human side, is right conduct taught and justified. But over 50,000,000 Americans out of a population of 110,000,000 belong to no Church, and seldom hear the Gospel; while millions more who are church members take their vows very

[8] Cf. Francis G. Peabody: "The Religious Education of an American Citizen"; John Dewey: "Democracy and Education"; Henry Frederick Cope: "Education for Democracy."

lightly. The antagonisms of thought, aim and situation existing in these incalculable numbers of highly individualized people, bent on taking their destinies into their own hands, cannot be removed by any single Church. The task would monopolize all the Churches and their efforts at their best. But they are unable to discharge it efficiently because less than one half of the 53,000,000 children and adolescents in this nation are enrolled in religious schools, and three out of every five Protestant children receive no definite religious training. In 1916 the enrollment in Protestant Bible Schools was 21,886,521; in 1920 it had shrunk to 15,617,060, a decrease of 6,269,461 in four years. The children of orthodox Jews get upon the average 354 hours of religious instruction annually; Roman Catholic children receive 200 hours annually; Protestant children 24 hours annually, or less than half an hour a week.[9] The problem is a moral one, and cannot be stated in statistics. They show, however, that Protestantism is the heaviest contributor to the secular policy in national education. Admirable efforts to overcome its menace are made by the Bible Schools and kindred organizations. The Universities, Colleges, Young Men's Christian Associations, Young Women's Christian Associations, Summer Schools and Conferences have done valiantly. But notwithstanding their exertions, secularism has stormed every defense and spread throughout the land. The marked absence of wise restraint in certain sections of society is usually charged to neglect of religion, and is commented upon by numerous clergymen and other public servants. It is not clearly determined how much or little of the havoc which the lack of such restraint causes is due to Protestant concessions to secularism for the sake of democracy. But that serious evils exist compatible with those concessions is demonstrated by the facts.

[9] Cf. "The Religious Education of Protestants in an American Commonwealth." The Indiana Survey of Religious Education made under the direction of Professor Walter S. Athearn.

There are many things to be said for secular education. Its defenders assert that the vitality and freedom of the public school depend upon its absolute independence of religious control. The cure for the ills of its liberty is more liberty; for the ills of its knowledge, is more knowledge. Under this plea, secularists annex institutions in which casual references to religion are still made. Colleges and schools founded by churchmen have passed beyond denominational supervision; others endeavor to get rid of it. Those that remain under it are prone to apologize for their position. Their critics speak of denominational institutions of learning as though they were necessarily inferior. The consciousness of a crippling sectarianism rankles in some of these foundations. The parochial schools of Roman Catholicism are quoted as standing examples of educational backwardness due to clerical supervision. The stigma is denied by those who have charge of the parochial schools, which they assert must comply with the tests and requirements fixed by the State, and applying to all public schools. Why religious teaching should dwarf the intellectual life, either of children or adults, is not apparent at a glance. But Catholics and Protestants who insist that their doctrines must be regarded as Christianity's most perfect forms, with which no secular learning can be allowed to interfere, help to explain the disparagement. The unwillingness of Christians to agree upon the truths of their Faith further complicates the issue, and strengthens the position of those who would exclude religious teaching from the schools. Scholars and scientists who regard all creeds as negligible lay the shortcomings of society at the door of sheer ignorance. Cleanse education, they say, of exploded traditions and antiquated ways of thinking, and the unfettered mind will bring in a better era. Not a few of these authorities maintain that the late war demonstrated the incompetency of nearly all the older methods of instruction. This is an assumption not generally admitted. Many believe that a Christianized educational system might have prevented the war, and it is certain that the scientific knowledge of advanced States greatly augmented its horrors. Nor were some of those States ignorant of the meanings of modern war, but they rushed into it under the delusion that it could be made profitable to them.

A further objection to religious education at the expense of the State is taken from past enormities done in the name of religion. For years the sword was scarcely laid aside in France, or in the low Provinces; nor in the Rhine Palatinate for a single month. In the streets of Paris; at Arques, Coutras and Ivry, blood flowed in torrents to expiate the infamies of St. Bartholomew's massacre. The animus behind the Thirty Years' War, and behind that of the Puritans against the Stuarts, was religious as much as political in its essence. The heroical struggle of Holland to throw off Spain's religious tyranny is engraved on the memory of freedom-loving peoples. Frequently these conflicts left no faith, no honor, no mercy, in the States they ravaged. Italian treachery grafted on French daring, or Spanish dourness matched against Dutch tenacity, proved capable of dreadful deeds. The Cromwellians who swept the field of battle did not govern constitutionally. The divine right of kings, taught for centuries in nearly every Protestant and Roman Catholic school of Europe, was the curse of freedom till it finally wore itself out. If, therefore, we would forestall the possibility of a revival of these complications, which filled men with a bestial ingenuity for vengeance, we are urged to keep the American public school entirely separate from all religious systems and their agents. These, it is said, should impart their instruction through the Churches, the home, and other domestic channels.

The appeal to history is well taken, provided there has been no change in the relation of the Churches since the seventeenth century. Do Christians still hate each other for the love of God as they did then? Is every advocate of religious instruction given in the public schools a disguised enemy seeking to secure State funds for divisive ends? Then the only thing to do is to exclude them from the public schools. But Americans of the highest character, Protestants, Catholics, laymen and clerics, are exceedingly anxious that religious instruction shall become a part of the educational program of the Republic. Their differences arise, not from the principle at stake, but from the methods of its application. Until they can agree upon what to teach, and who shall teach it, it is better to continue the present system, than it would be to precipitate a renewed fight about what some of us believe to be non-essentials of religion. Whichever policy may eventually obtain, neither the good nor the harm predicted by partisans is likely to ensue. Quiet discussion, with less heat and more light, would brighten the prospect for a settlement of this prolonged controversy. But prejudice still spins its process, and many harbor sectarian beliefs only to confuse them with universal principles; while the children, who should be our first concern, are untaught in the truths that have made the moral eminence of America. One can well believe that its democracy is equal to the emergency. For a hundred and fifty years it has stood for equality as resolutely as for freedom. It has mitigated ancient enmities, guaranteed intelligent intercourse, and promoted the interchange of opinions on controverted matters. Our citizens have reached a common mind on major questions about which they formerly differed, and even fought. The Union is one and indissoluble; it rests on the fealty and good-will of forty-eight sister Commonwealths. Its citizens heartily believe in education, though they do not always appreciate, as they should, its true nature and purposes. But the majority understand that it is given primarily for the foundation of character; for the moral discipline which should come before all knowledge; for the spiritual culture to which scholarship is but an accessory, for the truer insight and broader vision that see behind learning the wisdom it is meant to inculcate.

If these ends are to receive, without coercion of any man's conscience, the aid of religious instruction, those who accept them must arrive at a definite agreement which is not yet in sight. Nor will it be sighted so long as they remain within the confines of their several creeds. Protestants who are opposed to the whims and fancies of formalists and theorists upon education, should defend their deposit of the Christian Faith in the spirit of charity toward all men. How can they do this successfully, however, while reactionaries nurse a useless feud against scientific learning, and assail truths which are taught in every self-respecting school and college? No mediæval prelate was ever more rampant against non-conforming believers than are the men to whom I refer, against scholars and teachers who dare to differ with them. Competent instructors have been harassed, cross-examined, and in some instances, summarily dismissed, because they would not deny themselves, nor submit to the behests of eloquent ignorance, or of legislatures and boards of management susceptible to its sophisticated utterances. A more detestable wrong has seldom been inflicted upon American education by sincere but mistaken zealots, nor is their conscientiousness an extenuating plea. What has made bigots and persecutors dangerous to their fellow men if not their conviction that they were always right? The unrighteous sin and go to their own place. But who shall estimate the iniquity which the righteous do? Will those who in this case seek to stifle knowledge display the leadership which national education requires today? Can they deliver it from skepticism on the one hand, and from superstition on the other? They are far more likely to pervert it with creedal futilities and untutored emotionalism.

The responsibility for Christian education, and for the intellectual progress inseparable from it, is upon Protestantism as a whole so far as its own constituency is concerned. That responsibility is being met by the long list of its institutions and agencies, which are as opposed to godless knowledge as they are to pious obscurantism. Those who sustain them understand that one brainy rascal is a greater menace to the State than a thousand simple but honest and industrious citizens. They maintain that faith can be blended with learning to the enrichment of both. They teach lawfulness as the realization of liberty. They convey the advantages of religious education to hundreds of thousands of graduates who, in their turn, communicate those advantages to the Republic. It is not shut up to the extremes of secularism or reactionism. It is large enough to encompass all knowledge contributory to wisdom and character. It has not even the remotest idea of submission to a combination of Church and State in education or in aught else, such as paralyzed Mediæval Imperialism. Its present mind seems to be that religious education in the public schools must be predetermined by religious unity in the Churches. Until this is advanced, the *status quo* will obtain. And unless Protestants and Roman Catholics would open a Pandora's box, they must adjust their differences before they attempt any extensive changes in the nation's educational system.

V

Perhaps the highest evidence which Protestantism can offer that New Testament Christianity is its sustaining authority, is in its spirit and temper toward the non-Protestant world. No intellectual outlook, however ardent, furnishes a sufficient incentive for a conquering Faith. This must be rooted and grounded in love for those who are beyond the pale. Hate of anything save sin is the gangrene of religion. One is forcibly reminded of these verities in dealing with that ancient rival whose challenge ceaselessly resounds everywhere: the Roman Catholic Church against which our fathers revolted. Here a unique opportunity is presented for what the Apostle calls "truthing it in love," especially in the

United States, where a very vigorous Protestantism and Catholicism exist side by side, and share the same civic duties and responsibilities. Both these divisions of Western Christianity are fortunate enough to have far-sighted leaders who, when deeply touched by the greatest concerns, feel and think alike about them. Love of God, of Christ, of the Church, of the Bible; and a warm response to the appeal of holy living, characterize the best Protestants and Catholics. Could they be multiplied indefinitely, the rapprochement which now seems too remote to be practicable might be materially advanced. As the facts are, Catholics and Protestants are separated by a formidable barrier of varying beliefs which give proposals for their union a doctrinaire tang. In English-speaking nations there has been a diminution of the difficulties between them. The Anglo-Catholic Movement, its forerunner, Oxford Tractarianism, and the renaissance of Mediæval ideas now prevalent in Europe and America, have done much to overcome ecclesiastical insularity. But these two great bodies of Christians meet everywhere without any instinctive contact of spirit. Their prolonged quarrel strikes the depressing note of an almost permanent dislocation of institutional Christianity. Combative partisans of both kinds describe one another in George Meredith's lines:

> "Trim swordsmen they push forth; yet by thy steel,
> Thou, fighting for poor human kind, wilt feel
> The strength of Roland in thy wrist, to hew
> A chasm sheer into the barrier rock,
> And bring the army of the faithful through."

Since no church is a pure precipitate of New Testament teaching, Protestants can be content to let the militancy of this stanza subside. God reigns in the Churches; their purity or impurity, strength or weakness, are more evenly distributed than many concede. Catholicism is so completely organized that it is sensitive to the least rupture. Protestantism is so loosely organized that its fabric dissolves into the more than two hundred sects which bear its name in this nation alone. Yet how much Catholicism is latent in Protestantism, how much Protestantism is reciprocal in Catholicism, and how greatly indebted both are to Hebraism! When the corporate life of Christianity is viewed in its relation to the human race, it is apparent that the Faith we hold could not dispense with either of its two great Western divisions, and that the destruction of one would probably entail that of the other. The enforced tolerance which does not become them should give place to a cordial intercourse in which controversies can be amicably entertained. Before both lies the non-Christian world, with its countless antagonisms and agonies, always there, eagerly waiting for the Gospel of Redemption and Brotherhood, which these Churches have received from the Saviour of mankind and which they are under a solemn obligation to proclaim. In that world, and not in theological or ecclesiastical warfare, is the theater, as it seems to me, of any approximate agreements between them.[10]

Their divergencies are created by opposing estimates. The Protestant looks upon Catholicism as an inexplicable system, entangled in a mesh of inconsistencies and erroneous assumptions. He conceives it stultified by the spirit of progress, opposed to scientific inquiry, to advanced civilization, and to the independence of the State. The Catholic, on the other hand, regards his religion as the only one having the plenitude of divine authority. For him, it is peerless in spiritual sanction, in loveliness and in vision. He points to its worship in all countries through the medium of a classic language, as an evidence of its universality and antiquity. By means of that worship nations are welded into one Faith, despite the separative forces of race and temperament, climate and speech. Their various characters and political organizations are not the sole determinants of their

[10] Cf. Charles R. Brown: "The Larger Faith," p. 157 ff.

destiny. The missionary activities of his Church, from the time of Europe's conversion to the present propaganda of the Jesuits, are eulogized by him. She has also founded charitable institutions in every land, and her priesthood has never been known to retreat when any peril threatened the flock. These and other proofs of her divine nature and mission as the solely sufficient Church satisfy Roman adherents. Such a system, they aver, must eventually overcome all opposition and govern the religious beliefs of the earth. Its doctrines, as they apprehend them, are a closely woven yet comprehensive development of Biblical teaching in which no flaw can be found. The Spirit of God has inspired their symmetrical philosophy of the supreme religion. He still presides over its necessities, and speaks through the voice of the Sovereign Pontiff on all questions of faith and order.

Students of comparative religion, who are not of Rome, refer to the mingled firmness and flexibility of Catholicism, and to its remarkable knowledge of human needs and infirmities. Its representative teachers remind us that it does not forbid the right of private judgment, except when such judgment trespasses upon the supremacy of the Church in matters of dogma. She condemns Modernism because it does so trespass, as an offense, not in itself alone, but still more for its tacit resistance to the Holy See. Here the Catholic, though he be as learned as Acton or Döllinger, or as brilliant as Tyrrell, arrives at the terminus.[11] He is relieved of any necessity to find for himself the way to eternal life for which the Church is his one and only guide. "My brethren," said Cardinal Mercier, in his pastoral issued for the enforcement of the Papal Encyclical of 1907, "we have here merely the question of honesty: yes, or no? Do you believe the divine authority of the Church? Do you accept exteriorly and interiorly what in the Name of Jesus Christ she proposes to your belief: yes, or no? If yes, then she puts

[11] Cf. George Tyrrell: "Christianity at the Cross Roads"; M. D. Petrie: "Modernism."

the Sacraments at your disposal, and undertakes your safe conduct to Heaven. If no, you deliberately break the bond that united you to her, of which she had tied and blessed the knot. Before God and your conscience you belong to her no more." These words are explicitness itself. They have the refreshing lucidity of a first class mind. The discipline they exact could not exist for its own sake. Were it not prolific of spiritual compensations, men and women would not submit to its regimen.

Its inhibitions are viewed by Protestants as an unwarranted invasion of intellectual and moral rights. But to the Catholic, they present an unanswerable argument for the surrender of those rights. Obedience to the Church is synonymous with his soul's deliverance and purification from sin. Her infallibility throws its ægis around his errors; her conservation of doctrine is forever superior to those which individual or sectarian opinions supply. Hence the rewards of Catholicism are mystical and eternal; it emphasizes the unseen; it enunciates a creed of life rather than of thought. Its human side is more advanced than its literary side; it chastens the mind to enrich the heart. Theological speculations once nearly wrecked the Pontificate, so they are now beneath its edicts. Other interests of mortal existence are carefully economized in behalf of its transcendental aspects. Souls given either to misanthropy or to ecstasy, to submission or to worship, find Catholicism congenial to their longings and emotions. Those who have grown weary of efforts to formulate their own beliefs; those also who fear the overweening pressure of materialism; and the lesser natures which are drawn to elaborate rites, flee to Catholicism as their city of refuge and temple of devotion.[12]

Protestants complain of the rank undergrowth of Catholic communities, in which, as they assert, there is no breadth

[12] Cf. Cardinal Newman: "Apologia Pro Vita Sua"; "Life of Cardinal Gibbons" by Allen Sinclair Will; "Ignatius Loyola" by Henry Dwight Sedgwick.

of survey, no courageous criticism, no intellectual idealism: nothing but a drudgery of routine in prescribed ordinances. Yet many Catholics whom I have known, and who are charitably disposed toward Protestantism, have testified to the certitude, the joy, the peace and consolation, which their beliefs inspire in them. Whatever may be urged against the static condition of Catholic dogma, since the Pontificate of Leo XIII, a notable series of Encyclicals against greed, social oppression and war, or in behalf of lawfulness and sobriety, has come out of the Vatican. The Catholic Church, notwithstanding her innate conservatism, and her instinctive dislike of Communism, has ranged herself against arbitrary class privilege and influence. For reasons which Rome has doubtless carefully weighed, she deems the betterment of the people more important for her and for the world than the preservation of its plutocracies. Yet in the complexity of her vast organization, with its multitudinous concerns, she also acts for the stabilization of society, and for the protection of property rights.

Protestantism, in the main, is sundered as the poles from Catholicism's ideals and methods of religious propaganda. Its informed members tolerate every school of thought in its denominational range, and give preëminence to freedom of inquiry and statement. Its intellectualism is at once its strength and its weakness. Emphatically, it is the religion of liberty, and in its advanced phases, of the open mind. But with equal emphasis, *it is a religion.* It penetrates behind the sciences which are caviare to the general; behind metaphysics and their schools, first, into the realm of ethics, and next, into that of faith. Its approved moral standards are untainted by casuistry; austerely insistent upon what is just; and, as such, are recognized, even when not obeyed, as final. Spiritual realities are dealt with directly and simply. Every Protestant is his own priest, and himself makes the offering of his heart to his Maker. Immediate contact with God through Christ is obtained by repentance and faith. These evangelical traits are by no means characteristic of all Protestants, but they are the norm by which their religion should be judged. Nor are they confined to denominations which assume the name Evangelical as though they had a patent for it. On the contrary, they prevail in all the sects, and some minor ones are conspicuous for their possession. As in the well-known instance of the Moravian Brethren, their spirituality is fragrant, and their numbers are by no means commensurate with the wide and salutary influence which they exert. It is perhaps clear to us that the basis of the Reformed Faith is not a mediating Church, but a mediating Redeemer; not a book nor an organization, but a Person and a Life. Believers who obey that Person have a religious freedom conducive to some of the divinest meanings of that Life. They show the "ineffability", which Professor James noted as one of the four hall-marks of a mystical Faith.[13] Their experience of religion is verified by the witness of the Church at large. Underneath denominational varieties, as the earth's strata are underneath its fauna and flora, is a consciousness of God in Jesus Christ which is the invincible citadel of Protestantism.

Saints have hallowed Catholicism and Protestantism in every period of their history. The modern age has been illuminated by their lives shining like a golden path across the sea; a path for angels to walk upon, that led straight into the City of the Blessed One. I have but to mention Josephine Butler of London, S. F. Collier of Manchester, A. J. Lyman of Brooklyn, James M. Thoburn of India, David Hill of China, James W. Bashford of the farther East, Father Damien of the leper colony of Molokai, and Cardinal Gibbons of our country, to assure you that according to Cardinal Newman's argument, the Church that produces sanctified souls still stands in the Apostolic Succession. The beauty of their holiness casts its spell over old and young, and over

[13] Cf. "The Varieties of Religious Experience," p. 380.

the quickest or the slowest intelligences. Their spontaneous grace and goodness check the disputatious mind. In them we see the promise of better things ahead, when the non-Christian world now buried in darkness shall know that Christ came forth from God to give it light because His Church is one and indivisible in Him. While the generations of believers await that triumph, let us hold the truth in love, and state our reasons for difference with dignified fidelity, but without churlishness. "There will come a time," said a great Anglican divine, "when three words uttered in charity shall receive a more blessed reward than three thousand volumes written with disdainful sharpness of wit." [14] Have that time in mind, when the one flock shall be enfolded by the one Shepherd. Resolve that while brave for beliefs dear to you, it shall be yours to say at the last that wheresoever the divine spark glowed on other altars than your own, there your prayers were breathed to fan it to a still higher flame.

VI

To an impartial observer it would seem that Christianity's schisms could well be ignored, in the presence of atheistical Socialism, and of the aggressiveness of Moslem religion in the world. The challenge of Gandhi, the Hindu Reformer, is likewise heard, not only in India, but throughout the East, and also in Christian lands. Reverenced by his countrymen as a hero and a prophet, he bids them avoid Western civilization as they would a plague. Its medicine is black art, its surgery is butchery, its material benefits asphyxiate the spiritual values of Hinduism, its scientific achievements are a mockery, and its religion fatally deficient in moral concepts.[15]

[14] Richard Hooker: "Ecclesiastical Polity," (Everyman's Library Edition) p. 94.

[15] Cf. Sir Valentine Chirol: "India Old and New"; J. N. Farquhar: "Modern Religious Movements in India;" Dhan Lopal Mukerji: "Caste and Outcast"; R. Tagore: "Creative Unity."

But Gandhi has to give way for hyperbolic denunciations to Stepanoff, the Russian Red, who insists that Christianity's creeds cast a halo around the ever present hell of human misery. The Hindu's polemic is more persuasive than the wild ravings of the Marxian Soviet. Yet the evaluations of Sovietism and of Gandhi's refined Hinduism are jaded. They will run their course and disappear. Before this happens, however, they may prove to be the parents of a long progeniture, which will challenge Protestantism's future in the East.

The contingencies set forth here do not come from a world of shadowy abstractions, but from one of ponderable things, which must be clearly understood by those who take definite action upon them. Not a few people doubt if any action can be taken. Others question if institutional religion can survive the universal disaffection and its momentous changes. And the cynic who tells us that "we are all brothers now: all Cains and Abels," is vocal with libels upon the whole race. What feasible measures can be pushed ahead? First of all, Protestants should ascertain to what degree their religion is responsible for those breaches and divisions of organized society which have created its chronic feeling of insecurity. For if Christianity means anything it means the brave acceptance of life in the earnest expectation of more and better life to come. The strife that fills society today is the result, to a large degree, of the insufficiency of Christian Churches as vehicles of that saving grace which is pent up behind the scanty outlets they have hitherto furnished for it. But before attempting to answer the question of Protestant responsibility for this insufficiency, it should be said that the deepest separation between human beings is made by their possession or non-possession of the believing mind. This mind owes no fealty to the empirical distinctions for which men shed blood, save as those distinctions help it to prevail. It is a voluntary mind, self-imposed, confined to no race and to no creed. Christian and non-Christian are included within its scope. All who accept the Fatherhood of God, the Brotherhood of man, and the spiritual interpretation of life, belong to it. They compose the inner society of love, of service and of sacrifice, which we must steadily keep before us. Should Protestants who regard their sectarian peculiarities as supreme, attempt to act as though such a society does not and cannot exist outside their little bounds, they will discover that the healing of mankind is not assigned by God to them.

In this connection, it cannot be denied that Protestantism has had its disintegrating side. It has built up States, founded Churches, missionized distant and dark territories, and led the educational developments of the past four hundred years, But it has also split institutional religion into many fragments, and some Protestants assert that this is its most admirable deed. Yet if the failure of Mediævalism is traceable to its attempts to transform the Church into a secular society, the failure of Protestanism is not less traceable to its attempts to make the Church subservient to secular society. If the Mediæval Church consciousness exceeded legitimate boundaries, the Church consciousness of Protestantism has retreated too far from the ideal of the New Testament. How could that retreat be avoided in view of the origin and history of Protestantism? Its founders never agreed about the essential nature of the Church, nor has any unanimous agreement been reached since their day.

The first conception of her being as invisible, consisting of the redeemed whose union is mystical, the visible ministry of the preached Word, and the due observance of the Sacraments, soon became a bone of contention. Luther's scholasticism found vent in Consubstantiation, which made the Church an elevated but scarcely an efficient agent of God. As we have seen, Lutheranism showed marked inferiority to Calvinism as a virile form of Protestantism. Zwingli's rationalism was at variance with Luther's mysticism. The German Reformer stood for the believer's privileges through Justification by Faith, and insisted that there was no necessity for a visible Head of the Church. The Swiss Reformer maintained that Church and State were one in aim, and would have merged both in the State. The former claimed that the New Testament sanctioned the Real Presence in the Eucharist; the latter that all such allusions were purely metaphorical. Luther's theory submitted the Church to the control of temporal princes; Zwingli's theory saddled their criminal acts upon a participating Church. Their differences lay partly in temperament and partly in circumstances. Luther was conservative, suspicious of the Renaissance, always aware of his own past; Zwingli was radical, greatly attached to the Renaissance, and in a sense, the father of present liberalism. Calvin's genius rose like the eagle above the plain in his doctrine of Predestination. But his theory of a Church-State, as exemplified at Geneva, soon declined, although it had experimental values which greatly accelerated the growth of free States.

The disagreement noted in these three decisive cases was fatal to the unity of sixteenth-century Protestantism. Its quarrels involved the nations and multiplied the sects. Excessive individualism, as the rebound from an overbearing corporate life, produced Nationalism, and Nationalism widened the divisions of Protestanism. Erastianism came in to give monarchs governance over the now separated Churches. They often nominated their chief pastors, and even ratified their doctrinal forms. The achievement of a consolidated international Protestantism was postponed for centuries. So humiliating a subordination of the spiritual to the temporal rule outraged the *Communio Sanctorum*, "the company of the faithful," whose members drew apart into Independency. Thus other breaches were made, and the national Churches that had defied Rome were themselves defied by a segment of their more devout membership.

The chaos that followed is the most adequate explanation of the loss of Protestant authority in international affairs. Its inability consisted, not only in its controversial temper, but in its unwillingness to "see life steadily, and see it whole." Its religious revolts against the State were animated by otherworldiness; its conformity was wanting in the historic sense of an unbroken stream of human consciousness and effort. So it lay, stranded between two extremes. In the process we may observe a hesitancy about convictions, a tampering with them because of penalties or rewards, and a general absence of straight forward dealing in sacred affairs. These characteristics were most noticeable in State Churches, which were in the secular bondage that politics had fastened on them. False perspectives, unreal values, the pursuit of minor ends, were the outcome of their entombment "within the four walls of Acts of Parliament." The ideal of the Ecclesia as forever one, holy and indivisible, the creation of God in Christ Jesus, withered under the glare of national arrogance and self-determination. Old tyrannies were revived by those Churchmen who worshipped State authority as the Parsees worship the sun, without explaining it. The tendency of huge impersonal organizations to domineer over believers who dared to reassert the supremacy of the New Testament Church, was constantly exhibited by the State, which appropriated many Church rights and privileges.

The story of Protestant disintegration need not be recited at further length. It is now accomplished, and many Protestants are more deeply attached to their denominations than to the Universal Ecclesia. But it has bred in outsiders an aloofness which deepens at intervals into contempt. Walter Hobhouse declares that thus "the effective force of the Church as an instrument for the conversion of the world is half paralyzed by its internal incoherence." [16] Furthermore, the Scriptural vision of God's world-empire has disappeared from Protestantism, by reason of the absorbing claims and ecstasies of individualistic pieties. These have the detachment from the race tragedy of Browning's "Lazarus," without his supreme experience.[17] A recapitulation against sectarianism

[16] "The Church and the World in Idea and in History," p. 260.

[17] Cf. Frank I. Paradise: "The Living Church," in "The Hibbert Journal," April, 1907. p. 535.

charges it with intensifying the Nationalism that prevents the peace of Christendom; hindering industrial, economic and social progress; failing to furnish society with any impulse or pattern for its wider fellowship. It is also accused of stressing arbitrary social distinctions, and yielding to State absolutism. Whatever may be said for or against the indictment of our constitutional defects, those who know Protestantism from within will realize how unjust some of these animadversions are. In the past, its sons have withstood the State, broken the despotism of powerful Monarchs, and organized lawful freedom. Today, multitudes of Protestants realize that there is a higher love than love of democracy; a greater commandment than that of the State; a nobler obedience and a purer service than any political rule can rightly demand. From the ranks of such men and women our best citizenship is recruited. They abound everywhere to identify State and Church with the Divine Order, and to idealize both as the executants of that Order. The strength they inherit from their traditions of truth and justice is not frittered away, as some of their critics would have us believe. It is assuming new forms in a Protestant Catholicity, that shall reoccupy ground too long abandoned to a type of Catholicity which they cannot conscientiously accept.

The movements mentioned here can be regarded as phases of one presiding and intelligent evolution, in which the beliefs and institutions that survived its ordeals were preserved for further use and benefit. Justifiable reasons for the present existence of many sects have vanished. Some were never valid; others have become anachronisms; all are subjected to the sifting that separates their grain from their chaff. As surely as the signs of the sixteenth century pointed to the disunion of the Church, so surely do those of the twentieth century point to the union of all Christian believers. Whatever in this history, so multiform and complex, we lament or hail, it has a significance arising out of a sovereignty beyond our comprehension. Beneath its rough and troubled annals, its conflicts and schisms, its wretched episodes and its thrilling heroisms, there ever has been the true union of hearts that beat for God's honor.

No Fabian tactics can delay the incoming tide of a divine purpose which bears Protestantism onward to its future Catholicity. But competent leadership is required to guide its living forces in their best directions, and to intelligently apply them. Those forces are allied with the world's order and security, with the various Church federations that have been inaugurated during the past thirty years, with the advance of organized knowledge, and with the growing social and industrial consciousness of mankind. The revolt against the unconditioned Church has happened; the revolt against the unconditioned State has begun. The results of these movements run concurrently and demand the wisest superintendence if they are to yield the peaceable fruits of righteousness.[18] Church and State must reciprocate afresh for the approaching internationalism of which Protestant union should be the forerunner and the pledge. Its larger denominations contribute to the Catholicity we have in mind. They teach the lessons of collective responsibility in religious enterprises. They show that religious reconstruction is not an easy process because it deals with the most susceptible side of human nature. But they inculcate the patience of hope, and stimulate that love which surpasses knowledge. Their adherents undertake gigantic tasks for the good of the human race, not at ecclesiastical behest, but as the Lord's freemen. In the several Churches, merging as they constantly are by gradual degrees into a wider Church, we find the prototypes of a living unity, the organs of its expression, and the standards of its faith and practice. Yet these must be universally understood and accepted if outward unity is to be. Conventions may assemble and pass resolutions favoring such a unity until the crack of doom. But it will be realized in one way

[18] Cf. Charles A. Ellwood: "Christianity and Social Science," Chapter VIII on "The Problem of Leadership," p. 189 ff.

alone. When all Protestants who confess Christ as Lord are willing to abide by what that confession implies as the sole standard of Christian discipleship, then, and not till then, a renewed and a more glorious Protestantism shall prevail.

BIBLIOGRAPHY

The following books are arranged in five divisions, not in any exclusive sense but for the sake of convenience.

I. *General*

Ante-Nicene, Nicene and Post Nicene Fathers, The
AYER, J. C.: A Source Book for Ancient Church History.
Catholic Encyclopædia, The.
Encyclopædia Britannica, Eleventh Edition.
GWATKIN, H. M., and WHITNEY, J. P. (Editors): The Cambridge Mediæval History.
HASTINGS, JAMES (Editor): Encyclopædia of Religion and Ethics.
MOELLER, W., and SCHUBERT, HANS VON: A History of the Christian Church.
New International Encyclopædia, The.
SCHAFF, PHILIP: History of the Christian Church.
WALKER, WILLISTON: A History of the Christian Church.
WARD, A. W., PROTHERO, G. W., LEATHES, S. (Editors): The Cambridge Modern History.

II. *Philosophical and Sociological*

ACTON, LORD: The History of Freedom and other Essays.
ADAMS, HENRY: The Degradation of the Democratic Dogma.
ADLER, FELIX: An Ethical Philosophy of Life.
BAGEHOT, WALTER: Physics annd Politics.
BOSANQUET, BERNARD: The Philosophical Theory of the State.
BROWN, PHILIP M.: International Society, Its Nature and Interests.
BRYCE, VISCOUNT: International Relations.
BURGESS, J. W.: Political Science and Comparative Constitutional Law.
BURY, J. B.: The Idea of Progress.
BUTLER, NICHOLAS MURRAY: Building the American Nation.
CARLYLE, R. W., and CARLYLE, A. J.: A History of Mediæval Political Theory.
CROCE, BENEDETTO: History: Its Theory and Practice.
DICKINSON, EDWIN DEWITT: The Equality of States in International Law.

ELLWOOD, CHARLES A.: The Reconstruction of Religion.
EUCKEN, RUDOLF: The Problem of Human Life.
FIGGIS, J. N.: The Divine Right of Kings.
FOLLETT, M. P.: The New State.
FULLERTON, W. M.: Problems of Power.
GIDDINGS, FRANKLIN H.: Studies in the Theory of Human Society.
GRANT, MADISON: The Passing of the Great Race.
GREEN, THOMAS HILL: Principles of Ethical Obligation.
GREEN, THOMAS HILL: Prolegomena to Ethics.
HADLEY, ATTHUR T.: Economic Problems of Democracy.
HALL, THOMAS C.: History of Ethics within Organized Christianity.
HALLIDAY, WILLIAM R.: The Growth of the City State.
HATCH, EDWIN: The Influence of Greek Ideas and Usages upon the Christian Church.
HEARNSHAW, F. J. C. (Editor): The Social and Political Ideas of Some Great Mediæval Thinkers.
HENSON, H. HENSLEY: Moral Discipline in the Christian Church.
HERGENROETHER, CARDINAL: Catholic Church and Christian State.
HERTZLER, JOYCE O.: The History of Utopian Thought.
HOBHOUSE, L. T.: The Elements of Social Justice.
HOBHOUSE, L. T.: The Metaphysical Theory of the State.
HOBHOUSE, L. T.: The Rational Good.
HOBHOUSE, WALTER: The Church and the World in Idea and in History.
HUDSON, JAY WILLIAM: The Truths we Live By.
INGE, R. W.: Outspoken Essays, First and Second Series.
JACKS, L. P.: Realities and Shams.
JONES, SIR HENRY: Idealism as a Practical Creed.
JONES, SIR HENRY: The Principles of Citizenship.
JONES, SIR HENRY: The Working Faith of the Social Reformer.
JOSEY, CHARLES CONANT: Race and National Solidarity.
KIDD, B.: The Science of Power.
LECKY, W. E. H.: A History of the Rise and Influence of the Spirit of Rationalism in Europe.
MAINE, SIR HENRY: Popular Government.
MAINE, SIR HENRY: Ancient Law.
MARCHANT, SIR JAMES (Editor): The Coming Renaissance.
MARTINEAU, JAMES: Types of Ethical Theory.
MATHEWS, SHAILER: The Spiritual Interpretation of History.
MCDOUGALL, WILLIAM: The Group Mind.
MCDOUGALL, WILLIAM: Social Psychology.
MORLEY, VISCOUNT: On Compromise.
MORLEY, VISCOUNT: Oracles on Man and Government.

Morley, Viscount: Politics and History.
Muirhead, J. H. (Editor): Contemporary British Philosophy.
Oppenheim, L.: International Law.
Palmer, George Herbert: Altruism, Its Nature and Varieties.
Partridge, G. E.: The Psychology of Nations.
Penman, John Simpson: The Irresistible Movement of Democracy.
Rashdall, Hastings: Conscience and Christ.
Rauschenbusch, Walter: Christianizing the Social Order.
Ritchie, D. G.: Natural Rights.
Robinson, J. H.: The Mind in the Making.
Robinson, Norman L.: Christian Justice.
Rogers, Arthur Kenyon: English and American Philosophy Since 1800.
Russell, Bertrand: Mysticism and Logic.
Ryan, John A., and Millar, M. F. X.: The State and the Church.
Schweitzer, Albert: The Philosophy of Civilization. Part I, The Decay and the Restoration of Civilization; Part II, Civilization and Ethics.
Suguimori, Kojiro: The Principles of the Modern Empire.
Tawney, R. H.: The Acquisitive Society.
Taylor, Henry Osborn: Freedom of the Mind in History.
Troeltsch, Ernst: Protestantism and Progress.
Viallate, Achille: Economic Imperialism.
Wallace, William: Lectures and Essays on Natural Theology and Ethics.
Wallace, William Kay: The Trend of History.
Wallas, Graham: The Great Society.
Ward, Harry F.: The New Social Order.
Westermarch, E. A.: The Origin and Development of the Moral Ideas.
Westlake, John: International Law.
Willoughby, W. W.: The Nature of the State.
Wilson, Woodrow: Constitutional Government in the United States.
Wilson, Woodrow: The State: Elements of Historical and Practical Politics.
Wolfe, A. B.: Conservatism, Radicalism, and Scientific Method.

III. *Historical*

Acton, Lord: Historical Essays and Studies.
Acton, Lord: Lectures on Modern History.
Adeney, Walter F.: The Greek and Eastern Churches.
Angus, S.: The Environment of Early Christianity.
Asquith, Herbert H.: The Genesis of the War.

Bailey, Cyril (Editor): The Legacy of Rome.
Baird, H. M.: The Rise of the Huguenots in France.
Bartlett, J. V., and Carlyle, A. J.: Christianity in History.
Beet, W. Ernest: The Early Roman Episcopate.
Beet, W. Ernest: Rise of the Papacy.
Bryce, Viscount: Modern Democracies.
Bryce, Viscount: The Holy Roman Empire.
Butler, Dom Cuthbert: Benedictine Monarchism.
Cadman, S. Parkes: The Three Religious Leaders of Oxford.
Church, R. W.: Beginning of the Middle Ages.
Clark, Henry W.: History of English Nonconformity.
Coulton, G. G.: Five Centuries of Religion, Vol. I.
Creighton, Mandell: History of the Papacy from the Great Schism to the Sack of Rome, 1378–1527.
Dill, Samuel: Roman Society from Nero to Marcus Aurelius.
Dill, Samuel: Roman Society in the Last Century of the Western Empire.
Eusebius: Church History, translated by A. C. McGiffert.
Fleming, D. H.: The Reformation in Scotland.
Foakes-Jackson, F. J.: An Introduction to the History of Christianity, A. D. 590–1314.
Fowler, W. Warde: The City-State of the Greeks and Romans.
Gairdner, James: The English Church in the Sixteenth Century.
Gairdner, James: Lollardy and the Reformation.
Gardner, Percy: The Growth of Christianity.
Gasquet, Cardinal F. A.: The Eve of the Reformation.
Green, John Richard: A History of the English People.
Gregorovius, F.: History of the City of Rome in the Middle Ages.
Gwatkin, H. M.: Early Church History to A. D. 313.
Hardman, O., The Ideals of Asceticism.
Harnack, Adolf von: The Mission and Expansion of Christianity.
Harrison, Frederic: The Meaning of History.
Horne, C. Silvester: A Popular History of the Free Churches.
Hulme, Edward M.: The Renaissance, the Protestant Revolution and the Catholic Reformation.
Jones, Rufus M.: Spiritual Reformers in the 16th and 17th Centuries.
Jones, Rufus M.: Studies in Mystical Religion.
Kidd, B. J.: A History of the Church to A. D. 461.
Lagarde, André: The Latin Church in the Middle Ages.
Lea, H. C.: A History of the Inquisition in the Middle Ages.
Lea, H. C.: A History of Auricular Confession and Indulgence in the Latin Church.
Lindsay, T. M.: A History of the Reformation.

Livingstone, R. W. (Editor): The Legacy of Greece.
MacLaurin, C.: Post Mortem.
McGiffert, A. C.: History of Christianity in the Apostolic Age.
Mozley, J. R.: The Divine Aspect of History.
Pastor, L.: History of the Popes from the Close of the Middle Ages.
Plummer, Alfred: The Continental Reformation.
Ponsonby, Arthur: English Diaries.
Pullan, Leighton: Religion since the Reformation.
Rainy, Robert: The Ancient Catholic Church.
Ranke, L. von: History of the Popes during the Last Four Centuries.
Rashdall, Hastings: The Universities of Europe in the Middle Ages.
Sedgwick, Henry Dwight: Ignatius Loyola.
Seebohm, Frederick: The Oxford Reformers.
Sihler, Ernest G.: From Augustus to Augustine.
Smith, Preserved: The Age of the Reformation.
Stawell, F. Melian, and Marvin, F. S.: The Making of the Western Mind.
Symonds, J. A.: The Catholic Reaction.
Taylor, Henry Osborn: The Mediæval Mind.
Taylor, Henry Osborn: Thought and Expression in the Sixteenth Century.
Watkins, O. D.: The History of Penance.
Wells, H. G.: The Outline of History.
White, A. D.: The Warfare of Science and Theology.
Wilson, Woodrow: History of the American People.
Workman, H. B.: Persecution in the Early Church.
Workman, H. B.: The Evolution of the Monastic Ideal.
Workman, H. B.: The Dawn of the Reformation.
Workman, H. B.: The Foundation of Modern Religion.

IV. *Ecclesiastical*

Allen, Alexander V. G.: Christian Institutions.
Bennett, L. E.: The Realm of God.
Brown, Charles R.: The Larger Faith.
Brown, William Adams: The Church in America.
Brown, William Adams: Imperialistic Religion and the Religion of Democracy.
Campbell, Thomas J.: The Jesuits, 1534–1921.
Carlyle, A. J. and Others: Towards Reunion.
Cox, W. L. Paige (Editor): Anglican Essays.
Dale, R. W.: Essays and Addresses.

Döllinger, J. J. von: Declarations and Letters on the Vatican Decrees.
Drake, Durant: Shall We Stand by the Church?
DuBose, W. P.: The Ecumenical Councils.
Fairbairn, A. M.: Catholicism, Roman and Anglican.
Figgis, J. N.: Churches in the Modern State.
Forsyth, P. T.: The Church and the Sacraments.
Gore, Charles: The Church and the Ministry.
Gore, Charles (Introduction): The Return of Christendom, by A Group of Churchmen.
Hatch, Edwin: The Organization of the Early Christian Churches.
Headlam, Arthur C.: The Doctrine of the Church and Christian Union.
Henson, H. Hensley: The National Church.
Hodgkin, Henry T.: The Christian Revolution.
Hooker, Richard: Ecclesiastical Polity.
Hort, F. J. A.: The Christian Ecclesia.
Huss, John: The Church, translated by David S. Schaff.
Innes, A. Taylor: Church and State.
Joseph, Oscar L.: The Dynamic Ministry.
Lightfoor, Joseph Barber: Ignatius and Polycarp.
Lindsay, T. M.: The Church and the Ministry in the Early Centuries.
Lynch, Frederick (Editor): The Problem of Christian Unity.
MacGregor, W. M.: Christian Freedom.
McComas, Henry C.: The Psychology of Religious Sects.
Manning, Cardinal: The Vatican Decrees and their Bearing on Civil Allegiance.
Micklem, Nathaniel, and Morgan, Herbert: Christ and Caesar.
Micklem Nathaniel: God's Freemen.
Newman, Cardinal: Lectures on Certain Difficulties felt by Anglicans in Submitting to the Catholic Church.
Oman, John: The Church and the Divine Order.
Parks, Leighton: The Crisis of the Churches.
Petrie, M. D.: Modernism.
Robertson, A.: Regnum Dei.
Scott, C. A. Anderson: The Fellowship of the Spirit.
Scott, E. F.: The Beginning of the Church.
Simpson, P. Carnegie: Church Principles.
Söderblom, Nathan: Christian Fellowship.
Spencer, Malcolm and Others: Pathways to Christian Unity. A Free Church View.
Swete, H. B.: The Holy Catholic Church.

SWETE, H. B. (Editor): The Early History of the Church and the Ministry.
TEMPLE, WILLIAM: Church and Nation.
WILLIAMS, CHARLES D.: The Gospel of Fellowship.

V. *Theological*

ABBOTT, LYMAN: What Christianity Means to Me.
ALLEN, A. V. G.: The Continuity of Christian Thought.
ATKINS, GAIUS GLENN: Modern Religious Cults and Movements.
BALFOUR, ARTHUR J.: Theism and Humanism.
BALFOUR, ARTHUR J.: Theism and Thought.
BURROUGHS, E. A.: The Valley of Decision.
CADMAN, S. PARKES; Ambassadors of God.
CADOUX, A. T.: Essays in Christian Thinking.
CAIRNS, D. S.: The Reasonableness of the Christian Faith.
CLARK, HENRY W.: Liberal Orthodoxy: A Historical Survey.
CLARK, WILLIAM N.: An Outline of Christian Theology.
DAVISON, W. T. (Editor): The Chief Corner-stone.
DEARMER, PERCY: The Church at Prayer.
FISHER, GEORGE P.: History of Christian Doctrine.
FORSYTH, P. T.: The Principle of Authority.
FOSDICK, HARRY E.: Christianity and Progress.
GALLOWAY, GEORGE: Religion and Modern Thought.
GARDNER, PERCY: The Practical Basis of Christian Belief.
GLOVER, T. R.: Progress in Religion to the Christian Era.
HARNACK, ADOLF VON: History of Dogma.
HEADLAM, ARTHUR C.: The Life and Teachings of Jesus the Christ.
HOCKING, WILLIAM E.: Human Nature and Its Remaking.
HOCKING, WILLIAM E.: The Meaning of God in Human Experience.
HORTON, ROBERT F.: The Mystical Quest of Christ.
INGE, W. R.: Faith and Its Psychology.
JACKS, L. P.: Religious Perplexities.
JAMES, WILLIAM: The Varieties of Religious Experience.
JONES, SIR HENRY: A Faith that Enquires.
JOSEPH, OSCAR L.: Freedom and Advance.
JOSEPH, OSCAR L.: The Faith and the Fellowship.
MACKINTOSH, H. R.: The Originality of the Christian Message.
MACKINTOSH, H. R.: Some Aspects of Christian Belief.
MALDEN, R. H.: Problems of the New Testament To-day.
MCCONNELL, FRANCIS J.: Public Opinion and Theology.
MCGIFFERT, A. C.: The God of the Early Christians.
MCGIFFERT, A. C.: Protestant Thought before Kant.

McGiffert, A. C.: The Rise of Modern Religious Ideas.
Moore, E. C.: History of Christian Thought since Kant.
Moore, George Foot: History of Religions.
Moore, George Foot: The Birth and Growth of Religion.
Newman, Cardinal: Essay on the Development of Christian Doctrine.
Oman, John: Grace and Personality.
Oman, John: The Problem of Faith and Freedom.
Paterson, W. P.: The Rule of Faith.
Peabody, Francis G.: The Christian Life in the Modern World.
Poole, Reginald Lane: Illustrations of the History of Mediæval Thought.
Pratt, James B.: The Religious Consciousness.
Pringle-Pattison, A. Seth: The Idea of God.
Rawlinson, A. E. J.: Authority and Freedom.
Rogers, T. Guy (Editor): Liberal Evangelicalism: An Interpretation.
Royce, Josiah: The Problem of Christianity.
Sabatier, Auguste: Religions of Authority and the Religion of the Spirit.
Schaff, P.: The Creeds of Christendom.
Scott, E. F.: The Spirit in the New Testament.
Scott, A. Boyd: Nevertheless We Believe.
Simpson, J. Y.: Man and the Attainment of Immortality.
Simpson, J. Y.: The Spiritual Interpretation of Nature.
Smith, Gerald B. (Editor): A Guide to the Study of the Christian Religion.
Somervell, D. C.: A Short History of Our Religion.
Streeter, B. H. (Editor): Foundations. A Statement of Christian Belief in terms of Modern Thought.
Temple, William: Mens Creatrix.
Wood, H. G.: From George Fox to Bertrand Russell.
Workman, H. B.: Christian Thought to the Reformation.

INDEX